Edward Adolf Sonnenschein

**A Latin Grammar for Schools**

Based on the principles and requirements of the grammatical society

Edward Adolf Sonnenschein

**A Latin Grammar for Schools**
*Based on the principles and requirements of the grammatical society*

ISBN/EAN: 9783337302887

Printed in Europe, USA, Canada, Australia, Japan

Cover: Foto ©Paul-Georg Meister /pixelio.de

More available books at **www.hansebooks.com**

# PARALLEL GRAMMAR SERIES

EDITED BY

E. A. SONNENSCHEIN, M.A. (Oxon.)

———

# LATIN

"Almost every grammatical system has its *rationale*, capable of being comprehended by the mind, if the mind is kept steadily to it, and of serving as a clue to the facts; but . . . every one of the grammars following a different system" the student "masters the *rationale* of none of them; and in consequence, after all his labour, he often ends by possessing of the science of grammar nothing but a heap of terms jumbled together in inextricable confusion."—MATTHEW ARNOLD.

The PARALLEL GRAMMAR SERIES includes the following volumes:

**ENGLISH GRAMMAR**, by J. HALL, M.A., Head Master of the Hulme Grammar School, Manchester; A. J. COOPER, F.C.P., Head Mistress of the Edgbaston High School for Girls; and the Editor of the Series.

**ENGLISH EXAMPLES AND EXERCISES.** Part I., by M. A. WOODS, Head Mistress of the Clifton High School for Girls. Part II. by A. J. COOPER, F.C.P., Head Mistress of the Edgbaston High School for Girls.

**FRENCH GRAMMAR**, by L. M. MORIARTY, M.A. (Oxon.), Assistant Master in Harrow School; late Professor of French in King's College, London; Taylorian Scholar in French.

**FIRST FRENCH READER AND WRITER**, by R. J. MORICH, Chief Modern Language Master in the Manchester Grammar School, and W. S. LYON, M.A. (Oxon.), Assistant Master in Manchester Grammar School.

**GERMAN GRAMMAR**, by KUNO MEYER, PH.D., Lecturer in German in University College, Liverpool.

**FIRST GERMAN READER AND WRITER**, by E. A. SONNENSCHEIN.

**GREEK GRAMMAR**, by F. HAVERFIELD, M.A. (Oxon.), Sixth Form Master in Lancing College. [*In active preparation.*]

**LATIN GRAMMAR**, by E. A. SONNENSCHEIN, M.A. (Oxon.), Professor of Classics in the Mason College, Birmingham.

**FIRST LATIN READER AND WRITER**, by C. M. DIX, M.A., Assistant Master in the Oratory School, Birmingham.

[*This book contains the essential rules of Elementary Syntax, and thus forms, together with the Latin Accidence, a Complete Course for Beginners.*]

**SECOND LATIN READER AND WRITER**, by C. M. DIX.

**SPANISH GRAMMAR**, by H. B. CLARKE, B.A. (Oxon.), Taylorian Scholar in Spanish. [*In active preparation.*]

**ITALIAN GRAMMAR**, by C. M. C. BÉVENOT, Professor in the Mason College, Birmingham, late Assistant Master in Clifton College, Taylorian Exhibitioner in Italian. [*In active preparation.*]

☞ Other "*READERS and WRITERS*" *to follow the above will be shortly produced.*

SWAN SONNENSCHEIN & CO.

*PARALLEL GRAMMAR SERIES*

A
# LATIN GRAMMAR,
## FOR SCHOOLS

BASED ON THE PRINCIPLES AND REQUIREMENTS
OF THE
GRAMMATICAL SOCIETY

BY
E. A. SONNENSCHEIN, M.A. (Oxon.)
PROFESSOR OF CLASSICS
IN THE
MASON COLLEGE, BIRMINGHAM

*Subtilitas naturæ subtilitatem sensus et intellectus multis partibus superat.*—BACON

STEREOTYPED  EDITION

LONDON
SWAN SONNENSCHEIN & CO.
PATERNOSTER SQUARE

1892

# PARALLEL GRAMMAR SERIES.

The following are the distinguishing features of this Series:

### 1.—Uniformity of Classification and Terminology.

The same grammatical phenomenon is classified alike and named alike wherever found. Slightly different phenomena are described by slightly different but not inconsistent names. A pupil using these Grammars will therefore not be distracted by discordant grammatical views or puzzled by divergent formulæ where a single formula would suffice.

The order of the various Grammars being identical, mastery of one involves mastery of the principles and methods of the others.

These important results are attained **without any revolution in terminology**. It has been found that the existing stock of names, if used economically, is sufficient or very nearly sufficient.

Syntax is based on Analysis of Sentences; and the principle of **Comenius**, "Per exempla," as distinct from "Per praecepta," is followed: *i.e.*, rules are based upon a preceding set of selected examples, from which they may be inductively inferred.

### 2.—Uniformity of Scope.

The Series is designed to meet the needs of High Schools and Grammar Schools. Each Grammar is therefore of sufficient scope to cover the whole school course. Experience has shown the importance of utilising the local memory, but this advantage is sacrificed if the pupil passes from book to book and from one arrangement of the page to another.

On the other hand, this series is designed to supplement and not to supplant the teacher. Exposition and discussion are therefore confined to narrow limits. The object of the promoters has been to present in as brief space as possible a conspectus of the main features of the languages.

### 3.—Uniformity of Size and Type.

All the Grammars are printed in three sizes of type—Small Pica, Long Primer, and Brevier—corresponding to three stages of learning. A line down the margin gives additional prominence to the elementary matter. Great care has been bestowed upon making the pages as pictorial as possible, in order thereby to aid the local memory.

It is hoped that these volumes may fairly claim the title of a **Series of Parallel Grammars**. No labour has been spared in making them uniform, not merely externally, but also in principle and method.

---

SWAN SONNENSCHEIN & CO., PATERNOSTER SQUARE, LONDON.

# PREFACE
## TO THE STEREOTYPED EDITION.

IT would be easy to write a volume—it is difficult not to write a volume—in explanation of the principles by which my coadjutors and myself have been guided in our work. But in grammar, if anywhere, it is true that " A good wine needs no bush"; and the general aim of securing uniformity will probably commend itself to the judgment of practical teachers. The evils of anarchy are indeed only too obvious: either the pupil has to keep a separate compartment of his mind for each of his various grammars, or he has to spend his energy in translating the formulæ of one grammar into those of another: a readjustment of mental attitude altogether beyond his strength. It has been our task to find for the pupil a *common* point of view from which he may regard the different languages that he learns, and to present their grammatical structure to him in a system which shall do no violence to any of them. Thus we have adopted throughout the same classifications and terminology for the sounds, the parts of speech, the tenses, the rules of gender, and so forth. Paradigms have been presented so far as possible in the same form. In Syntax we start with the *sentence*, and, after a preliminary analysis, which sets forth the precise sense in which terms are used and is intended chiefly for reference, we ask the question, " How does such and such a language express such and such *meanings*, and to what extent does it leave the lines of demarcation between meanings confused?"* The second part of Syntax supplements the first by giving a conspectus of the uses of *forms* (cases, tenses, moods, etc.).

Nor have we neglected the more general question of

* Here the numeration of paragraphs in the Latin, French, and German syntaxes is identical. The table of Contents of Syntax is given on p. 220 of the complete book.

simplifying grammar, and making it more easily assimilable by the pupil. It is our hope that in more ways than one our method may effect a saving of time and energy; but especially by showing how the study of an ancient language may be helpful in the acquisition of a modern language, and *vice versâ*. Thiersch considered that two-thirds of the labour of learning languages might be saved by a parallel treatment of their grammars.

The method of teaching Latin Accidence here adopted is neither embarrassed by the discussion of difficult problems as to the historical origin of forms (e.g., *urbi-um* from *urbi-*, but *amant-ium* from *amant-*), nor liable to constant revision with every advance in philological science. In relegating the Protean 'stem' to a subordinate position (§§ 14, 210, for more advanced pupils), I find myself in agreement with the most approved recent school grammars of Germany. What the teacher is concerned with in the early stages of teaching is the part of the word which is *constant in a whole group of forms:* u*RB-* (cf. § 35), ama*NT-*, *dūr-* (cf. § 109), *laud-*, *laudāv-*, *laudāt-*. That such a division of words was recognised by the Roman consciousness is shown by the working of analogy: *dūr-ior* 'hard-er,' *moll-ior* 'soft-er,' *dūr-issimus* 'hard-est,' *moll-issimus* 'soft-est,' presuppose *dūr-* 'hard,' *moll-* 'soft'; *amant-ium* (for *amant-um*) shows that *-ium* had come to be felt as an 'ending' in *urb-ium* and other Genitive Plurals of i-stems. By avoiding the word 'stem' in the early stages, the pupil is saved confusion when he comes to study the question philologically.

The Nouns of the Third Declension have been carefully classified according to their affinities of form and gender. The gender rules for the Third Declension have been simplified by the omission of rare words, and also remodelled on an entirely new basis (§§ 64, 74-78).

In the marking of quantities I have followed a method first suggested by Ritschl, but never yet, so far as I know, carried out consistently in all parts of a grammar. To mark everything is to mark nothing. The essence of Ritschl's plan is *to leave naturally short vowels unmarked*. All vowels long by position— whether naturally short or long—are also unmarked; for here mere inspection of the word determines the quantity of the syllable. The pupil who studies a grammar systematically marked on this plan receives at the same time lessons in applied prosody. The Exercise books which accompany this grammar are marked on the same plan.

An Appendix gives a conspectus of the new pronunciation, in which a rigid and uncompromising attitude on disputed points has been carefully avoided. The grammar may be used equally well by adherents of the 'new' and of the 'old' pronunciation.

The alphabetical list of Principal Parts is given in addition to the classified list in deference to the wishes of many teachers, among whom I may mention Mr. Colbeck of Harrow and Miss Beale of Cheltenham.

It only remains to acknowledge obligations. My cordial thanks are due to Dr. Reid of Cambridge, Prof. Seyffert of Berlin, and Mr. Haverfield of Lancing College, for valuable hints on my provisional issue (September, 1887): and last, but not least, to the Grammatical Society—a body called into existence by the desire to arrive at a grammatical *concordat*. From the discussions in this Society I have gained many practical suggestions, and become acquainted with the views of teachers representing very various kinds of schools. Among books I have learnt most as to method from Perthes, in his grammar and his great work on the Reform of Latin Teaching, and from the grammars of Holzweissig, Harre, Stegmann, and Lattmann: as to points of scholarship I have consulted the standard authorities in English and German, including the valuable work of Stolz and Schmalz, and have been enabled to correct many a traditional error.

E. A. S.

MASON COLLEGE, BIRMINGHAM,
*June*, 1889.

# CONTENTS.

|  | PAGE |
|---|---|
| Introduction | 1—2 |
| Accidence | 3—107 |
|   Parts of Speech | 3 |
|   Nouns | 3—24 |
|     Declension of Nouns | 4—19 |
|     Gender of Nouns | 20—24 |
|   Adjectives | 25—31 |
|     Declension of Adjectives | 25—28 |
|     Comparison of Adjectives | 29—31 |
|     Declension of Comparatives, etc. | 31 |
|   Numerals (Adjectives and Adverbs) | 32—34 |
|   Pronouns and Adjectives connected therewith | 35—42 |
|     Personal | 35 |
|     Possessive | 36 |
|     Demonstrative | 37—39 |
|     Interrogative and Indefinite | 39—40 |
|     Relative | 41 |
|     Definitive | 41—42 |
|   Adverbs | 42—43 |
|     Comparison of Adverbs | 43 |
|   Verbs | 44—107 |
|     The verb *sum* | 47—49 |
|     Conjugations I—IV, Active Voice | 50—57 |
|     Conjugations I—IV, Passive Voice | 58—65 |
|     Table of Endings | 66—67 |
|     Verbs of Conjugation III in *iō* | 71 |
|     Deponent verbs | 73—75 |
|     Anomalous verbs | 77—80 |
|     Defective verbs | 80—82 |
|     Impersonal verbs | 82—83 |
|     Classified List of Principal Parts | 83—97 |
|     Alphabetical List of Principal Parts | 97—107 |
| Prepositions | 108 |
| Appendix (Pronunciation of Latin) | 108—112 |

# INTRODUCTION.

## Alphabet.

**1** Latin spelling was mainly phonetic, *i.e.* according to sound (not etymological, like English). Words must, therefore, be pronounced as spelled (*e.g. regere*, three syllables).

The Latin alphabet in Cicero's time contained only twenty-three letters, including Y and Z, which were called 'Greek letters' and used only in spelling words borrowed from the Greek: it had no J, no V (as distinct from U), and no W. On the other hand, its I and its U had each *two sounds*, being used sometimes as vowels, sometimes as consonants.

Nowadays the letters J, V are mostly written for I, U, when used as consonants, *i.e.* when standing before a vowel at the beginning of a word or between two vowels, *e.g. jam, victor, major* (for *iam, uictor, maior*). The most modern texts, however, do not employ J.

Y is always a vowel, as in the English 'mystery,' 'my' (never like the *y* in 'you,' 'year').

K is used only in a very few words (*e.g. Kalendae*, Calends, the first day of the month), its work being mostly done by C.

Qu is pronounced Kw, as in English (not like qu- in French): -ngu- before a vowel is pronounced -ngw- (*e.g. anguis*, two syllables; but *arguō* is three syllables); su- is pronounced sw- in *suāvis, suādeō, suescō*, and in compounds and derivatives of these words; but in all other words as su- (*e.g. su-us, censu-it*).

Two vowels coming together and so pronounced as to form one syllable are called a diphthong [δι-, φθόγγος, double sound]. The vowels *ae, oe,* and *au* are diphthongs (*e.g. mensae, moenia, aufert*), except where the contrary is indicated (*e.g. āēr, poēta*); the vowels *ui, ei, eu* are generally to be pronounced as two syllables (*e.g. fuī, meī, meum, eundem*); where they form a diphthong, a ⌢ is printed over them in this grammar: *e.g. hui͡c, cu͡, hei͡, seu͡, neu͡, neu͡ter*.

On the pronunciation of Latin by the Romans see Appendix I.

## Quantity and Accent.

**2** By the **quantity** of a syllable is meant the amount of time which is taken to pronounce it. A long syllable is one on which the voice rests; a short syllable is one over which the voice passes quickly: *e.g.* in the English *unanimous* and the Latin *ūnanimus* the first syllable is long, the others are short. A long syllable is considered equal in time to two short ones.

## QUANTITY AND ACCENT.

**3** The vowels *a, e, i, o, u, y* are sometimes long by nature, sometimes short by nature; *i.e.* these symbols stand for either a long or a short sound. But diphthongs are always long by nature.

A **syllable** is long when it contains a **naturally short** vowel followed by two consonants or a double consonant (*x* or *z*), even when the one consonant stands at the end of a word and the other at the beginning of the next : *e.g.* **doc**tus (from *dŏceō* ), in**cip**e (from *ĭn-*), **dux** (from *dŭc-*), am**at nōs** (*amăt*). In such cases the naturally short vowel is said to be 'long by position.'

**4** A syllable containing a **naturally long** vowel (or diphthong) followed by two consonants or a double consonant, is doubly long : *e.g.*, **rēx** (gen. *rēg-is*), am**ās nōs**.

The letter *h* and the *u* in *qu* (§ 1) do not count as consonants; accordingly, the second syllable of *stomachus, colloquor, amat hostem* is short.

**5** A mute[1] (*p, b ; t, d ; c, g*) or *f*, followed by a liquid[1] (*l, r*) was not felt to make so much of a *block* in the word, and, therefore, does not always form a position.[2] The poets use words like *tenebrae, volucris, multiplex* with the middle syllable either short or long; but, of course, the mute and liquid cannot *make* the syllable short if the vowel is naturally long.

In this Grammar all **vowels long by nature, except when long by position also, are marked** (*ā, ē, ī, ō, ū, ȳ*); **vowels short by nature are not marked at all** (*a, e, i, o, u, y*), unless for some special reason, when they bear the sign ˘. The sign ≍ means 'generally long, but sometimes shortened'; the sign ≎ means 'generally short, but sometimes lengthened.'

**6** A vowel standing before another vowel or *h* in words of Latin origin is generally short : *omnia, vehor, pius, vidua* (but cf. § 56).

**7** By the **accent** of a syllable is meant the stress or pitch of voice by which it is made more prominent than other syllables of the word : *e.g. unánimus* has its accent on the second syllable.

In words of two syllables the accent is always (or with rare exceptions) on the first : *e.g. máter, páter, díscit.*

In words of three or more than three syllables, if the last vowel but one is long, either by nature or position, it is accented ; if short, the accent is on the last syllable but two : *e.g., amā́mus, amātúrus, honéstus ; pérfidus, hóminis, ténebrae* (or *tenébrae*).

**8** In having no words of more than one syllable accented on the last syllable (with rare exceptions), Latin differs from Greek and modern languages.

---

[1] On the meaning of the words 'mute' and 'liquid' see Appendix.
[2] When the liquid introduces the second part of a compound, the preceding syllable is always long, *e.g.* in *ab-ripiō* the first syllable is long by position.

## ACCIDENCE.

**9** Accidence is the part of Grammar which tells how words change their *form* according to the part which they play in the sentence.

The Parts of Speech in Latin may be divided into two classes :—

1. Those which admit of changes of form :—
    **Nouns, Adjectives, Pronouns.** These may be *declined*. Adjectives may be also *compared*.
    **Adverbs.** These may be *compared*.
    **Verbs.** These may be *conjugated*.
2. Those which do not admit of changes of form :—
    **Prepositions, Conjunctions, Interjections.**

## NOUNS.

**10** In Latin there are two numbers, and six cases in each: The Cases are :—

The Nominative
Vocative

Oblique Cases.
{ Accusative
Genitive, generally translated by '**of**' or the possessive ending '**s**.
Dative, generally translated by '**to**' or '**for**.'
Ablative { generally translated by {
 '**with**' (*gladiō*, with a sword);
 '**from**' (*Rōmā*, from Rome);
 '**by**' (*vī*, by force);
 '**in**' (*mense Maiō*, in the month of May).

In nouns denoting a person, the Abl. is, as a rule, preceded by a preposition: *ā poētā* '**by** (**from**) the poet.'

**11** These English prepositions are merely a rough way of translating the Latin cases, the exact meanings of which will be explained in the *Syntax*. It must be remembered that Latin too has many prepositions, which have the meanings 'to,' 'from,' 'with,' 'by,' etc.

The Vocative is the Case of Address, *e.g. Dīc, Marce Tullī*, Speak, Cicero. It should *not* as a rule be translated by 'O,' still less by 'Oh,' which is used to express emotion (= Latin *ō*).

**12** The Numbers are the Singular and the Plural:—

The Singular speaks of *one*.

The Plural speaks of *more than one*.

### THE FIVE DECLENSIONS.

**13** There are five declensions of Nouns (*i.e.* five ways of 'declining' them), to be known by the ending of the Genitive Singular (which may be found in the dictionary).

| Ending of Gen. Sing. | Declension. | Ending of Nom. Sing. |
|---|---|---|
| -ae | I | -a |
| -ī | II | -us, -um |
| -is | III | -s, -is, -ēs, -e |
| -ūs | IV | -us, -ū |
| -ēī (two syllables) | V | -ēs |

The endings of the various cases are added to the **trunk:** *i.e.* **that part of the noun which remains when the ending of the Genitive Singular is removed:**

Gen. Sing.: *mens-ae, domin-ī, vōc-is, grad-ūs, faci-ēī*.

Trunk: *mens-, domin-, vōc-, grad-, faci-*.

In many words of the 3rd Decl., and in several of the 2nd Decl., the Nom. Sing. has no special ending of its own (e.g. *dolor*, Trunk *dolōr-*; *puer*, Trunk *puer-*).

The trunk **conveys the meaning of the word;** the case-endings show the part which that meaning plays in the sentence.

**14** The 'Trunk,' as above defined, must not be confused with the **stem;** nor the '**Ending**' with the '**Inflection.**' Historically the various cases are formed by adding a suffix, called the inflection (literally 'bending') to the crude form of the word, called the Stem; but when the stem ends in a vowel, and the inflection begins with a vowel, the resulting contraction often makes it difficult to say where the stem leaves off and the suffix begins. Thus, for example, the Genitive Singular of *mensa* was formed from the stem *mensā-* + the inflection -*i*; but this form was then contracted into two syllables *mensae*, in which the inflection is no longer separable from the stem. Similarly the Genitive *domini* comes from *domino-* (stem) + *i* (inflection), *dominoi* being contracted to *domini*. It happens that all stems that end in a vowel exhibit that vowel in the Genitive Plural: mensĀ-rum, dominŌ-rum, civĪ-um, gradŪ-um, faciĒ-rum; and vowel-stems are sometimes said to belong to the A, the O, the I, the U, and the E Declension respectively. (The Third Declension also includes a number of stems that end in a consonant. When the stem ends in a consonant, it is identical with the 'trunk;' and the inflection with the 'ending.' In other cases the trunk is the stem *minus* its final vowel, and the ending is the inflection *plus* the final vowel of the stem.)

## General Rules for Case-Formation.

**15** The Vocative is of the same form as the Nominative, except in the Singular Number of words of the Second Declension in -*us*, and in some words of Greek origin.

All Nouns have the same form in the Dative and Ablative Plural.

Neuter Nouns have the same form for the Nominative, Vocative, and Accusative, both in Singular and Plural.

## Genders.

**16** Rules for gender will be given hereafter. Meanwhile let it be observed that all nouns denoting a person follow the law of **natural gender,** *i.e.* those denoting a **male person** are **masculine,** and those denoting a **female person** are **feminine.** The gender of such words, therefore, can be found out by the **meaning.**—The letter *m.* stands for *masculine, f.* for *feminine, n.* for *neuter, i.e. neither* masculine nor feminine.

## First Declension.

**17** Mensa *f.* 'table.'

| Singular | | | Plural | | |
|---|---|---|---|---|---|
| N., V. | mens-a | } table | mens-ae | } tables | |
| Ac. | mens-am | | mens-ās | | |
| G. | mens-ae | of a table | mens-ārum | of tables | |
| D. | mens-ae | to a table | mens-īs | to tables | |
| Ab. | mens-ā | with a table | mens-īs | with tables | |

Examples for Declension.

**18**
agricol-a,* husbandman
Agripp-a*, Agrippa
āl-a *f.* wing
barb-a *f.* beard
cēn-a *f.* dinner
cūr-a *f.* care

hōr-a *f.* hour
insul-a *f.* island
īr-a *f.* anger
naut-a*, sailor
poēt-a*, poet

port-a *f.* gate
rip-a *f.* bank
sagitt-a *f.* arrow
vi-a *f.* road
victōri-a *f.* victory

* For the genders of Nouns denoting persons see § 16.

### PECULIARITIES.

**19** *Fīlia*, daughter, and *dea*, goddess, form the Dat. and Abl. Plur. in *-ābus* (in order to distinguish these forms from the same cases of *fīlius*, son, *deus* God).

*Fīliīs et filī*ābus, 'for (ā, from) sons and daughters.'
*Dīs et de*ābus, 'for (ā, from) gods and goddesses.'

Note the gen. sing. in the phrase *pater familiās*, 'father of the household' (otherwise the word *familia* has the regular genitive *familiae*).

### GREEK NOUNS ACCORDING TO THE FIRST DECLENSION.

**20** Greek Nouns corresponding to Latin Nouns of the 1st Decl. are declined in the Plural like Latin Nouns; in the Singular as follows (Italics indicate Latin endings) :—

| *Epitomē f.* ' *epitome.*' | *Aenēās* ( *proper name*). | *Spartiātēs,* ' *Spartan.*' |
|---|---|---|
| N. epitom-ē | Aenē-ās | Spartiāt-ēs |
| V. epitom-ē | Aenē-ā | Spartiāt-a(-ē) |
| Ac. epitom-ēn | Aenē-ān(-*am*) | Spartiāt-ēn(-*am*) |
| G. epitom-ēs | Aenē-*ae* | Spartiāt-*ae* |
| D. epitom-*ae* | Aenē-*ae* | Spartiāt-*ae* |
| Ab. epitom-ē | Aenē-ā | Spartiāt-ā(-ē) |

## Second Declension.

**Dominus** *m.* 'owner'  **Bellum** *n.* 'war'

| | Singular | Plural | | Singular | Plural |
|---|---|---|---|---|---|
| N. | domin-us | } domin-ī | N. | } bell-um | bell-a |
| V. | domin-e | | V. | | |
| Ac. | domin-um | domin-ōs | Ac. | | |
| G. | domin-ī | domin-ōrum | G. | bell-ī | bell-ōrum |
| D. | } domin-ō | domin-īs | D. | } bell-ō | bell-īs |
| Ab. | | | Ab. | | |

Examples for Declension.

ann-us *m.* year  
hort-us *m.* garden  
numer-us *m.* number  
serv-us, slave  
gladi-us *m.* sword } cf. §§ 27,  
soci-us, partner } 28.

dōn-um *n.* gift  
regn-um *n.* kingdom  
tect-um *n.* roof  
templ-um *n.* temple  
vin-um *n.* wine  
ingeni-um *n.* genius (§ 28)

In several nouns whose trunks end in *r*, the endings of the Nominative and Vocative Singular (-*us*, -*e*,) have disappeared. Trunks in *r* preceded by a consonant insert an *e* in the Nom. Sing. for convenience of pronunciation.

**Liber** *m.* 'book.'  **Puer** *m.* 'boy.'

| | Singular | Plural | | Singular | Plural |
|---|---|---|---|---|---|
| N., V. | liber | libr-ī | N., V. | puer | puer-ī |
| Ac. | libr-um | libr-ōs | Ac. | puer-um | puer-ōs |
| G. | libr-ī | libr-ōrum | G. | puer-ī | puer-ōrum |
| D. | } libr-ō | libr-īs | D. | } puer-ō | puer-īs |
| Ab. | | | Ab. | | |

Examples for declension like 'liber.'

ag*er* (agr-) *m.* field  
ap*er* (apr-) *m.* boar  
cap*er* (capr-) *m.* goat  
fab*er* (fabr-), smith  
magist*er* (magistr-), teacher

Four nouns are declined like 'puer.'

gener, son-in-law  
līberī *m.* (*pl.*) children (properly 'free ones,' from *līber*, adj., 'free,' as opposed to *vernae*, 'young slaves').  
socer, father-in-law  
vesper[1] *m.* evening

---

[1] No Plur.; Abl. Sing. vespere or vesperī (originally Locative : § 59).

## SECOND DECLENSION.

### PECULIARITIES.

**25** Note the words vir *m.* 'man'; deus *m.* 'God.'

|       | Singular | Plural              |       | Singular | Plural              |
|-------|----------|---------------------|-------|----------|---------------------|
| N., V.| vir      | vir-ī               | N., V.| de-us    | de-ī, *or* dī       |
| Ac.   | vir-um   | vir-ōs              | Ac.   | de-um    | de-ōs               |
| G.    | vir-ī    | vir-ōrum *or* vir-um| G.    | de-ī     | de-ōrum *or* de-um  |
| D. Ab.| vir-ō    | vir-īs              | D. Ab.| de-ō     | de-īs, *or* dīs     |

**26** *Vulgus,* n. common people, *vīrus,* n. poison, and *pelagus,* n. sea, form (in the singular) the Nom., Voc., and Acc. in -us, the Gen. in -ī, the Dat. and Abl. in -ō. They have no plural. For the Acc. *vulg-um* see § 73.

*Locus,* m. place, has two plurals: *locī* = places in books, topics (in the poets sometimes = localities), *loca* = localities.

*Jūgerum,* n. acre, forms pl. *jūgera, iūgerum, iūgeribus* (according to the 3rd Decl.).

**27** Proper names of Roman origin in *-ius* (which were more constantly on men's lips than the Vocatives of other words in *-ius,* and consequently got shortened) form the Vocative in -ī:

Vergilī, Gāī, Pompēī from *Vergilius, Gāius, Pompēius.* So too *filius;* e.g., *mi filī,* my son!

Contrast such vocatives as *Dēlie, Dārie,* from *Dēlius* (a Greek name), *Dārius* (a Persian name).

☞ The Vocative of other words in *-ius* (*e.g. gladius, socius*) is not found.

**28** The Gen. Sing. of all words in *-ius, -ium* is more correctly written -ī than -iī: so *ingenī* for *ingeniī, filī* for *filiī, Vergilī carmina,* the poems of Virgil.

Note that the Gen. Plur. of weights, measures, money, etc., ends in -*um* (instead of *-orum*); *modium* (*modius,* m. peck), *nummum* (*nummus,* m. silver coin), *sestertium* (*sestertius,* m. sesterce, a Roman coin worth 2¼d.).

## Third Declension.

**29** The nouns of this declension fall into three principal classes :—

I. Those which form the Ablative Singular in -e, and the Genitive Plural in -um; Neuters of this class form the Nominative Plural in -a. (See §§ 30, 32.)

II. Those which form the Ablative Singular in -e, and the Genitive Plural in -ium. (See §§ 35, 37.)

III. Those Neuters which form the Ablative Singular in -i, the Genitive Plural in -ium, and the Nominative Plural in -ia. (See § 39.)

**30** CLASS I.—**Characteristic endings: -e, -um, (-a).**

(a) Nominative Singular = Trunk (ending in one consonant) + s.

Vox f. 'voice.'

| | Singular | | Plural |
|---|---|---|---|
| N., V. | vox (= vōc-s) | N., V. | vōc-ēs |
| Ac. | vōc-em | Ac. | |
| G. | vōc-is | G. | vōc-um |
| D. | vōc-ī | D. | vōc-ibus |
| Ab. | vōc-e | Ab. | |

Examples for Declension.

**31**
pax (pāc-) f. peace
rex (rēg-), king
jūdex (jūdic-)[1], judge
rādix (rādīc-) f. root
dux (duc-), leader
trabs (trab-) f. beam
plebs (plēb-) f. commons
princeps (princip-),[1] chief
hiems (hiem-) f. winter
*Trunks ending in* d *or* t, *and one in* n *drop their final letter before* s *of the Nom. Sing. ; e.g.*
aetās (aetāt-) f. age
voluptās (voluptāt-) f. pleasure

vās (vad-) surety
quiēs (quiēt-) f. quiet
hērēs (hērēd-), heir
mīles (mīlit-)[1], soldier
obses (obsid-)[1], hostage
sacerdōs (sacerdōt-), priest(ess)
custōs (custōd-), guardian
juventūs (juventūt-), f. youth
virtūs (virtūt-) f. virtue
palūs (palūd-) f. swamp
pecus (pecud-) f. animal
laus (laud-) f. praise

sanguis (sanguin-), m. blood

[1] In this and many other trunks in ic-, ip-, it-, id-, the last vowel is changed in the Nom. Sing.

## THIRD DECLENSION.

**32** (*b*) Nominative Singular formed without any addition to the trunk.

MASCULINES AND FEMININES.
Dolor *m.* 'pain.'

|       | Singular | Plural |
|-------|----------|--------|
| N.,V. | dolor    | dolōr-ēs |
| Ac.   | dolōr-em |        |
| G.    | dolōr-is | dolōr-um |
| D.    | dolōr-ī  | dolōr-ibus |
| Ab.   | dolōr-e  |        |

NEUTERS.
Nōmen *n.* 'name.'

|       | Singular | Plural |
|-------|----------|--------|
| N.,V. | nōmen    | nōmin-a |
| Ac.   |          |        |
| G.    | nōmin-is | nōmin-um |
| D.    | nōmin-ī  | nōmin-ibus |
| Ab.   | nōmin-e  |        |

**33** Mōs *m.* 'custom.'

|       | Singular | Plural |
|-------|----------|--------|
| N.,V. | mōs      | mōr-ēs |
| Ac.   | mōr-em   |        |
| G.    | mōr-is   | mōr-um |
| D.    | mōr-ī    | mōr-ibus |
| Ab.   | mōr-e    |        |

Genus *n.* 'race.'

|       | Singular | Plural |
|-------|----------|--------|
| N.,V. | genus    | gener-a |
| Ac.   |          |        |
| G.    | gener-is | gener-um |
| D.    | gener-ī  | gener-ibus |
| Ab.   | gener-e  |        |

The final *s* of *mōs, genus* is not an *addition* to the trunk: the trunk originally ended in *s*, and this letter was changed to *r* in the oblique cases (*mōr-em* for *mōs-em*, etc.).

## THIRD DECLENSION.

**34**

### Like 'DOLOR.'

Caesar (Caesar-), Caesar
lār (lar-), household god
anser (anser-) *m.* goose (gander)
carcer (carcer-) *m.* prison
mulier (mulier-), woman
amor (amōr-) *m.* love
conditor (conditōr-), founder
imperātor (imperātōr-), general
labor (labōr-) *m.* labour
nitor (nitōr-) *m.* brilliance
pastor (pastōr-), shepherd
prōditor (prōditōr-), traitor
rector (rectōr-), guider
victor (victōr-), conqueror

*A few words drop an e in the oblique cases:—*

pater (gen. patr-is), father
māter (gen. mātr-is), mother
frāter (gen. frātr-is), brother

Model for Declension.

|        | Singular | Plural |
|--------|----------|--------|
| N., V. | pater    | patr-ēs |
| Ac.    | patr-em  |         |
| G.     | patr-is  | patr-um |
| D.     | patr-ī   | patr-ibus |
| Ab.    | patr-e   |         |

*For the Gen. Plur. of* imber, linter, ūter, venter, *see* § 42.

sāl (sal-) *m.* salt
sōl (sōl-) *m.* sun
consul (consul-), consul
tubicen (tubicin-), trumpeter
tībīcen (tībicin-), piper

**Words which drop the final n of the trunk.**

(i) *Nom. in* ō, iō: *Trunk in* ōn-, iōn-
(*about* 280 *words*).

Cicerō (Cicerōn-), Cicero
latrō (latrōn-), robber
leō (leōn-) *m.* lion
sermō (sermōn-) *m.* talk
centuriō (centuriōn-), centurion
conjūrātiō(conjūrātiōn-)*f.* conspiracy
dominātiō (dominātiōn-)*f.* dominion
exercitātiō (exercitātiōn-)*f.* practice
legiō (legiōn-) *f.* legion

Examples for Declension.

ōrātiō (ōrātiōn-) *f.* speech
petītiō (petītiōn-) *f.* candidature
ratiō (ratiōn-) *f.* calculation
regiō (regiōn-) *f.* region, direction
(ii) *Nom. in* ō; *Trunk in* in-: *three words:* cf. nēmō (nēmin-), § 63.
Apollō (Apollin-), Apollo
homō (homin-) *m.* man, human being
turbō (turbin-) *m.* whirlwind
(iii) *Nom. in* dō, gō; *Trunk in* din-, gin- (*about* 90 *words*).
fortitūdō (fortitūdin-) *f.* courage
magnitūdō (magnitūdin-) *f.* size
grandō (grandin-) *f.* hail
cālīgō (cālīgin-) *f.* mist
imāgō (imāgin-) *f.* image
orīgō (orīgin-) *f.* origin
virgō (virgin-), maiden

### Like 'NŌMEN.'

crīmen (crīmin-) *n.* charge
lūmen (lūmin-) *n.* light

bacchar (bacchar-) *n.* berry
jubar (jubar-) *n.* radiance
nectar (nectar-) *n.* nectar
cadāver (cadāver-) *n.* corpse
rōbur (rōbor-) *n.* oak wood
fulgur (fulgur-) *n.* lightning
caput (capit-) *n.* head

### Like 'MŌS.'

flōs (flōr-) *m.* flower
cinis (ciner-) *m.* ashes
pulvis (pulver-) *m.* dust
Venus (Vener-), Venus

### Like 'GENUS.'

mūnus (mūner-) *n.* gift
vulnus (vulner-) *n.* wound
onus (oner-) *n.* burden
opus (oper-) *n.* work
scelus (sceler-) *n.* crime
decus (decor-) *n.* grace
pecus (pecor-) *n.* flock
frigus (frigor-) *n.* cold
tempus (tempor-) *n.* time
crūs (crūr-) *n.* leg
jūs (jūr-) *n.* right
rūs (rūr-) *n.* country
ōs (ōr-) *n.* mouth

} Note short vowel of trunk

## THIRD DECLENSION.

**35** CLASS II.—**Characteristic endings : -e, -ium.**

(*a*) Nominative Singular = Trunk (ending in two consonants) + s.

Urbs *f.* 'city.'

| Singular | | Plural | |
|---|---|---|---|
| N., V. | urb-s | N., V. | urb-ēs |
| Ac. | urb-em | Ac. | |
| G. | urb-is | G. | urb-ium |
| D. | urb-ī | D. | urb-ibus |
| Ab. | urb-e | Ab. | |

**36** Examples for Declension.

nox (noct-) *f.* night
arx (arc-) *f.* citadel
ars (art-) *f.* art
adulescens (adulescent-), young man
cohors (cohort-) *f.* cohort

cliens (client-), client
frons (front-) *f.* forehead
frons (frond-) *f.* leafy branch
gens (gent-) *f.* clan
mors (mort-) *f.* death

**37** (*b*) Nominative Singular = Trunk + -is or -ēs.

Cīvis *m.* or *f.* 'citizen.'    Nūbēs *f.* 'cloud.'

| Singular | Plural | | Singular | Plural | |
|---|---|---|---|---|---|
| N., V. | cīv-is | cīv-ēs | N., V. | nūb-ēs | nūb-ēs |
| Ac. | cīv-em | | Ac. | nūb-em | |
| G. | cīv-is | cīv-ium | G. | nūb-is | nūb-ium |
| D. | cīv-ī | cīv-ibus | D. | nūb-ī | nūb-ibus |
| Ab. | cīv-e | | Ab. | nūb-e | |

Like 'cīvis'

**38** av-is *f.* bird
class-is *f.* fleet
pest-is *f.* plague
rat-is *f.* bark (boat)
vest-is *f.* garment
vīt-is *f.* vine
amn-is *m.* river
ax-is *m.* pole (sky)
coll-is *m.* hill
ens-is *m.* sword

fīn-is *m.* boundary (*sometimes f.*)
aedīl-is, ædile
rīvāl-is, rival
host-is, enemy

Like 'nūbēs
aed-ēs *f.* temple (*Plur.* = 'house')
caed-ēs *f.* slaughter
clād-ēs *f.* disaster
mōl-ēs *f.* mass
prōl-ēs *f.* offspring (*no Plur.*)

## THIRD DECLENSION.

**39** CLASS III.—**Characteristic endings: -ī, -ium, -ia.**
Nominative Singular = Trunk + e. (In some words this e is dropped).
The words of Class III are **all neuter**, and have one form for the Dative and Ablative Singular. The trunks mostly end in *āl-, īl-, ār-*.[1]

Ovīle *n.* 'sheepfold.'

|  | Singular | Plural |
|---|---|---|
| N., V., Ac. | ovīl-e | ovīl-ia |
| G. | ovīl-is | ovīl-ium |
| D., Ab. | ovīl-ī | ovīl-ibus |

**40** Examples for Declension.

ancīl-e, oval shield
cubīl-e, bed, lair
hastīl-e, spear-shaft
sedīl-e, seat

fōcāl-e, comforter (for the neck)
penetrāl-e, sanctuary
animal (animāl-), animal
tribūnal (tribūnāl-), platform

vectigal (vectigāl-), tax
calcar (calcār-), spur
exemplar (exemplār-), copy
 (24 *Neut. in* al, āl-; ar, ār-)

*So also are declined the words:—*
**mar-e**, sea
**rēt-e**, net
**conclāv-e**, chamber

**41** The words with trunks in *āl-, īl-, ār-* were originally adjectives; thus *ovīle*, 'sheepfold,' meant 'of or belonging to sheep'; *fōcāle*, 'neck-cloth,' meant 'of or belonging to the throat' [*faucēs* = throat] : so, too, *animal* (orig. *animāle*) meant 'living (thing),' *calcar* (orig. *calcāre*) 'of or belonging to the heel' [*calx*]. Some of the nouns of Class II (*b*) were originally masculine adjectives, *e.g. aedīlis*, an officer 'connected with buildings' [*aedēs*], *rivālis*, a person 'belonging to the same stream [*rivus*] as another,' hence 'rival': see too § 46.

### PECULIARITIES.
#### *Genitive Plural.*

**42** (i) The **Genitive Plural ends in -ium** in the following words belonging to Class I :—

vis (vīr-) *f.* violence (§§ 44, 46, 49), *Plur.* strength
līs (līt-) *f.* dispute
faucēs, *Plur.* (fauc-) *f.* jaws
nix (niv-) *f.* snow

Penātēs, *Plur.* (Penāt-), household gods
optimātēs, *Plur.* (optimāt-), aristocrats

---
[1] Contrast the trunks in ăl-, ăr- of Class I. *b* (§ 34).

and also in tribal names ending in -*is* (-*ĭtis*), -*ās* (-*ātis*), *e.g.*, *Samnīs* (*Samnīt-*), Samnite; *Quirītēs*, Romans (in the capacity of civilians); *Arpīnās* (*Arpīnāt-*), inhabitant of Arpinum.

**vīrium, lītium, faucium, Penātium,
nivium, Samnītium, Quirītium, optimātium.**

Also in the following words (belonging to Class I. *b*):—

imber (imbr-) *m.* rain | ūter (ūtr-) *m.* skin-bag
linter (lintr-) *f.* wherry | venter (ventr-) *m.* belly

**imbrium, lintrium, ūtrium, ventrium.**

Mūs (mūr-) *m.* mouse, forms mūrium in the best MSS.
Cīvitās (cīvitāt-) *f.* state, forms both cīvitātum and cīvitātium.

(ii) The **Genitive Plural ends in -um** in the following words belonging to Class II:—

canis (can-), *m.* or *f.*, dog | juvenis (juven-), young man

Parens (parent-), parent, forms both parentium and (more commonly) parentum. Horace uses both forms.

**parentum, canum, juvenum.**

Compare also § 34 (**patrum, mātrum, frātrum**) and § 49 (**senum**)

A few other words belonging to Class II (*b*) are occasionally found with
43 Gen. Plur. in -*um*, as *apis* (*ap-*) f. bee; *volucris* (*volucr-*) f. (properly fem. of Adj. *volucer*, § 99, used as a Noun) bird; *mensis* (*mens-*) m. month; *sēdēs* (*sēd-*) f. seat; *vātēs* (*vāt-*) seer.

*Accusative Singular.*

The **Accusative Singular ends in -im** in the following words
44 in -*is* belonging to Class II (*b*):—

(*a*) Names of places and rivers, *e.g. Tiberis* m. Tiber, *Neāpolis* f. Naples, *Ligeris* m. Loire, *Charybdis* f. a whirlpool off Sicily, etc.

(*b*) The words *vīs* f. violence, *secūris* f. axe, *sitis* f. thirst, *puppis* f. stern (of a vessel).

**Tiberim, vim, Neāpolim; secūrim, sitim, puppim.**

A few words in -*is* belonging to Class II (*b*) have two forms of the Acc.
45 Sing., one in -*im*, the other in -*em*, as *turris* f. tower, *febris* f. fever.

*Ablative Singular.*

The **Ablative Singular ends in -ī:**—

46 (*a*) in all words that form the Acc. Sing. in -*im*;
(*b*) in the names of months in -*is* and -*er*, and some other words, originally adjectives, which have come to be used as nouns,

*e.g. Aprīlis* (originally *mensis aprīlis*, 'the month of opening'—RUSKIN), m. ; *September* (*Septembr-*), m. ; *aequālis*, contemporary; *familiāris*, familiar friend ; *affīnis*, relative ; *nātālis* (originally *diēs nātālis*) m. birthday.

**Tiberī, vī, Neāpolī ; secūrī, sitī, puppī :**
**Aprīlī and Septembrī ; add aequālī and nātālī.**

**47** A few other words in *-is* belonging to Class II (*b*) occasionally form the Abl. Sing. in *-ī* ; thus we have :—

| *turr-e* | from | *ign-e* | from | *nāv-e* | from |
|---|---|---|---|---|---|
| *turr-ī* | *turris*, tower. | *ign-ī* | *ignis*, fire. | *nāv-ī* | *nāvis*, ship. |

*Accusative Plural.*

**48** An **Accusative Plural in -īs** is found as a by-form (for *-ēs*) in all Masc. and Fem. words (Nouns and Adjs.) that form the Genitive Plural in *-ium*;

*e.g. angustōs* { *fīnēs* / *fīnīs*    *duās* { *partēs* / *partīs*

**IRREGULAR NOUNS.**

**49**

| Juppiter 'Jove'<br>[Juppiter = Jov- pater<br>'Father Jove'] | | jūsjūrandum *n.* 'oath'<br>(a compound word with no Plural, the last part acc. to II Decl.) | Sāturnālia *n.* 'festival of Saturn' |
|---|---|---|---|
| | *Singular* | *Singular* | *Plural* |
| N.,V. | Juppiter | } jūsjūrand-**um** | } Sāturnāl-**ia** |
| Ac. | Jov-**em** | | |
| G. | Jov-**is** | jūrisjūrand-**ī** | Sāturnāli-**ōrum**[1] |
| D. | Jov-**ī** | jūrījūrand-**ō** | } Sāturnāl-**ibus** |
| Ab. | Jov-**e** | jūrejūrand-**ō** | |

| bōs *m.* or *f.* 'ox' | | sūs *m.* or *f.* 'pig' | |
|---|---|---|---|
| *Singular* | *Plural* | *Singular* | *Plural* |
| | | | |

| | | | | |
|---|---|---|---|---|
| N.,V. | bōs | } bov-**ēs** | sūs | } su-**ēs** |
| Ac. | bov-**em** | | su-**em** | |
| G. | bov-**is** | bo-**um** | su-**is** | su-**um** |
| D. | bov-**ī** | } bū**bus** or | su-**ī** | } sŭ**bus** |
| Ab. | bov-**e** | bō**bus** | su-**e** | |

[1] As if from Nominative Singular *Sāturnālium* (2nd Declension); but sometimes the Genitive Plural is formed regularly (*Sāturnālium*, from trunk *Sāturnāl-*).

## THIRD DECLENSION.

| vīs *f.*(*Sing.* 'violence,' *Pl.* 'strength') | | | vās *n.* ' vessel,' ' dish ' | |
|---|---|---|---|---|
| | *Singular* | *Plural* | *Singular* | *Plural* |
| N., V. | vīs | } vir-ēs | } vās | } vās-a |
| Ac. | vim | | | |
| G. | — | vir-ium | vās-is | vās-ōrum |
| D. | — | }vir-ibus | vās-ī | } vās-īs |
| Ab. | vī | | vās-e | |

| os *n.* ' bone ' | | | senex ' old man ' | |
|---|---|---|---|---|
| | *Singular* | *Plural* | *Singular* | *Plural* |
| N., V. | } os | } oss-a | sen-ex | } sen-ēs |
| Ac. | | | sen-em | |
| G. | oss-is | oss-ium | sen-is | sen-um |
| D. | oss-ī | } oss-ibus | sen-ī | } sen-ibus |
| Ab. | oss-e | | sen-e | |

Observe the trunk of the following words :—

iter (**itiner-**) *n.* journey

jecur {jecor- / jecinor- / jocinor-} *n.* liver

supellex (**supellectil-**) *f.* furniture

### GREEK NOUNS ACCORDING TO THE 3RD DECLENSION.

**50** Greek Nouns corresponding to Latin Nouns of the 3rd Decl. are for the most part declined (in prose) like Latin words : the following are some of their chief peculiarities :—

(1) The words *āēr* (ἀήρ), m., lower air, atmosphere, *aethēr* (αἰθήρ), m., upper air, sky, and occasionally other words like *crātēr* (κρατήρ), m., mixing bowl, *Salamis*, Salamis, form their Accus. in *-a* (*āer-a*, *aether-a*, *crātēr-a*, *Salamīn-a*).

(2) The Neuters in *-ma* end in *-is* (for *-ibus*) in the Dat. and Abl. Plur., *e.g.* poēma (Trunk *poēmat-*), poem, forms *poēmat-is*.

(3) Proper names in *-ēs* sometimes form the Gen. in *-ī*, as well as in *is ; e.g. Sōcratēs* forms *Sōcratis* and *Sōcratī*.

(4) Feminine Proper Names in *-ō* (*-ώ*) form the Gen. in *-ūs* (*-οῦς*), the other cases in *-ō ; e.g.* Nom., Voc., Acc., Dat., Abl. *Dīd-ō,* Gen. *Dīd-ūs.*

(5) Proper Names with Nom. in *-eus* (*-εύς*) form Voc. in *eu*, but in other cases are treated like words of the 2nd Decl. in *e-us* (two syllables. *e.g. de-us*) : thus *Orpheus* forms Acc. *Orphe-um*, Gen. *Orphe-ī*. Dat. and Abl. *Orphe-ō*. The Greek hero Ulysses ('Ὀδυσσεύς) appears as *Ulix-ēs*, Gen. sometimes *Ulix-is*, sometimes *Ulixe-ī* (Horace).

(6) Many Proper Names omit the nominatival *s* in the Voc. ; *e.g. Daphnis* (V. *Daphni*), *Cotys* (V. *Coty*), *Atlās* (V. *Atlā*), *Orpheus* (V. *Orpheu*).

## Fourth Declension.
Gradus *m.* 'step.'  Cornū *n.* 'horn.'

**51**

|  | Singular | Plural |  | Singular | Plural |
|---|---|---|---|---|---|
| N.,V. | grad-us | } grad-ūs | N.,V. | } corn-ū | corn-ua |
| Ac. | grad-um | | Ac. | | |
| G. | grad-ūs | grad-uum | G. | corn-ūs | corn-uum |
| D. | grad-uī | } grad-ibus | D. | corn-uī | } corn-ibus |
| Ab. | grad-ū | | Ab. | corn-ū | |

**52**

Examples for Declension.

MASCULINES, like 'gradus.'
curr-us, chariot
exercit-us, army
fluct-us, wave
mōt-us, movement
ūs-us, use

FEMININES, like 'gradus.'
an-us, old woman
īd-ūs (Plur.), Ides (a day of the month)
man-us, hand
portic-us, portico

NEUTERS, like 'cornū.'
gen-ū, knee
ver-ū, spit

PECULIARITIES.

**53** The Dative Singular sometimes ends in -*ū* (for -*uī*), especially in neuters. The Dative and Ablative Plural of words of two syllables in *cus*—

*e.g.* acus *f.* needle | lacus *m.* lake, tank
arcus *m.* bow | quercus *f.* oak tree

and also of *tribus f.* tribe, end in -*ubus* (for -*ibus*): *e.g. lacubus, tribubus; artus* limb, and *partus* birth, form *artubus, partubus* (to distinguish these forms from cases of *ars* art, *pars* part).

**54** *Domus* f. 'house' follows the 2nd Decl. in certain cases :—

|  | Singular | Plural |
|---|---|---|
| N.,V. | dom-us | dom-ūs |
| Ac. | dom-um | dom-ōs |
| G. | dom-ūs | dom-uum *or* dom-ōrum |
| D. | dom-uī | } dom-ibus |
| Ab. | dom-ō | |

Note the form
dom-ī 'at home'(Locative, § 59).

With verbs of motion—

dom-um = 'homewards, home.'
dom-ō = 'from home.'

## Fifth Declension.

**55**

Faciēs *f*. 'face,' 'form.'

| Singular | | Plural | |
|---|---|---|---|
| N., V. | faci-ēs | N., V. | faci-ēs |
| Ac. | faci-em | Ac. | faci-ēs |
| G. | faci-ēī | G. | faci-ērum |
| D. | faci-ēī | D. | faci-ēbus |
| Ab. | faci-ē | Ab. | faci-ēbus |

**56**  In the Gen. and Dat. Sing. the *e* is generally regarded as long when a vowel precedes it (*faci-ēi, di-ēi*), short when a consonant precedes it (*fid-ĕi, sp-ĕi, r-ĕi*). But there is some doubt about the quantity.

**57**  The ending -*ei* is often contracted into -*ē, e.g. aci-ēi* into *aci-ē, fid-ei* into *fid-ē;* sometimes into -*i, e.g. plēb-ei* (from the archaic Nom. *plēbēs* f. commons) into *plēb-i* (which is also the Dat. of *plebs*, § 31).

**58**                         Examples for Declension.

    aci-ēs *f*. edge                                 fid-ēs *f*. fidelity
    di-ēs [1] *m.* day (in Sing. sometimes *f*. = time)    r-ēs [1] *f*. thing
    pernici-ēs *f*. ruin                            sp-ēs *f*. hope
    speci-ēs *f*. show, class (species)

Rēs publica (rēspublica) *f*. 'the common interest,' 'the state, is declined in both its parts (*publica* is an Adjective, cf. § 92). The Plural *rēs publicae* means 'states' or 'constitutions,' and must not be used in the sense of 'common interests,' 'public affairs.'

| Singular | | | Plural | | |
|---|---|---|---|---|---|
| N., V. | r-ēs | public-a | N., V. | r-ēs | public-ae |
| Ac. | r-em | public-am | Ac. | r-ēs | public-ās |
| G. | r-eī | public-ae | G. | r-ērum | public-ārum |
| D. | r-eī | public-ae | D. | r-ēbus | public-īs |
| Ab. | r-ē | public-ā | Ab. | r-ēbus | public-īs |

Each of these forms may be written as one word, *e.g. rērumpublicārum, rēbuspublicīs.*

---

[1] *Diēs* and *rēs* are the only words of this Declension in which all cases of the Plural are actually found in classical authors.

## REMARKS ON THE FIVE DECLENSIONS.

**59** In very early times, before the beginning of Latin literature, all nouns possessed two additional cases, the **Locative in** -ī, denoting the place *at* which, and the **Instrumental**, denoting the instrument *with* which, or the means *by* which, an action was performed. The Instrumental disappeared entirely as a separate case (the Ablative being used instead), but the Locative survived in a few common nouns :—

*mīlitĭ*-ae (for *mīlitiā-ī*), on service, from *mīliti-a* 1st Decl.
*hum*-ī, on the ground, from *hum-us* 2nd Decl.
*rūr*-ī, in the country, from *rūs* 3rd Decl.
*dom*-ī, at home, from *dom-us* 2nd and 4th Decl. (§ 54);

and it is also regularly used to express 'place at which' with the names of towns and small islands—

*Rōm*-ae, at Rome  *Carthāgin*-e, at Carthage
*Corinth*-ī, at Corinth  *Syrăcūs*-īs (Nom. -*ae* Plur.), at Syracuse

☞ In Singulars of 1st and 2nd Decl., Locative = Genitive : In Singulars of 3rd Decl. (except *rūs*) and all Plurals, Locative = Ablative.

**60** Some words are **used only in the Plural** :—

*arma*, arms              *idūs*, Ides              *mānēs*, spirits of the dead
*divitiae*, riches        *insidiae*, ambush        *minae*, threats
*epulae*, banquet         *liberī*, children        *moenia*, walls (of a town)
*fasti*, calendar (§ 86)  *mājōrēs*, ancestors      *tenebrae*, darkness

**61** Some words **change their meaning in the Plural** :—

*aedēs* (sing.), shrine      *cōpia*, abundance              *littera*, letter (of alphabet)
*aedēs* (plur.), house       *cōpiae*, troops                *litterae*, letter (=*epistola*)
*auxilium*, aid              *finis*, end                    *opem*, help (*Ops*, a goddess)
*auxilia*, allied forces     *fīnēs*, territory              *opēs*, wealth, resources
*castrum*, fort              *impedīmentum*, hindrance       *vis*, violence
*castra*, camp               *impedīmenta*, baggage          *vīrēs*, strength

**62** Some words **suffer a slight change of meaning in the Plural**: *ars*, art, *artēs*, works of art (pictures, statues, etc.); *ira*, anger, *irae*, angry passions; *virtūs*, manliness, *virtūtēs*, virtues ; *Caesar*, Caesar, *Caesarēs*, men like Caesar (emperors, the family of the Caesars); *frūmentum*, corn, *frūmenta*, different kinds of corn ; *aes*, bronze, *aera*, articles made of bronze (bronzes).

**63** Some words are **defective in case**, *i.e.* do not form all their cases :—

No Plur. { *nēmō* m., f. has Acc. and Dat. Sing., *nēminem* and *nēminī*; the Gen. and Abl. are supplied by *nullīus, nullō* (from *nullus*). *nihil* n. (Nom. and Acc. ; originally *nihil-um*) has *nihilī, nihilō* but *nullīus reī, nullī reī, nullā rē* are generally used instead.

*vīs* f. has in the Sing. Acc. *vim*, Abl. *vī*, but no Gen. or Dat. (§ 49).

## Gender of Nouns.

☞ In the following paragraphs on Gender—
Masculine Nouns are printed in **Clarendon** type;
Feminine „ „ *Italics;*
Neuter „ „ SMALL CAPITALS.

**64** To discover the gender of a Noun, ask—
I. DOES THE NOUN DENOTE A PERSON? If so, it follows the law of NATURAL GENDER, *i.e.*—
Nouns that denote a Male are Masculine;
Nouns that denote a Female are Feminine.

EXAMPLES.

| | |
|---|---|
| **pater**, father | *māter*, mother |
| **agricola**, husbandman | *mulier*, woman |
| **Herculēs**, Hercules | *anus*, old woman |
| **Cupīdō**, the god Cupid | *Venus*, the goddess Venus |

Nouns that may denote either a Male or a Female are said to be Common, *i.e.* either Masc. or Fem. according to their application.

*e.g.* **sacerdōs**, priest   *sacerdōs*, priestess
   **conjux**, husband   *conjux*, wife

Note that the word **homō**, 'human being,' is always Masc.

But *homō* may be predicated of a feminine subject; *e.g.* of Cicero's daughter, Tullia, '*quoniam homō nāta fuerat*,' 'since she had been born a human being' (Fam. iv. 5. 4).

EXCEPTIONS.

**65** 1. This rule does not apply to Collective Nouns, *e.g.*:—
*plebs*   the commons
VULGUS   the vulgar

2. The following Nouns, which properly denote sexless things, obey the law of gender by ending (§ 70):—
*opera*   workman, properly 'work,' generally in Plur.: *operae*, 'a gang of workmen'
*cōpiae*   troops, Plural of *cōpia*, abundance
*dēliciae*   darling, properly 'delights' (Plur.)
*excubiae*   watch, properly 'watchings' (Plur.)
AUXILIA   auxiliary forces, Plural of *auxilium*, aid
MANCIPIUM   slave, properly 'chattel'

**66** II. DOES THE NOUN DENOTE A SEXLESS THING? If so, its gender may be known either by its ending, according to rules about to be given, or in a few classes of words by its meaning.

## GENDER BY MEANING.

**67** (*a*) Names of Rivers, Winds, and Months are Masculine; for rivers and winds were thought of as gods, and the month-names are really Adjectives, agreeing with **mensis** (Masc.) understood. Thus **Tiberis** Tiber, **Garumna** Garonne, **Albula** Albula, **Boreas** North Wind, **November, Aprilis**, are Masc. ; so, too, **Hadria** the Adriatic Sea (improbus **Hadria**, the violent Adriatic, *Horace*). But *Matrona* Marne, *Allia*, *Styx*, *Lēthē*, and a few others, follow the law of gender by ending, and are therefore Fem. (§ 71).

**68** (*b*) Names of Cities, Countries, Islands, and nouns denoting Trees are Feminine (corresponding to the gender of *urbs, terra, insula, arbor*) ; thus, dēlenda est *Carthāgō*. Captīva *Corinthus*. *Aegyptus, Cyprus, Dēlos, fāgus* beech, *īlex* (*ilic-*) holm-oak, *quercus* oak-tree.

**69** But the plural city-names in *-i* follow the law of gender by ending, and are therefore Masc. (§ 72), as **Delphī, Veiī** ; so too the names of cities in *-um, -e*, which are Neut. (§§ 72, 78), as TARENTUM, ĪLIUM, PRAENESTE.

## GENDER BY ENDING.

**70** The first rule applies to nouns which are indeclinable, and therefore cannot be said to belong to any of the five Declensions:—

Indeclinable nouns are Neuter, *e.g.* FĀS the lawful, NEFĀS the unlawful, sin. So too are all infinitives (verb-nouns) *e.g.* dulcE et decōrUM est prō patriā MORĪ, 'it is sweet and seemly to die for one's country' (*Horace*), and all other indeclinable parts of speech when *used as nouns, e.g.* VALĒ 'farewell' (imperative of valēre, 'to be in health :' suprēmUM VALĒ, 'a last farewell ').

The following rules apply to all nouns which are declinable (disregarding a few that are of comparatively rare occurrence):—

**71** Nouns denoting sexless things of 1st Decl. are Fem., *e.g. rosa* bell*a* 'a pretty rose,' *mensa* rotund*a* 'a round table.'

**72** Nouns denoting sexless things of 2nd Decl.

in **-us, -er** (Plur. **-ī**) are Masc.

in **-UM**, are Neut.

EXCEPTIONS.

**73**

| *Feminine.* | *Neuter.* |
|---|---|
| *humus* ārid*a*, the dry ground | VULGUS profānUM, the profane throng |
| *alvus* inglōri*a*, the ignoble belly | VĪRUS ātrUM, black poison |
| *colus* plēn*a*, a full distaff | PELAGUS apertUM, the open sea |

But **vulgus** is sometimes Masc., with Acc. Sing. vulgUM (*Caesar, Virgil*).

## GENDER OF NOUNS.

**Rules for Nouns denoting sexless things of 3rd Decl.**
☞ For exceptions see the opposite page.

**74** 1. Those which form the Nom. Sing. by adding -*s*, -*is*, or -*ēs* to the Trunk [Class I (*a*), Class II (*a*), Class II (*b*)] are **Feminine**:

e.g. *dap-s* (dap-) feast
*fax* (fac-) torch
*incū-s* (incūd-) anvil
*stirp-s* (stirp-) root
*falx* (falc-) scythe
*clāv-is*, key
*cut-is*, skin
*fid-is*, harpstring

*for-is*, door
*lu-ēs*, pestilence
*nāv-is*, ship

*mercē-s* (mercēd-) pay
*sege-s* (seget-) cornfield
*dō-s* (dōt-) dowry: cf. § 31
*gen-s* (gent-) clan
*men-s* (ment-) mind: cf. § 36
*secūr-is*, axe
*sēd-ēs*, seat
*turr-is*, tower: cf. § 38

**75** 2. Those which form the Nom. Sing. without any addition to the Trunk [Class I (*b*)] are, as a rule, **Masculine**:

e.g. **color** (colōr-) colour
**agger** (agger-) mound
**carcer** (carcer-) prison
**carbō** (carbōn-) coal

**tēmō** (tēmōn-) carriage-pole
**turbō** (turbin-) whirlwind
**cinis** (ciner-) ash
**pulvis** (pulver-) dust : cf. § 34

☞ The chief Masc. endings in Nom. Sing. are or, er.

but

**76 Feminine** if Nom. Sing. ends in *dō*, *gō*, or *iō* [1]—

e.g. *arundō* (arundin-) reed
*imāgō* (imāgin-) image

*contiō* (contiōn-) assembly :
cf. § 34 (i), (iii)

**77 Neuter** if Nom. Sing. ends in AR, UR, EN, US—

e.g. FAR (farr-) spelt
JUBAR (jubar-) radiance
MURMUR (murmur-) murmur

NŪMEN (nūmin-) divine will
GENUS (gener-) race

**78** 3. Those which form the Nom. Sing. by adding -*e* (dropped in some words) to the Trunk [Class III] are **Neuter**:

e.g. MONĪL-E, necklace
BIDENTAL, place struck by lightning (where a sheep, *bidens*, was sacrificed).

So Plural names of festivals
LIBERĀL-IA, LUPERCĀL-IA
(§ 49).
Cf. § 40

---

[1] Most of the Feminines in *iō* are derived from the Supine Trunk of verbs, e.g. *ōrāt-iō* (ōrātiōn-) speech [from ōrāt-, ōrāre, 'to plead '], *petīt-iō* (petītiōn-) candidature, request [from petīt-, petere, 'to ask '], *cōgitāt-iō* (cōgitātiōn-) thought, reflexion [from cōgitāt-, cōgitāre, 'to think ']. But some are from Present Trunks, e.g. *oblīv-iō* (oblīviōn-) forgetfulness [oblīviscī, 'to forget '], *obsid-iō* (obsidiōn-) siege [from obsidēre, 'to besiege '], *reg-iō* (regiōn-) direction [from regere, 'to direct '].—A few are used in a Collective sense, e.g. *leg-iō* (legiōn-) legion (lit. 'levying') [from legere, 'to pick '], *nāt-iō* (nātiōn-) tribe (lit. 'breed') [from nāt-, nascī, 'to be born '].

## GENDER OF NOUNS. 23

### EXCEPTIONS TO RULE 1: § 74.

**79** (*a*) Words in -ex, -icis } are Masc.
    -es, -itis }

*e.g.* apex (apic-) tip
caespes (caespit-) turf
cortex (cortic-) bark
gurges (gurgit-) whirlpool
latex (latic-) water

poples (poplit-) back of the knee
pūmex (pūmic-) pumice
stipes (stipit-) stock
vortex (vortic-) whirl
For *ilex* (ilic-) see § 68.

(*b*) The following 13 words are also Masc. :—
lapis, sanguis, fons and mons
rudens, torrens, dens and pons
grex and calix, fornix, pēs
(grāta *compēs*¹), pariēs

stone, blood, fount, mountain,
cable, torrent, tooth, bridge,
flock, cup, arch, foot,
house-wall.

**80** (*c*) Sixteen masculines are fīn-ĕs
(fīn-is hic or haec), and crīn-ĕs
amn-is, ax-is, orb-is, ens-is
pān-is, fasc-is, post-is, mens-is
fūn-is, fust-is, foll-is
ign-is, ungu-is, coll-is

territory (boundaries) *Plur.*
end (*Sing.* m. or f.), hair (generally Plur.)
river, sky, circle, sword
bread, bundle, post, month
rope, cudgel, leather bag (Plur. 'bellows')
fire, nail, hill

☞ In six of these words the trunk ends in n.

### EXCEPTIONS TO RULE 2: §§ 75-77.

**81**                         NEUTERS.

(The Plural ending, where it exists, is given in italics to mark the gender.)

CORD-*A*, VĒR, LĀC, CAPIT-*A*
ŪBER-*A*, PAPĀVER-*A*
MELL-*A*, FEL, ITINER-*A*
VERBER-*A*, CADĀVER-*A*
ŌR-*A*, OSS-*A*, AEQUOR-*A*
AER-*A*, VĀS-*A*, MARMOR-*A*.

heart (COR), spring, milk, head (CAPUT)
teat, poppy
honey (MEL), gall, journey (ITER § 49)
lash, corpse
mouth (OS), bone (§ 49), sea
bronze (AES), vessel (§ 49), marble.

**82**                         FEMININES.

*vīs* and *tellūs*, *arbor* nūda
*linter* cava, *carō* crūda

violence, land, naked tree
hollow boat, raw flesh.

**83**                         MASCULINES.

Several nouns ending in -*iō* and denoting material things, like pug-iō (pugiōn-) dagger, scīp-iō (scīpiōn-) staff, are Masc. So also are the three words or-dŏ (ordin-) row, mar-gŏ (margin-) brink, car-dŏ (cardin-) hinge.

Primus ordŏ, margine
extrēmō, versō cardine.

First row, on the extreme brink (Abl.),
on the hinge being turned (Abl.).

The word **pecten** (pectin-) comb is also Masc. (cf § 77); argūtus pecten, a shrill comb (here a weaver's instrument).

---

¹ That is: *Compēs* (though it comes from pēs) is Fem., *grātā compede vinctus*, bound with a pleasing fetter (*Horace*).

## GENDER OF NOUNS.

**84.** Nouns denoting sexless things of 4th Decl.
in -us are Masc.
in -ū are Neut.

### EXCEPTIONS.

**85.**
*tribus* urbāna, a city tribe
*acus* acūta, a sharp needle
*porticus* publica, a public walk

*idūs* (Plur.) Martiae, the Ides of March
*domus* mea, my house
*manus* impia, unholy hand (or band)

*Quercus* 'oak tree' is Fem. according to § 68.

*tribus, acus, porticus,
idūs, domus, manus.*

**86.** Nouns denoting sexless things of the 5th Decl. are Feminine, except diēs, which is Masc. in the sense 'day' (Sing. or Plur.), Fem. in the sense 'time' (only Sing.); thus **diēs** festus, 'a feast day,' **diēs** fastī (nefastī), 'lawful (unlawful) days,' damnōsa *diēs*, 'ruinous time' (*Horace*).

*Diēs* Fem. Sing. sometimes means 'day,' *e.g. certā diē* 'on a fixed day,' *post eam diem, ex eā diē,* etc.

**87.** III. DOES THE NOUN DENOTE AN ANIMAL? If so, it is either **Masc.** or **Fem.** according to the laws of gender by ending.

☞ No nouns denoting kinds of animals are Neuter.

**88.** 1. The word ANIMAL itself is Neut. (properly 'living thing,' § 41); so, too, is JŪMENTUM, beast of burden.

2. Nouns which, according to the rule of grammatical gender, we should expect to be Neut. are Masc., *e.g.*

vultur (vultur-) vulture
lepus (lepor-) hare

mūs (mūr-) mouse

3. The following (which would be Fem. according to rule) are Masc. :—

pisc-is fish
verm-is worm

All those in *iō, e.g.*
pāpiliō (pāpiliōn-) butterfly

**89.** 4. There are a few nouns denoting Male Animals which follow the law of natural gender, *e.g.* **verrēs** boar, **ariēs** ram, **vervex** wether. And others are Common ; *e.g.*—

| | | | |
|---|---|---|---|
| bōs | bull | bōs | cow |
| canis | dog | canis | bitch |
| anser | gander | anser | goose |
| sūs | boar | sūs | sow |

## ADJECTIVES.

**90** Some adjectives have separate endings for each of the three genders (Adjectives of Three endings); others have one form for the masc. and fem., and a second for the neut. (Adjectives of Two endings): a few have only one form for all three genders (Adjectives of One ending).

**91** CLASS I (according to 1st and 2nd Declensions of Nouns).

Adjectives of Class I have three endings; in the masc and neut. they follow the 2nd Decl. of nouns; in the fem. they follow the 1st Decl. of nouns.

**92** Dūrus, 'hard.' ☞ Nouns, §§ 21, 17.

| SING. | Masc. | Fem. | Neut. |
|---|---|---|---|
| N. | dūr-us | dūr-a | dūr-um |
| V. | dūr-e | dūr-a | dūr-um |
| Ac. | dūr-um | dūr-am | dūr-um |
| G. | dūr-ī | dūr-ae | dūr-ī |
| D. | dūr-ō | dūr-ae | dūr-ō |
| Ab. | dūr-ō | dūr-ā | dūr-ō |
| PLUR. | | | |
| N., V. | dūr-ī | dūr-ae | dūr-a |
| Ac. | dūr-ōs | dūr-ās | dūr-a |
| G. | dūr-ōrum | dūr-ārum | dūr-ōrum |
| D., Ab. | dūr-īs | dūr-īs | dūr-īs |

EXAMPLES FOR DECLENSION.

bon-us, -a, -um  good
cār-us, -a, -um  dear
mal-us, -a, -um  bad
magn-us, -a, -um  great

parv-us, -a, -um  small
pi-us, -a, -um  pious
tant-us, -a, -um  so great
quant-us, -a, -um  how great

So all Verb-adjectives in -us, *e.g.* cantāt-us, -a, -um 'sung' (§§ 201, 202)

## 93. Pulcher, 'beautiful.' ☞ Nouns, § 23 (e inserted).

| SING. | Masc. | Fem. | Neut. |
|---|---|---|---|
| N., V. | pulche*r* | pulchr-a | pulchr-um |
| Ac. | pulchr-um | pulchr-am | pulchr-um |
|  | etc. | etc. | etc. |

| PLUR. | | | |
|---|---|---|---|
| N., V. | pulchr-ī | pulchr-ae | pulchr-a |
| Ac. | pulchr-ōs | pulchr-ās | pulchr-a |
|  | etc. | etc. | etc. |

### Examples for Declension.

aege*r*, aegr-a, aegr-um sick
āte*r*, ātr-a, ātr-um black
crēbe*r*, crēbr-a, crēbr-um frequent
dexte*r*, dextr-a, dextr-um right
(or decl. like liber)

intege*r*, integr-a, integr-um whole
mace*r*, macr-a, macr-um lean
nige*r*, nigr-a, nigr-um black
sace*r*, sacr-a, sacr-um sacred
siniste*r*, sinistr-a, sinistr-um left

## 94. Liber, 'free.' ☞ Nouns, § 23 (e of trunk).

| SING. | Masc. | Fem. | Neut. |
|---|---|---|---|
| N., V. | liber | liber-a | liber-um |
| Ac. | liber-um | liber-am | liber-um |
|  | etc. | etc. | etc. |

| PLUR. | | | |
|---|---|---|---|
| N., V. | liber-ī | liber-ae | liber-a |
| Ac. | liber-ōs | liber-ās | liber-a |
|  | etc. | etc. | etc. |

### So Decline the Five Words

asper, -a, -um rough
lacer, -a, -um torn
miser, -a, -um wretched

prosper, -a, -um prosperous
tener, -a, -um tender

and all compounds in -fer and -ger:—
 pestifer, -a, -um plague-bringing | corniger, -a, -um horn-wearing
Note the word satur, -a, -um sated.

## DECLENSION OF ADJECTIVES.

**95** CLASS II (according to 3rd Declension of Nouns). Most adjectives of this class are of Two endings; but some are of Three, and some of only One ending.

**Characteristic Endings: -ī, -ium, -ia.**

**96** Tristis, 'sad.' ☞ Nouns, §§ 37, 39: note the Abl. Sing.

| SING. | Masc. and Fem. | Neut. | PLUR. M. and F. | Neut. |
|---|---|---|---|---|
| N., V. | trist-is | trist-e | trist-ēs | trist-ia |
| Ac. | trist-em | trist-e | | |
| G. | trist-is | | trist-ium | |
| D., Ab. | trist-ī | | trist-ibus | |

**97** Ācer, 'keen.'

| SING. | Masc. | Fem. | Neut. | PLUR. M. and F. | Neut. |
|---|---|---|---|---|---|
| N., V. | ācer | ācr-is | ācr-e | ācr-ēs | ācr-ia |
| Ac. | ācr-em | ācr-em | ācr-e | | |
| G. | ācr-is | | | ācr-ium | |
| D., Ab. | ācr-ī | | | ācr-ibus | |

**98** Prūdens, 'wise.' ☞ Nouns, § 35: note the Abl. Sing.

| SING. | Masc. and Fem. | Neut. | PLUR. M. and F. | Neut. |
|---|---|---|---|---|
| N., V. | prūden-s | | prūdent-ēs | prūdent-ia |
| Ac. | prūdent-em | prūden-s | | |
| G. | prūdent-is | | prūdent-ium | |
| D., Ab. | prūdent-ī | | prūdent-ibus | |

**99** EXAMPLES FOR DECLENSION.

Like tristis.
- facil-is — easy
- fort-is — brave
- moll-is — soft
- simil-is — like
- turp-is — base
- tāl-is — such
- quāl-is — of what kind

Like ācer.
- alacer (-cr-) lively
- celeber (-br-) famous
- equester (-tr-) equestrian
- puter (-tr-) rotten
- salūber (-br-) healthy
  (Also salūbris m. and f.)
- volucer (-cr-) winged

Like prūdens.
- ingens (-nt-) huge
- ēlegans (-nt-) elegant
- recens (-nt-) fresh
- audax (-āc-) bold
- fēlix (-ic-) lucky
- pār (par-) equal
- anceps (-cipit-) two-headed

## PECULIARITIES IN CLASS II.

**100** Present Participles are declined like *prūdens*, except that Abl. Sing. ends in *e*: *Tarquiniō regnante*, Tarquin being king = when Tarquin was king. (Characteristic endings: -e, -ium, -ia.)

**101** When used as Attributes, Present Participles, as a rule, follow *prūdens* in the Abl. Sing. as well as in other cases: *e.g.*, *in flūmine currentī*, in a running stream.

**102** Adjectives and participles in *-ns* occasionally form a Gen. Plur. in *-um* (only in the poets): *recentum, amantum, bellantum, silentum, venientum*.

**103** Some adjectives of one ending, whose trunk ends in a short syllable, take the characteristic endings -e, -um (the Neuter is not used). Most of these words were originally nouns.

caelebs (caelib-) bachelor
compos (compot-) having control
dēses (dēsid-) idle (idler)
dives (dīvit-)[1] rich
particeps (particip-) sharer

pauper (pauper-) poor
princeps (princip-) chieftain
pūbes (pūber-) adult
sospes (sospit-) saved
superstes (superstit-) survivor

**104** The following take -ī, -um :—

inops (inop-) helpless | memor (memor-) mindful

**105** *Vetus* (Trunk *veter-*) is an exceptional adjective of one ending, with the characteristic forms veter-e, veter-um, veter-a.

**106** *Celer, celeris, celere* (Trunk *celer-*) swift, keeps the *e* of the trunk throughout. It forms a Gen. Plur. *celerum*, which is used as a noun in the phrase *tribūnus celerum*, officer of the cavalry.

**107** *Plūs* n. (Trunk *plūr-*) more, the Comparative of *multus*, forms in the Plural

Nom., Acc. plūr-*ēs* plūr-*a*
Gen. plūr-*ium*
Dat., Abl. plūr-*ibus*

The singular *plūs* is used as a noun (*plūs vīnī*, more wine): Gen. *plūris*, at a higher price. The Dat. and Abl. are wanting.

**108** A few Adjectives are indeclinable, as *tot* so many, *quot* how many, *nēquam*, good for nothing, *frūgī*, worth one's salt [orig. a dat. of *frux* (*frūg-*)—lit. 'for fruit,' *i.e.* 'for use,' 'serviceable'].

---

[1] Gen. Plur. dīvĭt*um*, but dīt*ium* (with long syllable before ending).

## Comparison of Adjectives.

**109** The Comparative is formed by adding to the trunk of the Positive the endings *-ior* masc. and fem., *-ius* neut.

The Superlative is formed by adding to the trunk of the Positive the endings *-issimus* masc., *-issima* fem., *-issimum* neut.

|  | | Comparative | Superlative |
|---|---|---|---|
| *Trunk of Positive* | dūr-<br>hard | dūr-ior (-ius)<br>harder, too hard,<br>somewhat hard | dūr-issim-us (-a, -um)<br>hardest, very hard |
|  | trist- | trist-ior (-ius) | trist-issim-us (-a, -um) |
|  | fēlic- | fēlic-ior (-ius) | fēlic-issim-us (-a, -um) |

So too many Participles (Present and Perfect):
amant- *loving*   amant-ior(-ius) amant-issim-us(-a, -um)
remōt- *removed*  remōt-ior (-ius) remōt-issim-us(-a, -um)

**110** The Superlative of some adjectives is formed by doubling the last letter of the trunk of the Positive, and adding *-imus, -ima, -imum*. These are:—

1. Adjs. which end in the Nom. Sing. Masc. in *-er*, e.g.—
pulcher (pulchr-), *fine*   pulchr-ior   pulcher-r-imus
niger (nigr-), *black*      nigr-ior     niger-r-imus
līber (liber-), *free*      liber-ior    liber-r-imus
ācer (ācr-), *keen*         ācr-ior      ācer-r-imus
salūb<sup>.</sup>r or -bris, *healthy* salūbr-ior   salūber-r-imus
celer (celer-), *swift*     celer-ior    celer-r-imus

So also vetus (veter-), *old* (§§ 105, 119) veter-r-imus

Observe that the *e* of the Nominative, whether inserted (§ 93) or belonging to the trunk (§ 94), always appears in the Superlative.

**111** 2. The four adjectives :—
facil-is, gracil-is
simil-is, humil-is

i.e. *easy, slender, like, lowly,* together with the compounds dif-ficil-is, *hard,* dis-simil-is, *unlike;* thus :—

    facil-is        facil-ior        facil-l-imus

Other adjectives in *-il-is* form the Superlative regularly: ūtil-is, *useful,* ūtil-ior, ūtil-issimus.

**112**                    PECULIARITIES.

Irregular Comparison :—

| | | |
|---|---|---|
| bonus, *good* | mel-ior, -ius, *better* | opt-imus, *best* |
| malus, *bad* | pē-jor, -jus, *worse* | pess-imus, *worst* |
| magnus, *great* | mā-jor, -jus, *greater* | max-imus, *greatest* |
| parvus, *small* | min-or, -us, *less* | min-imus, *least* |
| multus, *much* | ——, plūs, *more* | plūr-imus, *most* |

(Trunk plūr- § 107.)

**113**    Note the Comp. and Superl. of the indeclinable adjectives :—

| | | |
|---|---|---|
| frūgī (§ 108) | frūgāl-ior | frūgāl-issimus |
| nēqu-am (§ 108) | nēqu-ior | nēqu-issimus |
| pot-is, *able* | pot-ior | pot-issimus |

**114**    The following are irregular in the Superlative :—

| | | | | | |
|---|---|---|---|---|---|
| (exter-us | *outer)* | exter-ior | *outer* | extrēmus / ext-imus | } *outmost* |
| infer-us | *lower* | infer-ior | *lower* | imus / inf-imus | } *lowest* |
| (poster-us | *later)* | poster-ior | *later* | post-umus / postrēmus | } *last* |
| super-us | *upper* | super-ior | *upper* | suprēmus / summus | } *highest* |

**115**    A few Comparatives and Superlatives have no corresponding positive adjective; but *adverbs* or *prepositions* of similar origin exist in some cases :—

| | | | | | | |
|---|---|---|---|---|---|---|
| | | dēter-ior | *worse* | | dēter-r-imus | *worst* |
| | | ōc-ior | *swifter* | | ōc-issimus | *swiftest* |
| intus | *within* | inter-ior | *inner* | | int-imus | *inmost* |
| prae | *before* | pr-ior | *former* | | prīmus | *first* |
| prop-e | *near* | prop-ior | *nearer* | | prox-imus | *nearest* |
| ultr-ā | *beyond* | ulter-ior | *farther* | | ult-imus | *farthest* |

## COMPARISON OF ADJECTIVES.

**116** The following Comparatives correspond to nouns:—
juven-is *young man*  jūn-ior  (nātū minimus)
sen-ex *old man*  sen-ior  (nātū maximus)

**117** Trunks ending in -*dic*-, -*fic*-, -*vol*- form the Comparative and Superlative from old participial trunks in -*dīcent*-, -*ficent*-, -*volent*- :
male-dic-us *abusive*  male-dīcent-ior  male-dīcent-issimus
magni-fic-us *noble*  magni-ficent-ior  magni-ficent-issimus
bene-vol-us *well-wishing*  bene-volent-ior  bene-volent-issimus

**118** Adjectives in -*us* preceded by a vowel making a separate syllable (-*e-us*, -*i-us*, -*u-us*) generally form the Comparative and Superlative by means of the adverbs *magis*, more, and *maximē*, most.
 pi-us *pious*  magis pius  maximē pius
Contrast antīqu-us *old*  antīqu-ior  antīqu-issimus

**119** The words *dīversus, falsus, novus, sacer, vetus* have no Comparative; the words *diūturnus, insignis, longinquus, propinquus*, together with most adjectives in -*bilis*, have no Superlative, though neither Comparative nor Superlative is excluded by the *meaning* of these adjectives. *Ēgregius* 'excellent' forms *ēgregior* (contrary to rule in § 118).

### DECLENSION OF COMPARATIVES AND SUPERLATIVES.

**120** Comparatives are declined like nouns of 3rd Decl., with the characteristic endings -e, -um, -a.
 Tristior, 'sadder.'  Dūrior, 'harder,' etc.
The neut. *tristius* is simply another form of the trunk *tristiōr*-, which originally ended in -*iōs* (cf. corpus, Trunk corpor-, § 33).

| SING. | Masc. and Fem. | Neut. | PLUR. M. and F. | Neut. |
|---|---|---|---|---|
| N., V. | tristior | tristius | tristiōr-ēs | tristiōr-a |
| Ac. | tristiōr-em | tristius | | |
| G. | tristiōr-is | | tristiōr-um | |
| D. | tristiōr-ī | | tristiōr-ibus | |
| Ab. | tristiōr-e | | | |

EXAMPLES FOR DECLENSION.
(ācer)  ācriōr-  keener  (locuplēs)  locuplētiōr-  richer
(prūdens)  prūdentiōr-  wiser  (sollers)  sollertiōr-  cleverer

**121** Superlatives are declined like *dūr*-us, -a, -um (§ 92).

## NUMERAL ADJECTIVES.

| | | CARDINAL<br>answering the question 'how many?'<br>(*quot?*) | ORDINAL<br>answering the question 'which in<br>numerical order?' (*quotus?*) |
|---|---|---|---|
| 1 | I | ūn-us, -a, -um | prīm-us, -a, -um |
| 2 | II | du-o, -ae, -o | secund-us, -a, -um (alter) |
| 3 | III | trēs, tria | terti-us, -a, -um |
| 4 | IV | quattuor | quart-us, -a, -um |
| 5 | V | quinque | quint-us, -a, -um |
| 6 | VI | sex | sext-us, -a, -um |
| 7 | VII | septem | septim-us, -a, -um |
| 8 | VIII | octō | octāv-us, -a, -um |
| 9 | IX | novem | nōn-us, -a, -um |
| 10 | X | decem | decim-us, -a, -um |
| 11 | XI | undecim | undecim-us, -a, -um |
| 12 | XII | duodecim | duodecim-us, -a, -um |
| 13 | XIII | tredecim | terti-us decim-us, etc. |
| 14 | XIV | quattuordecim | quart-us decim-us, etc. |
| 15 | XV | quindecim | quint-us decim-us, etc. |
| 16 | XVI | sēdecim | sext-us decim-us, etc. |
| 17 | XVII | septendecim | septim-us decim-us, etc. |
| 18 | XVIII | duodēvīgintī | duodēvīcēsim-us, etc. |
| 19 | XIX | undēvīgintī | undēvīcēsim-us, etc. |
| 20 | XX | vīgintī | vīcēsim-us, etc. |
| 30 | XXX | trīgintā | trīcēsim-us, etc. |
| 40 | XL | quadrāgintā | quadrāgēsim-us, etc. |
| 50 | L | quinquāgintā | quinquāgēsim-us, etc. |
| 60 | LX | sexāgintā | sexāgēsim-us, etc. |
| 70 | LXX | septuāgintā | septuāgēsim-us, etc. |
| 80 | LXXX | octōgintā | octōgēsim-us, etc. |
| 90 | XC | nōnāgintā | nōnāgēsim-us, etc. |
| 100 | C | centum | centēsim-us, etc. |
| 200 | CC | ducent-ī, -ae, -a | ducentēsim-us, etc. |
| 300 | CCC | trecent-ī, -ae, -a | trecentēsim-us, etc. |
| 400 | CCCC | quadringent-ī, -ae, -a | quadringentēsim-us, etc. |
| 500 | D(IƆ) | quingent-ī, -ae, -a | quingentēsim-us, etc. |
| 600 | DC | sexcent-ī, -ae, -a | sexcentēsim-us, etc. |
| 700 | DCC | septingent-ī, -ae, -a | septingentēsim-us, etc. |
| 800 | DCCC | octingent-ī, -ae, -a | octingentēsim-us, etc. |
| 900 | DCCCC | nongent-ī, -ae, -a | nongentēsim-us, etc. |
| 1,000 | M(CIƆ) | mille | millēsim-us, etc. |
| 2,000 | MM | duo mīlia | bis millēsim-us, etc. |
| 100,000 | CCCIƆƆƆ | centum mīlia | centiēs millēsim-us, etc. |
| 1,000,000 | CCCCIƆƆƆƆ | deciēs centēna mīlia | deciēs centiēs millēsim-us |

## NUMERALS.

| DISTRIBUTIVE<br>answering the question 'how many a-piece?' (*quotēni?*) | NUMERAL ADVERBS<br>answering the question 'how many times?' (*quotiens?*) |
|---|---|
| singul-ī, -ae, -a | semel |
| bīn-ī, -ae, -a | bis |
| tern-ī (trīn-ī), -ae, -a | ter |
| quatern-ī, -ae, -a | quater |
| quīn-ī, -ae, -a | quinquiēs |
| sēn-ī, -ae, -a | sexiēs |
| septēn-ī, -ae, -a | septiēs |
| octōn-ī, -ae, -a | octiēs |
| novēn-ī, -ae, -a | noviēs |
| dēn-ī, -ae, -a | deciēs |
| undēn-ī, -ae, -a | undeciēs |
| duodēn-ī, -ae, -a | duodeciēs |
| tern-ī dēn-ī, -ae, -a | ter deciēs |
| quatern-ī dēn-ī, -ae, -a | quater deciēs |
| quīn-ī dēn-ī, -ae, -a | quinquiēs deciēs |
| sēn-ī dēn-ī, -ae, -a | sexiēs deciēs |
| septēn-ī dēn-ī, -ae, -a | septiēs deciēs |
| duodēvīcēn-ī, -ae, -a | duodēvīciēs |
| undēvīcēn-ī, -ae, -a | undēvīciēs |
| vīcēn-ī, -ae, -a | vīciēs |
| trīcēn-ī, -ae, -a | trīciēs |
| quadrāgēn-ī, -ae, -a | quadrāgiēs |
| quinquāgēn-ī, -ae, -a | quinquāgiēs |
| sexāgēn-ī, -ae, -a | sexāgiēs |
| septuāgēn-ī, -ae, -a | septuāgiēs |
| octōgēn-ī, -ae, -a | octōgiēs |
| nōnāgēn-ī, -ae, -a | nōnāgiēs |
| centēnī, -ae, -a | centiēs |
| ducēn-ī, -ae, -a | ducentiēs |
| trecēn-ī, -ae, -a | trecentiēs |
| quadringēn-ī, -ae, -a | quadringentiēs |
| quingēn-ī, -ae, -a | quingentiēs |
| sexcēn-ī, -ae, -a | sexcentiēs |
| septingēn-ī, -ae, -a | septingentiēs |
| octingēn-ī, -ae, -a | octingentiēs |
| nongēn-ī, -ae, -a | nongentiēs |
| singula mīlia | mīliēs |
| bīna mīlia | bis mīliēs |
| centēna mīlia | centiēs mīliēs |
| deciēs centēna mīlia | deciēs centiēs mīliēs |

## NUMERALS.

**123** The Numeral Adjectives with endings marked in thicker type are declinable. (For decl. of *ūn-us*, see § 165.)

|  | Masc. | Fem. | Neut. |  | Masc. Fem. | Neut. |
|---|---|---|---|---|---|---|
| N. | du-o | -ae | -o | N. | tr-ēs | tr-ia |
| Ac. | du-o *or* du-ōs | -ās | -o | Ac. | tr-ēs | tr-ia |
| G. | du-ōrum | -ārum | -ōrum | G. | tr-ium | |
| D.,Ab. | du-ōbus | -ābus | -ōbus | D.,Ab. | tr-ibus | |

The Gen. Plur. of *duo* is sometimes du-**um**: cf. § 28.

Like *duo* is declined *amb-ō, -ae, -ō*, 'both.'

*Duo* and *ambō* are relics of an old dual number, *i.e.* a number that speaks of two.

**124** *Mille* is an indeclinable adjective in the Singular, e.g. *mille hominēs*, 1,000 men; but the Plural *mīlia* 'thousands,' is a neuter noun (3rd Decl., Class III), and is followed by the Genitive:—

duo mīl-**ia** homin-**um**, two thousands of men, *i.e.* 2,000 men.

**125** In Compound numbers from 20 to 100, place the smaller first (with *et*); above 100, place the larger number first (without *et*).

| Cardinal. | Ordinal. |
|---|---|
| 21 ūn**us** et vīgintī | ūnus et vīcēsimus. |
| 22 duo et vīgintī, *etc.* | alter et vīcēsimus, *etc.* |
| 101 centum ūnus, *etc.* | centēsimus prīmus, *etc.* |
| 133 centum trīgintā trēs | centēsimus trīcēsimus tertius |

**126** The Distributive Numerals are sometimes used in the sense of Cardinals (i) with Plurals that have Singular meaning, e.g. *bīnae litterae*, two epistles, *trīna castra*, three camps (but ' one epistle ' is *ūnae litterae*, cf. § 167); (ii) in multiplication, e.g. *bis bīna sunt quattuor*, $2 \times 2 = 4$; *deciēs* cent**ēna** *mīlia*, 1,000,000 (i.e. 100,000 × 10); *vīciēs* cent**ēna** *mīlia*, 2,000,000, etc.; (iii) *bīnī* = a pair, e.g. *bīnī scyphī*, a pair of cups.

**127** Note the adverbs—
    *prīmum* for the first time | *tertium* for the third time
    *iterum* for the second time | *postrēmum* for the last time
    (*semel, bis* = once, twice: *prīmō*, at first, *postrēmō*, at last).

## PRONOUNS AND ADJECTIVES CONNECTED THEREWITH.

### Personal Pronouns.

#### FIRST PERSON.

**128**

| | Singular | | REFLEXIVE | | Plural | | REFLEXIVE |
|---|---|---|---|---|---|---|---|
| N. | ego | *I* | | nōs | *we* | | |
| Ac. | mē | *me* | *myself* | nōs | *us* | | *ourselves* |
| G. | meī | *of me* | *of* ⎫ | nostrī[1] | *of us* | *of* ⎫ | |
| D. | mihĭ | *to me* | *to* ⎬ *myself* | nōbīs | *to us* | *to* ⎬ *ourselves* | |
| Ab. | mē | *from me* | *from* ⎭ | nōbīs | *from us* | *from* ⎭ | |

#### SECOND PERSON.

**129**

| | Singular | | REFLEXIVE | | Plural | | REFLEXIVE |
|---|---|---|---|---|---|---|---|
| N., V. | tū | *thou (you)* | | vōs | *you* | | |
| Ac. | tē | *thee* | *thyself* | vōs | *you* | | *yourselves* |
| G. | tuī | *of thee* | *of* ⎫ | vestrī[1] | *of you* | *of* ⎫ | |
| D. | tibĭ | *to thee* | *to* ⎬ *thyself* | vōbīs | *to you* | *to* ⎬ *yourselves* | |
| Ab. | tē | *from thee* | *from* ⎭ | vōbīs | *from you* | *from* ⎭ | |

**130** ☞ The Plural of formal intercourse, which is so common in modern languages, is not known in Latin. Thus strangers say to one another *tū*; *vōs* is used only when more than one person is addressed.

---

[1] Second forms of Gen. Plur. (cf. Syntax, §§ 558, 559):—
nostrum, *of us* (e.g. *multī nostrum, omnium nostrum*)
vestrum, *of you* (e.g. *duo vestrum*).

## Third Person.

**131**

|  | Singular | Plural | REFLEXIVE<br>Sing. and Plur. |
|---|---|---|---|
|  | he she it | they | himself, herself,<br>itself; themselves |
| N. | is   ea   id | eī (iī)   eae   ea |  |
| Ac. | eum eam id | eōs   eas   ea | Ac. sē |
| G. | ējus | eōrum eārum eōrum | G. suī |
| D. | eī | } eīs (iīs) | D. sibī |
| Ab. | eō   eā   eō | | Ab. sē |

**132** The forms called reflexive refer to the subject of the sentence (e.g. *Brūtus sē occīdit*, 'Brutus killed himself'; *Mē laesī*, 'I have hurt myself'), and have no Nominative Case. In the 1st and 2nd Persons they are the same as the forms which are not reflexive.

**133** CAUTION: Carefully distinguish the Reflexive Pronoun from the Definitive Adjective *ipse* (§ 163): e.g. *Ipse dixit*, 'He has said it himself;' *Ipse fēcī*, 'I did it myself.'

**134** When the preposition *cum* is used with *mē, tē, sē, nōbis* or *vōbis*, it stands as a suffix: e.g. *mēcum, sēcum, vōbiscum.* So often *quōcum, quibuscum*, 'with whom' (§ 160).

## Possessive Adjectives and Pronouns.

(declined like *aūr-us, -a, -um; pulcher, pulchr-a, pulchr-um*).

**135** Me-us, me-a, me-um 'my': as Pron. 'mine.'
Tu-us, tu-a, tu-um 'thy,' 'your': as Pron. 'thine,' 'yours.'
Su-us, su-a, su-um 'his (own),' 'her (own),' 'its (own),' 'their (own)': as Pron. 'his,' 'hers,' 'its,' 'theirs.'
Noster, nostr-a, nostr-um 'our': as Pron. 'ours.'
Vester, vestr-a, vestr-um 'your': as Pron. 'yours.'

**136** Note that the Vocative Masculine of *meus* is *mī*.

## DEMONSTRATIVE ADJECTIVES AND PRONOUNS. 37

**137** *Suus* is always, and *meus, tuus, noster, vester* are sometimes, reflexive (cf. § 132). Compare :—

He has lost his book, *Librum suum āmīsit.*
I have lost his book, *Librum ējus* (§ 131, 'of him') *āmīsī.*

## Demonstrative Adjectives and Pronouns.

**138** hīc m., haec f., hōc n. 'this (by me).'

|      | Singular |      |     | Plural |       |       |
|------|----------|------|-----|--------|-------|-------|
| N.   | hīc      | haec | hōc | hī     | hae   | haec  |
| Ac   | hunc     | hanc | hōc | hōs    | hās   | haec  |
| G.   |          | hūjus|     | hōrum  | hārum | hōrum |
| D.   |          | huic |     | hīs    |       |       |
| Ab.  | hōc      | hāc  | hōc | hīs    |       |       |

**139** *Hic* is short in two passages of Virgil (Aen. IV. 22, VI. 791).

**140** The Neut. Sing. *hōc* is shortened from *hod-ce.* This *-ce*, which appears as *-c* in most forms of the Sing. and in the Neut. Plur., is a demonstrative suffix: *hī-c* then = (in meaning) this-here, French ce-ci. *-ce* is sometimes added to *hūjus, hōs, hīs,* etc. (*hūjus-ce, hōs-ce, his-ce,* etc.).

**141** When the interrogative particle *-ne* is added, the demonstrative suffix appears as a separate syllable: *hici-ne, haeci-ne, hōci-ne,* 'this?'

**142** ille m., illa f., illud n., 'that (by him),' 'yon.'

|      | Singular |       |       | Plural  |         |         |
|------|----------|-------|-------|---------|---------|---------|
| N.   | ille     | illa  | illud | illī    | illae   | illa    |
| Ac.  | illum    | illam | illud | illōs   | illās   | illa    |
| G.   |          | illīus|       | illōrum | illārum | illōrum |
| D.   |          | illī  |       | illīs   |         |         |
| Ab.  | illō     | illā  | illō  | illīs   |         |         |

# 38 DEMONSTRATIVE ADJECTIVES AND PRONOUNS.

**143** **iste** m., **ista** f., **istud** n. 'that (by you)'
is declined like *ille*.

**144** *Hic* is the Demonstrative of the 1st Person, *iste* of the 2nd, *ille* of the 3rd.

**145** *Ille* and *iste* are found with a short *i* in the Gen. Sing. in verse (cf. § 166).

**146** The demonstrative suffix *-c* (*-ce*), which appears in *hīc*, is also sometimes found attached to several cases of *ille* and *iste;* e.g. *illic* (for *ille-ce*), *illunc* (for *illum-ce*), *illuc* (for *illud-ce*), *istic* (for *iste-ce*) (cf. the French celui-là, and the English vulgarism 'that *there*').

**147** **is** m., **ea** f., **id** n. 'that,' 'the' (Unemphatic): cf. § 131.

|   | Singular | | | Plural | | |
|---|---|---|---|---|---|---|
| N. | is | ea | id | eī (iī) | eae | ea |
| Ac. | eum | eam | id | eōs | eās | ea |
| G. |   | ējus |   | eōrum | eārum | eōrum |
| D. |   | eī |   | eīs (iīs) | | |
| Ab. | eō | eā | eō | | | |

**148** **īdem** m. [*is* + *-dem*], **eadem** f., **idem** n. 'same.'

|   | Singular | | | Plural | | |
|---|---|---|---|---|---|---|
| N. | īdem | eadem | idem | īdem | eaedem | eadem |
| Ac. | eundem | eandem | idem | eōsdem | eāsdem | eadem |
| G. |   | ējusdem |   | eōrundem | eārundem | eōrundem |
| D. |   | eīdem |   | īsdem | | |
| Ab. | eōdem | eādem | eōdem | | | |

**149** The Nom. Plur. Masc. is sometimes written *eīdem* or *iīdem*, and the Dat. and Abl. Plur. *eīsdem* or *iīsdem*.

## INTERROGATIVE AND INDEFINITE PRONOUNS, ETC.

**150** **alius** m., **alia** f., **aliud** n. 'other.'

| | Singular | | | Plural | | |
|---|---|---|---|---|---|---|
| N. | alius | alia | aliud | aliī | aliae | alia |
| Ac. | alium | aliam | aliud | aliōs | aliās | alia |
| G. | | alīus | | aliōrum | aliārum | aliorum |
| D. | | aliī | | { aliīs | | |
| Ab. | aliō | aliā | aliō | | | |

**151** Interrogative and Indefinite

| Pronoun. | Adjective. |
|---|---|
| **quis** m., f., **quid** n. 'who?' 'what?' (Interrog.), 'anyone,' 'anything' (Indef.). | **quī** m., **quae** f., **quod** n. 'which?' 'what?' (Interrog.), 'any' (Indef.). |

| | Singular | | | | | |
|---|---|---|---|---|---|---|
| | Masc. | Fem. | Neut. | Masc. | Fem. | Neut. |
| N. | quis | | quid | quī | quae | quod |
| Ac. | quem | quam | quid | quem | quam | quod |
| G. | | cūjus | | | cūjus | |
| D. | | cui | | | cui | |
| Ab. | quō | quā | quō | quō | quā | quō |

| | Plural. | | |
|---|---|---|---|
| | Masc. | Fem. | Neut. |
| N. | quī | quae | quae |
| Ac. | quōs | quās | quae |
| G. | quōrum | quārum | quōrum |
| D. Ab. | { quibus | | |

## 4c INTERROGATIVE AND INDEFINITE PRONOUNS, ETC.

**152** The indefinite *quis, qui*, is used after such words as *sī* if, *nē* lest (that not) ; *sī quis*, if anyone ; *nē quid*, lest anything (that nothing) ; *sī quem virum*, if any man.

**153** *Quī* when indefinite generally shortens the form *quae* in the Fem. Sing. and Neut. Plur. to *qua* (*si qua rēs*, if anything). So too in the compounds in which *quī* forms the last part (§ 158).

**154** *Quis* is sometimes used as an Adjective ; *e.g. quis puer?* 'what boy?'

☞ *Quis puer* asks after the boy's name.
*Qui puer* may mean 'what sort of a boy?'

**155** An old-fashioned Ablative Singular *quī* is employed in the sense 'how?' *e.g. quī fit?* 'how comes it?' : an old-fashioned Dat. and Abl. Plur. is *quīs* (*queis*), for *quibus*.

**156** The following are compounded of *quis, quid*, and an indeclinable part. In the neut., *quid* becomes *quic-* before *qu,*} *quip-* before *p.*

quis-nam *m., f.*, quid-nam *n.* 'who (what) in the world?'
quis-que *m., f.*, quic-que (quid-que) *n.* 'each one,' 'each thing.'
quis-quam *m., f.*, quic-quam *n.* 'anyone at all,' 'anything at all.'
quis-piam *m., f.*, quip-piam *n.* 'a man,' 'a thing.'
ali-quis *m., f.*, ali-quid *n.* 'some one,' 'something.'
ec-quis *m., f.*, ec-quid *n.* 'anyone?' 'anything?' (used in questions).

**157** One of the above compounds (*quis-que*) has also adjectival forms for the fem. and neut. :—
quis-que, **quae-que** f., **quod-que** n. 'each.

**158** The following are compounded of *quī* and an indeclinable part :—
qui-nam *m.*, quae-nam *f.*, quod-nam *n.* 'which (what) in the world?'
qui-dam *m.*, quae-dam *f.*, quod-dam *n.* 'a certain.'
    Plural : qui-dam *m.*, quae-dam *f.*, quae-dam *n.*
    In the oblique cases, *m* before *d* is changed into *n*, e.g. *quen-dam, quōrun-dam*.
qui-vis *m.*, quae-vis *f.*, quod-vis *n.* } 'any you like.'
qui-libet *m.*, quae-libet *f.*, quod-libet *n.*
    Plural : qui- *m.*, quae- *f.*, quae- *n.*
ali-qui *m.*, ali-qua *f.*, ali-quod *n.* 'some.'
    Plural : ali-qui *m.*, ali-quae *f.*, ali-qua *n.*
ec-qui *m.*, ec-qua *or* ec-quae *f.*, ec-quod *n.* 'any?' (in questions).

**159** Three of the above also form **pronouns** in the Neut. Sing.
    quid-dam n. 'a certain thing.'
    quid-vis n. } 'anything you like.'
    quid-libet n.

## Relative Pronoun and Adjective.

**160** quī m., **quae** f., **quod** n., 'who,' 'which,' 'that.'[1]

| | Singular | | | Plural | | |
|---|---|---|---|---|---|---|
| N. | quī | quae | quod | quī | quae | quae |
| Ac. | quem | quam | quod | quōs | quās | quae |
| G. | | cūjus | | quōrum | quārum | quōrum |
| D. | | cui | | } quibus | | |
| Ab. | quō | quā | quō | | | |

**161** Old-fashioned forms are :—
    Dat. and Abl. Plur. *quīs (quêis).*
    Abl. Sing. (all genders) *quī,* e.g. *quīcum* 'with whom.'

**162** The following compounds are called 'General Relatives' (Engl. -ever):

(1) quis-quis *m., f.,* quic-quid *n.* 'whoever,' 'whatever.'

Both parts are declined (like *quis, quid,* § 151), but the only form in common use besides the Nom. is *quōquō* (Abl.).

(2) quī-cumque *m.,* quae-cumque *f.,* quod-cumque *n.* 'whichever,' ('whoever'), 'whatever.'

The last part (-cumque) is indeclinable.

## Definitive Adjective and Pronoun.

**163** ipse m., ipsa f., ipsum n. 'self.'

| | Singular | | | Plural | | |
|---|---|---|---|---|---|---|
| N. | ips-e | ips-a | ips-um | ips-ī | ips-ae | ips-a |
| Ac. | ips-um | ips-am | ips-um | ips-ōs | ips-ās | ips-a |
| G. | | ips-īus | | ips-ōrum | ips-ārum | ips-ōrum |
| D. | | ips-ī | | } ips-īs | | |
| Ab. | ips-ō | ips-ā | ips-ō | | | |

---

[1] *Quod* may also be translated 'what' when it is used without an antecedent: *e.g. Quod factum est, infectum reddi nōn potest,* 'What has been done cannot be undone.'

**164** *Ipse* may be of the 1st, 2nd, or 3rd Pers.: *Caesar ipse*, Caesar himself, *mē ipsum*, me myself, *vōbīs ipsīs*, to (from) you yourselves: cf. § 133.

**165** The following are declined like *ipse* in the oblique cases:—

| | | |
|---|---|---|
| ūn-us | -a -um | 'one' |
| sōl-us | -a -um | 'alone' |
| tōt-us | -a -um | 'whole,' 'entire' |
| ull-us | -a -um | 'any (at all)' |
| null-us | -a -um | 'not any (at all),' 'no' |
| alter, alter-a, alter-um | | 'one (of two),' 'other (of two)' |
| uter, utr-a, utr-um | | 'which (of two)?' |
| neuter, neutr-a, neutr-um | | 'neither (of two)' |

ūnus, sōlus, tōtus, ullus,
alter, uter, neuter, nullus.

**166** All these adjectives, including *ipse*, are found in the poets with a short *i* in the Gen. Sing. (*-ius*), that form being more convenient for some kinds of verse.

**167** The Plural of *ūnus* is used with words whose Plurals have a Singular meaning, *e.g. ūna castra* 'one camp:' cf. § 126. Also in the sense 'alone,' *e.g. ūnīs Suēbis*, 'to the Suebi alone:' and in contrast to *alteri* (*ūni...alteri*).

**168** *Alteri* (Plur.), when used as a Pronoun, means 'one of two parties' (*alteri...alteri*, 'the one party...the other party).

**169** Like *uter* are declined the following compounds (the suffix is indeclinable):—

uter-que 'either of two,' 'both'; *utrique* 'both parties.'
uter-vis } 'either of the two'
uter-libet
uter-cumque 'whichever of the two' (Relative).

## ADVERBS.

**170** Adjectives that are declined according to the 2nd and 1st Decl. of Nouns form Adverbs by adding *-ē* to the trunk: *e.g.* jūcund-ē, *pleasantly*, līber-ē, *freely*.

Note: ben-ĕ, *well*, mal-ĕ, *badly* (from *bon-us, mal-us*).

171  Yet the following have -ō : falsō, meritō, necessāriō, perpetuō, rārō, sēdulō, sērō, subitō, tūtō, and a few others.
   Distinguish : certō, *for certain* ; certē, *at any rate*
   vērō, *truly, assuredly* ; vērē, *truly, veraciously*.

172  Adjectives that are declined according to the 3rd Decl. of Nouns form Adverbs by adding to the trunk -*iter* (-*er* when the trunk ends in *nt*) : *e.g.* fort-iter, *bravely*, ferōc-iter, *haughtily*, prūdent-er, *prudently*.

173  Note: audac-ter, *boldly* (from trunk audāc-).
   facil-e, *easily* (from trunk facil-).
   With *difficulty* is generally nōn facile.
   violent-er, *violently* (from violent-us. Contrast § 170).

## Comparison of Adverbs.

174  The Comparative is supplied by the Neut. Sing. of the Comparative Adjective : the Superlative is formed from the trunk of the Superlative Adjective by adding -*ē* :

*Pos.* jūcund-ē  *Comp.* jūcund-ius  *Sup.* jūcund-issim-ē
*pleasantly*   *more* (*too*) *pleasantly*   *most* (*very*) *pleasantly*
            *somewhat pleasantly*
fort-iter      fort-ius               fort-issim-ē.

175  The following are compared irregularly :—

bene, *well*          melius, *better*         optimē, *best*
male, *badly*         pējus, *worse*           pessimē, *worst*
multum, *much*        plūs, *more*             plūrimum, *most*
magnopere, *greatly*  magis, *more highly*     maximē, *most highly*
nōn multum, *little*  minus, *less*            minimē, *least*

176  Note : diū, *long* (of time) diūtius, *longer*    diūtissimē *most long*
      saepe, *often*           saepius, *oftener*    saepissimē *most often*
      [wanting]                ōcius (*more*) *quickly* ōcissimē *most quickly*
                               potius, *rather*      potissimum, *especially*
      nūper, *lately*          [wanting]             nūperrimē, *most lately*
      satis, *enough*          satius, *preferably*  [wanting]
      secus, *otherwise*       sētius, *less*        ,,

## VERBS.

**177** The Latin verb has—

(a) **Two voices:**
   The Active, *or* voice of 'doing' [*agere*, 'to do'].
   The Passive, *or* voice of 'suffering' [*pati*, 'to suffer'].

(b) **Three moods:**
   The Indicative.
   The Subjunctive.
   The Imperative.

(c) **Seven tenses** (of the Indicative Mood):

|  |  |  | NAME OF LATIN TENSE. |
|---|---|---|---|
| PRESENT TIME | *He sings* <br> *He is singing* | cantat | Present |
|  | *He has sung* <br> *He has been singing* | cantāvit | Perfect |
| PAST TIME | *He sang* | cantāvit | Past |
|  | *He was singing* | cantābat | Imperfect |
|  | *He had sung* <br> *He had been singing* | cantāverat | Pluperfect |
| FUTURE TIME | *He will sing* <br> *He will be singing* | cantābit | Future |
|  | *He will have sung* <br> *He will have been singing* | cantāverit | Future Perfect |

The name 'Perfect' stands for 'Present Perfect.'
   „    „   'Imperfect' stands for 'Past Imperfect' (= 'Past Continuous').
   „    „   'Pluperfect' stands for 'Past Perfect.'

A single Form serves in Latin for both Perfect and Past.

## CONJUGATION OF VERBS.

(d) **Two numbers** (Singular and Plural).

(e) **Three persons** (in each number), corresponding to the three Persons of Pronouns (§§ 128—131):

**178** A verb in the Indicative, Subjunctive, or Imperative Mood is said to be 'finite' [*finire*, 'to limit'] as contrasted with the 'Infinitive' (§ 179), because it is *defined* by its ending as belonging to a certain person and number.

**179** To the verb belong also—

(a) **Verb-adjectives:**

Three Participles (declinable: § 201).
The Gerundive (declinable: § 202).

(b) **Verb-nouns:**

The Infinitive (indeclinable: § 203).
The Gerund (declinable in the Sing.: § 204).
Two Supines (indeclinable: § 205).

### THE FOUR CONJUGATIONS.

**180** There are **four conjugations** of verbs (*i.e.* four ways of 'conjugating' them), to be known by the ending of the Present Infinitive Active:—

| Ending of Pres. Inf. Act. | Conjugation. | Example.[1] | First Pers. Sing Pres. Ind. Act. |
|---|---|---|---|
| -āre | I | laud-āre | laud-ō |
| -ēre | II | mon-ēre | mon-eō |
| -ĕre | III | reg-ere | reg-ō |
| -īre | IV | aud-īre | aud-iō |

---

[1] Other examples, which may be used for practice in conjugating, are:
Conj. I—armāre, damnāre, decorāre, ēducāre, jūdicāre, ornāre.
Conj. II—dēbēre, habēre, nocēre, praebēre, tacēre, terrēre.
Conj. III—tegere, dīcere, dūcere, jungere, carpere, sculpere.
Conj. IV—custōdīre, expedīre, fīnīre, mollīre, pūnīre, vestīre.

**181** About 1,000 verbs (360 uncompounded) belong to the I Conj.
„ 150 „ (120 uncompounded) „ II Conj.
„ 300 „ (170 uncompounded) „ III Conj.
„ 100 „ (60 uncompounded) „ IV Conj.

**182** A verb-form consists of two parts:—

1. The **trunk**, i.e. the part from which comes a whole group of forms (e.g. *laud-* in *laud-āre, laud-ō*, etc.).

2. The **ending**, i.e. the part which varies in different forms coming from the same trunk (e.g. *-āre, -ō,* etc.)

**183** The forms of the regular verb come from **three trunks**, and fall into three groups:—

1. The **Present trunk** may be found by removing the ending of the Present Infinitive, as given in the dictionary.

2. The **Perfect Active trunk** may be found by removing the ending (*-i*) of the 1st Pers. Sing. Perfect Indicative Active, as given in the dictionary.

3. The **Supine trunk** may be found by removing the ending (*-um*) of the Supine, as given in the dictionary.

Comparison of trunks in the regular Conjugations:—

| Conjugation | Present Trunk | Perfect Active Trunk | Supine Trunk |
|---|---|---|---|
| I | laud- | laudāv- | laudāt- |
| II | mon- | monu- | monit- |
| III | reg- | rex- (reg-s-) | rect- (reg-t) |
| IV | aud- | audīv- | audīt- |

The Present Trunk generally ends in a consonant, but not always: *statuere* gives *statu-*, *nuntiāre* gives *nunti-*.

**184** From the Present trunk comes the **Present group** of forms, in which each conjugation employs its own special endings. The endings of the 1st, 2nd, and 4th conjugation are marked by a characteristic vowel (called the Character).

## CONJUGATION OF VERBS.

From the Perfect Active trunk comes the **Perfect Active group** of forms, in which the four conjugations employ the same endings.

From the Supine trunk comes the **Supine group** of forms, in which the four conjugations employ the same endings.

**185** The **endings** (including those of Verb-adjectives and Verb-nouns) belonging to the three trunks in each conjugation are briefly summarized in §§ 198—200.

**186** The last part of the ending expresses person and number and is called the **personal suffix**. The following table shows the personal suffixes as they are found in the Indicative and Subjunctive moods throughout the verb, except in the 1st and 2nd Pers. Sing. and the 2nd Pers. Plur. of the Perfect Indic. Active (-ī, -stī, -stis).

|  | Active | | Passive | |
|---|---|---|---|---|
|  | Sing. | Plur. | Sing. | Plur. |
| 1st Pers. | m or ō | mus | r | mur |
| 2nd Pers. | s | tis | ris | minī |
| 3rd Pers. | t | nt | tur | ntur |

☞ The personal suffixes are clearly seen in the verb *sum*, § 189.

**187** The **Principal Parts** of a verb are the forms from which the three trunks may be found:—

| 1st Sing. Pres. Ind. Act. | Pres. Infin. | 1st Sing Perf. Ind. Act. | Supine |
|---|---|---|---|
| laud-ō | laud-āre | laudāv-ī | laudāt-um |

**188** The Perf., Pluperf. and Fut. Perf. Pass. are compound tenses, formed by combining the Perf. Part. Pass. with the **irregular verb** *sum*, I am, used as an **auxiliary** (Princ. Parts **sum, esse, fuī,** ———). This verb has no Supine (but forms a Fut. Part. as if from Supine trunk *fut-*), no Gerund, and no Pres. Part. (cf. however § 215). It does not, of course, admit of a Passive.

☞ For further remarks on the verb *sum*, and its compounds, see §§ 213—216.

## CONJUGATION of the Verb SUM.

| | | INDICATIVE | SUBJUNCTIVE | |
|---|---|---|---|---|
| **Present** | | S. 1. sum, *I am*<br>2. es, *thou art*<br>3. est, *he is*<br>P. 1. sumus, *we*<br>2. estis, *you* } *are*<br>3. sunt, *they* | sim, *I be*<br>sis, *thou be*<br>sit, *he be*<br>simus, *we be*<br>sitis, *you be*<br>sint, *they be* | |
| **Imperfect** | | S. 1. eram, *I was*<br>2. erās, *thou wast*<br>3. erat, *he was*<br>P. 1. erāmus, *we*<br>2. erātis, *you* } *were*<br>3. erant, *they* | essem, *I were*<br>essēs, *thou wert*<br>esset, *he were*<br>essēmus, *we*<br>essētis, *you* } *were*<br>essent, *they* | (forem, forēs, etc.; § 214) |
| **Future** | | S. 1. erō, *I shall be*<br>2. eris, *thou wilt be*<br>3. erit, *he will be*<br>P. 1. erimus, *we shall be*<br>2. eritis, *you will be*<br>3. erunt, *they will be* | | |

### IMPERATIVE

| | *Unemphatic* | | *Emphatic* | |
|---|---|---|---|---|
| | S. 2. es, *be (thou)*<br><br>P. 2. este, *be (ye)* | | S. 2. estō, *thou shalt be*<br>3. estō, *he shall be*<br>P. 2. estōte, *ye shall be*<br>3. suntō, *they shall be* | |

| VERB-NOUN : VERB-ADJ. | |
|---|---|
| | **Pres. Infin.** esse, *to be* |

## fu-

|  | INDICATIVE | | SUBJUNCTIVE | |
|---|---|---|---|---|
| **Perfect and Past** | S. 1. fu-ī, *I have been*<br>2. fu-istī, *thou hast been*<br>3. fu-it, *he has been*<br>P. 1. fu-imus, *we have been*<br>2. fu-istis, *you have been*<br>3. fu-ērunt, *they have been* | *or, I was, thou wast, etc.* | fu-erim, *I*<br>fu-eris, *thou*<br>fu-erit, *he*<br>fu-erimus, *we*<br>fu-eritis, *you*<br>fu-erint, *they* | *have been* |
| **Pluperfect** | S. 1. fu-eram, *I had been*<br>2. fu-erās, *thou hadst been*<br>3. fu-erat, *he had been*<br>P. 1. fu-erāmus, *we*<br>2. fu-erātis, *you*<br>3. fu-erant, *they* | *had been* | fu-issem, *I*<br>fu-issēs, *thou*<br>fu-isset, *he*<br>fu-issēmus, *we*<br>fu-issētis, *you*<br>fu-issent, *they* | *had been* |
| **Future Perfect** | S. 1. fu-erō, *I shall have been*<br>2. fu-eris, *thou wilt have been*<br>3. fu-erit, *he will have been*<br>P. 1. fu-erimus, *we shall have been*<br>2. fu-eritis, *you will have been*<br>3. fu-erint, *they will have been* | | | |

| | fu- | fut- |
|---|---|---|
| **Verb-Adj.** | | Fut. Part. fut-ūrus, *about to be* |
| **Verb-Nouns** | Perf. Infin. fu-isse, *to have been* | Fut. Infin. fut-ūrus esse, *to be about to be* (fore: § 214) |

## FIRST CONJUGATION—ACTIVE VOICE.

**190** — **laud-: Character A.**

| | INDICATIVE | SUBJUNCTIVE |
|---|---|---|
| **Present** | laud-ō, *I praise (I am praising)* | laud-em* |
| | laud-ās, *thou praisest (thou art praising)* | laud-ēs |
| | laud-at, *he praises (he is praising)* | laud-et |
| | laud-āmus, *we praise (we are praising)* | laud-ēmus |
| | laud-ātis, *you praise (you are praising)* | laud-ētis |
| | laud-ant, *they praise (they are praising)* | laud-ent |
| **Imperfect** | laud-ābam, *I was praising* | laud-ārem* |
| | laud-ābās, *thou wast praising* | laud-ārēs |
| | laud-ābat, *he was praising* | laud-āret |
| | laud-ābāmus, *we were praising* | laud-ārēmus |
| | laud-ābātis, *you were praising* | laud-ārētis |
| | laud-ābant, *they were praising* | laud-ārent |
| **Future** | laud-ābō, *I shall praise* | *The meanings of the Subjunctive in the various kinds of sentence and clause will be explained in Syntax.* |
| | laud-ābis, *thou wilt praise* | |
| | laud-ābit, *he will praise* | |
| | laud-ābimus, *we shall praise* | |
| | laud-ābitis, *you will praise* | |
| | laud-ābunt, *they will praise* | |

### IMPERATIVE

| | Unemphatic | | Emphatic |
|---|---|---|---|
| | laud-ā, *praise (thou)* | | laud-ātō, *thou shalt praise* |
| | | | laud-ātō, *he shall praise* |
| | laud-āte, *praise (ye)* | | laud-ātōte, *ye shall praise* |
| | | | laud-antō, *they shall praise* |

**VERB-ADJ.**    Pres. Part. laud-ans, *praising*

**VERB-NOUNS**
Pres. Infin. laud-āre, *to praise, to be praising*
Gerund
- N., Ac. laud-andum, *(the) praising*
- G. laud-andī, *of (the) praising*
- D., Ab. laud-andō, *for, by (the) praising*

# FIRST CONJUGATION—ACTIVE VOICE.

## laudāv-

| | INDICATIVE | | SUBJUNCTIVE |
|---|---|---|---|
| **Perfect and Past** | laudāv-ī, *I have praised*<br>laudāv-istī, *thou hast praised*<br>laudāv-it, *he has praised*<br>laudāv-imus, *we have praised*<br>laudāv-istis, *you have praised*<br>laudāv-ērunt, *they have praised* | or, *I praised, etc.* | laudāv-erim<br>laudāv-erīs<br>laudāv-erit<br>laudāv-erīmus<br>laudāv-erītis<br>laudāv-erint |
| **Pluperfect** | laudāv-eram, *I had praised*<br>laudāv-erās, *thou hadst praised*<br>laudāv-erat, *he had praised*<br>laudāv-erāmus, *we had praised*<br>laudāv-erātis, *you had praised*<br>laudāv-erant, *they had praised* | | laudāv-issem<br>laudāv-issēs<br>laudāv-isset<br>laudāv-issēmus<br>laudāv-issētis<br>laudāv-issent |
| **Future Perfect** | laudāv-erō, *I shall have praised*<br>laudāv-erĭs, *thou wilt have praised*<br>laudāv-erit, *he will have praised*<br>laudāv-erĭmus, *we shall have praised*<br>laudāv-erĭtis, *you will have praised*<br>laudāv-erint, *they will have praised* | | |

| | laudāv- | laudāt- | |
|---|---|---|---|
| **VERB. ADJ.** | | Fut. Part. laudāt-ūrus, *about to [praise* | |
| **VERB. NOUNS** | Perf. Infin. laudāv-isse, *[to have praised* | Fut. Infin. laudāt-ūrus esse, *to be [about to praise* | |
| | | Supines | laudāt-um, *a-praising*<br>laudāt-ū, *in the praising* |

## SECOND CONJUGATION—ACTIVE VOICE.

**191**   **mon-: Character E.**

| | INDICATIVE | SUBJUNCTIVE |
|---|---|---|
| **Present** | mon-eō, *I warn (I am warning)* <br> mon-ēs, *thou warnest (thou art warning)* <br> mon-et, *he warns (he is warning)* <br> mon-ēmus, *we warn (we are warning)* <br> mon-ētis, *you warn (you are warning)* <br> mon-ent, *they warn (they are warning)* | mon-eam <br> mon-eās <br> mon-eat <br> mon-eāmus <br> mon-eātis <br> mon-eant |
| **Imperfect** | mon-ēbam, *I was warning* <br> mon-ēbās, *thou wast warning* <br> mon-ēbat, *he was warning* <br> mon-ēbāmus, *we were warning* <br> mon-ēbātis, *you were warning* <br> mon-ēbant, *they were warning* | mon-ērem <br> mon-ērēs <br> mon-ēret <br> mon-ērēmus <br> mon-ērētis <br> mon-ērent |
| **Future** | mon-ēbō, *I shall warn* <br> mon-ēbis, *thou wilt warn* <br> mon-ēbit, *he will warn* <br> mon-ēbimus, *we shall warn* <br> mon-ēbitis, *you will warn* <br> mon-ēbunt, *they will warn* | |

### IMPERATIVE

| | | | |
|---|---|---|---|
| *Unemphatic* | mon-ē, *warn (thou)* <br> mon-ēte, *warn (ye)* | *Emphatic* | mon-ētō, *thou shalt warn* <br> mon-ētō, *he shall warn* <br> mon-ētōte, *ye shall warn* <br> mon-entō, *they shall warn* |

**VERB-ADJ.**  Pres. Part. **mon-ens**, *warning*

**VERB-NOUNS**
Pres. Infin. **mon-ēre**, *to warn, to be warning*
Gerund
- N., Ac. **mon-endum**, *(the) warning*
- G. **mon-endī**, *of (the) warning*
- D., Ab. **mon-endō**, *for, by (the) warning*

## SECOND CONJUGATION—ACTIVE VOICE.

| | monu- | | |
|---|---|---|---|
| | *INDICATIVE* | | *SUBJUNCTIVE* |
| **Perfect and Past** | monu-ī, *I have warned* <br> monu-istī, *thou hast warned* <br> monu-it, *he has warned* <br> monu-imus, *we have warned* <br> monu-istis, *you have warned* <br> monu-ērunt, *they have warned* | } *or, I warned, etc.* | monu-erim <br> monu-erĭs <br> monu-erit <br> monu-erĭmus <br> monu-erĭtis <br> monu-erint |
| **Pluperfect** | monu-eram, *I had warned* <br> monu-erās, *thou hadst warned* <br> monu-erat, *he had warned* <br> monu-erāmus, *we had warned* <br> monu-erātis, *you had warned* <br> monu-erant, *they had warned* | | monu-issem <br> monu-issēs <br> monu-isset <br> monu-issēmus <br> monu-issētis <br> monu-issent |
| **Future Perfect** | monu-erō, *I shall have warned* <br> monu-erĭs, *thou wilt have warned* <br> monu-erit, *he will have warned* <br> monu-erĭmus, *we shall have warned* <br> monu-erĭtis, *you will have warned* <br> monu-erint, *they will have warned* | | |

| | monu- | monit- | |
|---|---|---|---|
| **Verb-Adj.** | | Fut. Part. monit-ūrus, *about to [warn* | |
| **Verb-Nouns** | Perf. Infin. monu-isse, *[to have warned* | Fut. Infin. monit-ūrus esse, *to be [about to warn* | |
| | | Supines { monit-um, *a-warning* <br> monit-ū, *in the warning* | |

## THIRD CONJUGATION—ACTIVE VOICE.

### reg-

| | INDICATIVE | SUBJUNCTIVE |
|---|---|---|
| **Present** | reg-ō, *I rule (I am ruling)*<br>reg-is, *thou rulest (thou art ruling)*<br>reg-it, *he rules (he is ruling)*<br>reg-imus, *we rule (we are ruling)*<br>reg-itis, *you rule (you are ruling)*<br>reg-unt, *they rule (they are ruling)* | reg-am<br>reg-ās<br>reg-at<br>reg-āmus<br>reg-ātis<br>reg-ant |
| **Imperfect** | reg-ēbam, *I was ruling*<br>reg-ēbās, *thou wast ruling*<br>reg-ēbat, *he was ruling*<br>reg-ēbāmus, *we were ruling*<br>reg-ēbātis, *you were ruling*<br>reg-ēbant, *they were ruling* | reg-erem<br>reg-erēs<br>reg-eret<br>reg-erēmus<br>reg-erētis<br>reg-erent |
| **Future** | reg-am, *I shall rule*<br>reg-ēs, *thou wilt rule*<br>reg-et, *he will rule*<br>reg-ēmus, *we shall rule*<br>reg-ētis, *you will rule*<br>reg-ent, *they will rule* | |

### IMPERATIVE

| | Unemphatic | | Emphatic |
|---|---|---|---|
| | reg-e, *rule (thou)*<br><br>reg-ite, *rule (ye)* | | reg-itō, *thou shalt rule*<br>reg-itō, *he shall rule*<br>reg-itōte, *ye shall rule*<br>reg-untō, *they shall rule* |

**VERB. ADJ.**    Pres. Part. **reg-ens**, *ruling*

**VERB. NOUNS**
Pres. Infin. **reg-ere**, *to rule, to be ruling*
Gerund
{ N., Ac. **reg-endum**, *(the) ruling*
{ G.      **reg-endī**, *of (the) ruling*
{ D., Ab. **reg-endō**, *for, by (the) ruling*

## THIRD CONJUGATION—ACTIVE VOICE.

| | rex- | | |
|---|---|---|---|
| | *INDICATIVE* | | *SUBJUNCTIVE* |
| **PERFECT AND PAST** | rex-ī, *I have ruled* <br> rex-istī, *thou hast ruled* <br> rex-it, *he has ruled* <br> rex-imus, *we have ruled* <br> rex-istis, *you have ruled* <br> rex-ērunt, *they have ruled* | or, *I ruled*, etc. | rex-erim <br> rex-eris <br> rex-erit <br> rex-erimus <br> rex-eritis <br> rex-erint |
| **PLUPERFECT** | rex-eram, *I had ruled* <br> rex-erās, *thou hadst ruled* <br> rex-erat, *he had ruled* <br> rex-erāmus, *we had ruled* <br> rex-erātis, *you had ruled* <br> rex-erant, *they had ruled* | | rex-issem <br> rex-issēs <br> rex-isset <br> rex-issēmus <br> rex-issētis <br> rex-issent |
| **FUTURE PERFECT** | rex-erō, *I shall have ruled* <br> rex-eris, *thou wilt have ruled* <br> rex-erit, *he will have ruled* <br> rex-erimus, *we shall have ruled* <br> rex-eritis, *you will have ruled* <br> rex-erint, *they will have ruled* | | |

| | rex- | rect- |
|---|---|---|
| **VERB. ADJ.** | | FUT. PART. rect-ūrus, *about to [rule* |
| **VERB. NOUNS** | PERF. INFIN. rex-isse, *to [have ruled* | FUT. INFIN. rect-ūrus esse, *to be [about to rule* <br> SUPINES { rect-um, *a-ruling* <br> rect-ū, *in the ruling* |

## FOURTH CONJUGATION—ACTIVE VOICE.

**193** 

### aud-: Character I.

| | INDICATIVE | SUBJUNCTIVE |
|---|---|---|
| **PRESENT** | aud-īō, *I hear (I am hearing)* <br> aud-īs, *thou hearest (thou art hearing)* <br> aud-it, *he hears (he is hearing)* <br> aud-īmus, *we hear (we are hearing)* <br> aud-ītis, *you hear (you are hearing)* <br> aud-iunt, *they hear (they are hearing)* | aud-iam <br> aud-iās <br> aud-iat <br> aud-iāmus <br> aud-iātis <br> aud-iant |
| **IMPERFECT** | aud-iēbam, *I was hearing* <br> aud-iēbās, *thou wast hearing* <br> aud-iēbat, *he was hearing* <br> aud-iēbāmus, *we were hearing* <br> aud-iēbātis, *you were hearing* <br> aud-iēbant, *they were hearing* | aud-īrem <br> aud-īrēs <br> aud-īret <br> aud-īrēmus <br> aud-īrētis <br> aud-īrent |
| **FUTURE** | aud-iam, *I shall hear* <br> aud-iēs, *thou wilt hear* <br> aud-iet, *he will hear* <br> aud-iēmus, *we shall hear* <br> aud-iētis, *you will hear* <br> aud-ient, *they will hear* | |

#### IMPERATIVE

| | Unemphatic | | Emphatic |
|---|---|---|---|
| | aud-ī, *hear (thou)* <br> aud-īte, *hear (ye)* | | aud-ītō, *thou shalt hear* <br> aud-ītō, *he shall hear* <br> aud-ītōte, *ye shall hear* <br> aud-iuntō, *they shall hear* |

**VERB-ADJ.** PRES. PART. aud-iens, *hearing*

**VERB-NOUNS**
PRES. INFIN. aud-īre, *to hear, to be hearing*
GERUND
- N., Ac. aud-iendum, *(the) hearing*
- G. aud-iendī, *of (the) hearing*
- D., Ab. aud-iendō, *for, by (the) hearing*

# FOURTH CONJUGATION—ACTIVE VOICE.

## audīv-

| | INDICATIVE | | SUBJUNCTIVE |
|---|---|---|---|
| **PERFECT AND PAST** | audīv-ī, *I have heard* <br> audīv-istī, *thou hast heard* <br> audīv-it, *he has heard* <br> audīv-ĭmus, *we have heard* <br> audīv-istis, *you have heard* <br> audīv-ērunt, *they have heard* | *or, I heard, etc.* | audīv-erim <br> audīv-erĭs <br> audīv-erit <br> audīv-erĭmus <br> audīv-erĭtis <br> audīv-erint |
| **PLUPERFECT** | audīv-eram, *I had heard* <br> audīv-erās, *thou hadst heard* <br> audīv-erat, *he had heard* <br> audīv-erāmus, *we had heard* <br> audīv-erātis, *you had heard* <br> audīv-erant, *they had heard* | | audīv-issem <br> audīv-issēs <br> audīv-isset <br> audīv-issēmus <br> audīv-issētis <br> audīv-issent |
| **FUTURE PERFECT** | audīv-erō, *I shall have heard* <br> audīv-erĭs, *thou wilt have heard* <br> audīv-erit, *he will have heard* <br> audīv-erĭmus, *we shall have heard* <br> audīv-erĭtis, *you will have heard* <br> audīv-erint, *they will have heard* | | |

| | audīv- | audīt- | |
|---|---|---|---|
| **VERB-ADJ.** | | FUT. PART. audīt-ūrus, *about to [hear* | |
| **VERB-NOUNS** | PERF. INFIN. audīv-isse, *[to have heard* | FUT. INFIN. audīt-ūrus esse, *to be [about to hear* <br> SUPINES { audīt-um, *a-hearing* <br> audīt-ū, *in the hearing* | |

## FIRST CONJUGATION—PASSIVE VOICE.

### laud-: Character A.

| | INDICATIVE | SUBJUNCTIVE |
|---|---|---|
| **Present** | laud-or, *I am (being) praised* | laud-er |
| | laud-āris, *thou art (being) praised* | laud-ēris |
| | laud-ātur, *he is (being) praised* | laud-ētur |
| | laud-āmur, *we are (being) praised* | laud-ēmur |
| | laud-āminī, *you are (being) praised* | laud-ēminī |
| | laud-antur, *they are (being) praised* | laud-entur |
| **Imperfect** | laud-ābar, *I was being praised* | laud-ārer |
| | laud-ābāris, *thou wast being praised* | laud-ārēris |
| | laud-ābātur, *he was being praised* | laud-ārētur |
| | laud-ābāmur, *we were being praised* | laud-ārēmur |
| | laud-ābāminī, *you were being praised* | laud-ārēminī |
| | laud-ābantur, *they were being praised* | laud-ārentur |
| **Future** | laud-ābor, *I shall be praised* | |
| | laud-āberis, *thou wilt be praised* | |
| | laud-ābitur, *he will be praised* | |
| | laud-ābimur, *we shall be praised* | |
| | laud-ābiminī, *you will be praised* | |
| | laud-ābuntur, *they will be praised* | |

#### IMPERATIVE

| | | | |
|---|---|---|---|
| *Unemphatic* | laud-āre, *be (thou) praised* | *Emphatic* | laud-ātor, *thou shalt be praised* |
| | | | laud-ātor, *he shall be praised* |
| | laud-āminī, *be (ye) praised* | | laud-antor, *they shall be [praised* |

| VERB. ADJ. | Gerundive laud-andus, (*fit*) *to-be-praised* |
|---|---|
| **VERB. NOUN** | Pres. Infin. laud-ārī, *to be praised* |

# FIRST CONJUGATION—PASSIVE VOICE.

## laudāt-

| | INDICATIVE | | SUBJUNCTIVE |
|---|---|---|---|
| **Perfect and Past** | laudāt-us* sum, *I have been praised* | | laudāt-us* sim |
| | laudāt-us es, *thou hast been praised* | or *I was praised,* etc. | laudāt-us sīs |
| | laudāt-us est, *he has been praised* | | laudāt-us sit |
| | laudāt-ī sumus, *we have been praised* | | laudāt-ī sīmus |
| | laudāt-ī estis, *you have been praised* | | laudāt-ī sītis |
| | laudāt-ī sunt, *they have been praised* | | laudāt-ī sint |
| **Pluperfect** | laudāt-us* eram, *I had been praised* | | laudāt-us* essem |
| | laudāt-us erās, *thou hadst been praised* | | laudāt-us essēs |
| | laudāt-us erat, *he had been praised* | | laudāt-us esset |
| | laudāt-ī erāmus, *we had been praised* | | laudāt-ī essēmus |
| | laudāt-ī erātis, *you had been praised* | | laudāt-ī essētis |
| | laudāt-ī erant, *they had been praised* | | laudāt-ī essent |
| **Future Perfect** | laudāt-us* erō, *I shall have been praised* | | |
| | laudāt-us eris, *thou wilt have been praised* | | |
| | laudāt-us erit, *he will have been praised* | | |
| | laudāt-ī erimus, *we shall have been praised* | | |
| | laudāt-ī eritis, *you will have been praised* | | |
| | laudāt-ī erunt, *they will have been praised* | | |

\* Declined in all three genders (Nominative Case):
    Sing. laudāt-us, -a, -um.    Plur. laudāt-ī, -ae, -a.

| | |
|---|---|
| **VERB-ADJ.** | Perf. Part. laudāt-us, *(having been) praised* |
| **VERB-NOUNS** | Perf. Infin. laudāt-us esse, *to have been praised*<br>Fut. Infin. laudāt-um īrī, *to be about to be praised* |

## SECOND CONJUGATION—PASSIVE VOICE.

### mon-: Character E.

| | INDICATIVE | SUBJUNCTIVE |
|---|---|---|
| **Present** | mon-eor, *I am (being) warned* | mon-ear |
| | mon-ēris, *thou art (being) warned* | mon-eāris |
| | mon-ētur, *he is (being) warned* | mon-eātur |
| | mon-ēmur, *we are (being) warned* | mon-eāmur |
| | mon-ēminī, *you are (being) warned* | mon-eāminī |
| | mon-entur, *they are (being) warned* | mon-eantur |
| **Imperfect** | mon-ēbar, *I was being warned* | mon-ērer |
| | mon-ēbāris, *thou wast being warned* | mon-ērēris |
| | mon-ēbātur, *he was being warned* | mon-ērētur |
| | mon-ēbāmur, *we were being warned* | mon-ērēmur |
| | mon-ēbāminī, *you were being warned* | mon-ērēminī |
| | mon-ēbantur, *they were being warned* | mon-ērentur |
| **Future** | mon-ēbor, *I shall be warned* | |
| | mon-ēberis, *thou wilt be warned* | |
| | mon-ēbitur, *he will be warned* | |
| | mon-ēbimur, *we shall be warned* | |
| | mon-ēbiminī, *you will be warned* | |
| | mon-ēbuntur, *they will be warned* | |

#### IMPERATIVE

| | Unemphatic | | Emphatic |
|---|---|---|---|
| | mon-ēre, *be (thou) warned* | | mon-ētor, *thou shalt be warned* |
| | | | mon-ētor, *he shall be warned* |
| | mon-ēminī, *be (ye) warned* | | |
| | | | mon-entor, *they shall be warned* |

| VERB. ADJ. | GERUNDIVE mon-endus, *(fit) to-be-warned* |
|---|---|
| VERB. ADJ. | Pres. Infin. mon-ērī, *to be warned* |

## SECOND CONJUGATION—PASSIVE VOICE.

### monit-

| | INDICATIVE | SUBJUNCTIVE |
|---|---|---|
| **PERFECT AND PAST** | monit-**us*** sum, *I have been warned*<br>monit-**us** es, *thou hast been warned*<br>monit-**us** est, *he has been warned*<br>monit-**ī** sumus, *we have been warned*<br>monit-**ī** estis, *you have been warned*<br>monit-**ī** sunt, *they have been warned*   *or, I was warned, etc.* | monit-**us*** sim<br>monit-**us** sīs<br>monit-**us** sit<br>monit-**ī** sīmus<br>monit-**ī** sītis<br>monit-**ī** sint |
| **PLUPERFECT** | monit-**us*** eram, *I had been warned*<br>monit-**us** erās, *thou hadst been warned*<br>monit-**us** erat, *he had been warned*<br>monit-**ī** erāmus, *we had been warned*<br>monit-**ī** erātis, *you had been warned*<br>monit-**ī** erant, *they had been warned* | monit-**us*** essem<br>monit-**us** essēs<br>monit-**us** esset<br>monit-**ī** essēmus<br>monit-**ī** essētis<br>monit-**ī** essent |
| **FUTURE PERFECT** | monit-**us*** erō, *I shall have been warned*<br>monit-**us** eris, *thou wilt have been warned*<br>monit-**us** erit, *he will have been warned*<br>monit-**ī** erimus, *we shall have been warned*<br>monit-**ī** eritis, *you will have been warned*<br>monit-**ī** erunt, *they will have been warned* | |

\* Declined in all three genders (Nominative Case):
SING. monit-**us, -a, -um.**    PLUR. monit-**ī, -ae, -a.**

| VERB-ADJ. | PERF. PART. monit-**us**, *(having been) warned* |
|---|---|
| **VERB-NOUNS** | PERF. INFIN. monit-**us** esse, *to have been warned*<br>FUT. INFIN. monit-**um** īrī, *to be about to be warned* |

## THIRD CONJUGATION—PASSIVE VOICE.

**196** — **reg-**

| | | INDICATIVE | SUBJUNCTIVE |
|---|---|---|---|
| **Present** | | reg-**or**, *I am (being) ruled* | reg-**ar** |
| | | reg-**eris**, *thou art (being) ruled* | reg-**āris** |
| | | reg-**itur**, *he is (being) ruled* | reg-**ātur** |
| | | reg-**imur**, *we are (being) ruled* | reg-**āmur** |
| | | reg-**iminī**, *you are (being) ruled* | reg-**āminī** |
| | | reg-**untur**, *they are (being) ruled* | reg-**antur** |
| **Imperfect** | | reg-**ēbar**, *I was being ruled* | reg-**erer** |
| | | reg-**ēbāris**, *thou wast being ruled* | reg-**erēris** |
| | | reg-**ēbātur**, *he was being ruled* | reg-**erētur** |
| | | reg-**ēbāmur**, *we were being ruled* | reg-**erēmur** |
| | | reg-**ēbāminī**, *you were being ruled* | reg-**erēminī** |
| | | reg-**ēbantur**, *they were being ruled* | reg-**erentur** |
| **Future** | | reg-**ar**, *I shall be ruled* | |
| | | reg-**ēris**, *thou wilt be ruled* | |
| | | reg-**ētur**, *he will be ruled* | |
| | | reg-**ēmur**, *we shall be ruled* | |
| | | reg-**ēminī**, *you will be ruled* | |
| | | reg-**entur**, *they will be ruled* | |

| | | IMPERATIVE | | |
|---|---|---|---|---|
| *Unemphatic* | reg-**ere**, *be (thou) ruled* | | *Emphatic* | reg-**itor**, *thou shalt be ruled* |
| | | | | reg-**itor**, *he shall be ruled* |
| | reg-**iminī**, *be (ye) ruled* | | | |
| | | | | reg-**untor**, *they shall be ruled* |

| VERB-ADJ. | Gerundive reg-**endus**, (*fit*) *to-be-ruled* |
|---|---|

| VERB-NOUN | Pres. Infin. reg-**ī**, *to be ruled* |
|---|---|

## THIRD CONJUGATION—PASSIVE VOICE.

### rect-

| | INDICATIVE | | SUBJUNCTIVE |
|---|---|---|---|
| **Perfect and Past** | rect-us * sum, *I have been ruled* | | rect-us* sim |
| | rect-us es, *thou hast been ruled* | | rect-us sis |
| | rect-us est, *he has been ruled* | or, *I was ruled*, etc. | rect-us sit |
| | rect-ī sumus, *we have been ruled* | | rect-ī sīmus |
| | rect-ī estis, *you have been ruled* | | rect-ī sītis |
| | rect-ī sunt, *they have been ruled* | | rect-ī sint |
| **Pluperfect** | rect-us* eram, *I had been ruled* | | rect-us* essem |
| | rect-us erās, *thou hadst been ruled* | | rect-us essēs |
| | rect-us erat, *he had been ruled* | | rect-us esset |
| | rect-ī erāmus, *we had been ruled* | | rect-ī essēmus |
| | rect-ī erātis, *you had been ruled* | | rect-ī essētis |
| | rect-ī erant, *they had been ruled* | | rect-ī essent |
| **Future Perfect** | rect-us* erō, *I shall have been ruled* | | |
| | rect-us eris, *thou wilt have been ruled* | | |
| | rect-us erit, *he will have been ruled* | | |
| | rect-ī erimus, *we shall have been ruled* | | |
| | rect-ī eritis, *you will have been ruled* | | |
| | rect-ī erunt, *they will have been ruled* | | |

\* Declined in all three genders (Nominative Case):
    Sing. rect-us, -a, -um.    Plur. rect-ī, -ae, -a.

| VERB-ADJ. | Perf. Part. rect-us, *(having been) ruled* |
|---|---|
| **VERB-NOUNS** | Perf. Infin. rect-us esse, *to have been ruled*<br>Fut. Infin. rect-um īrī, *to be about to be ruled* |

## FOURTH CONJUGATION—PASSIVE VOICE.

**197**

### aud-: Character I.

| | INDICATIVE | SUBJUNCTIVE |
|---|---|---|
| **PRESENT** | aud-ior, *I am (being) heard* <br> aud-īris, *thou art (being) heard* <br> aud-ītur, *he is (being) heard* <br> aud-īmur, *we are (being) heard* <br> aud-īminī, *you are (being) heard* <br> aud-iuntur, *they are (being) heard* | aud-iar <br> aud-iāris <br> aud-iātur <br> aud-iāmur <br> aud-iāminī <br> aud-iantur |
| **IMPERFECT** | aud-iēbar, *I was being heard* <br> aud-iēbāris, *thou wast being heard* <br> aud-iēbātur, *he was being heard* <br> aud-iēbāmur, *we were being heard* <br> aud-iēbāminī, *you were being heard* <br> aud-iēbantur, *they were being heard* | aud-īrer <br> aud-īrēris <br> aud-īrētur <br> aud-īrēmur <br> aud-īrēminī <br> aud-īrentur |
| **FUTURE** | aud-iar, *I shall be heard* <br> aud-iēris, *thou wilt be heard* <br> aud-iētur, *he will be heard* <br> aud-iēmur, *we shall be heard* <br> aud-iēminī, *you will be heard* <br> aud-ientur, *they will be heard* | |

### IMPERATIVE

| | Unemphatic | | Emphatic |
|---|---|---|---|
| | aud-īre, *be (thou) heard* <br> aud-īminī, *be (ye) heard* | | aud-ītor, *thou shalt be heard* <br> aud-ītor, *he shall be heard* <br> aud-iuntor, *they shall be heard* |

| VERB-ADJ. | GERUNDIVE | aud-iendus, *(fit) to-be-heard* |
|---|---|---|
| **VERB-NOUN** | PRES. INFIN. | aud-īrī, *to be heard* |

# FOURTH CONJUGATION—PASSIVE VOICE.

## audīt-

| | INDICATIVE | SUBJUNCTIVE |
|---|---|---|
| **PERFECT AND PAST** | audīt-us* sum, *I have been heard* <br> audīt-us es, *thou hast been heard* <br> audīt-us est, *he has been heard* <br> audīt-ī sumus, *we have been heard* <br> audīt-ī estis, *you have been heard* <br> audīt-ī sunt, *they have been heard* <br> *or, I was heard, etc.* | audīt-us* sim <br> audīt-us sīs <br> audīt-us sit <br> audīt-ī sīmus <br> audīt-ī sītis <br> audīt-ī sint |
| **PLUPERFECT** | audīt-us* eram, *I had been heard* <br> audīt-us erās, *thou hadst been heard* <br> audīt-us erat, *he had been heard* <br> audīt-ī erāmus, *we had been heard* <br> audīt-ī erātis, *you had been heard* <br> audīt-ī erant, *they had been heard* | audīt-us* essem <br> audīt-us essēs <br> audīt-us esset <br> audīt-ī essēmus <br> audīt-ī essētis <br> audīt-ī essent |
| **FUTURE PERFECT** | audīt-us* erō, *I shall have been heard* <br> audīt-us eris, *thou wilt have been heard* <br> audīt-us erit, *he will have been heard* <br> audīt-ī erimus, *we shall have been heard* <br> audīt-ī eritis, *you will have been heard* <br> audīt-ī erunt, *they will have been heard* | |

\* Declined in all three genders (Nominative Case):
    SING. audīt-us, -a, -um.    PLUR. audīt-ī, -ae, -a.

| | | |
|---|---|---|
| **VERB-ADJ.** | PERF. PART. | audīt-us, *(having been) heard* |
| **VERB-NOUNS** | PERF. INFIN. <br> FUT. INFIN. | audīt-us esse, *to have been heard* <br> audīt-um īrī, *to be about to be heard* |

## Table of Endings.

**PRESENT TRUNK GROUP**

|  |  | I<br>laud- | II<br>mon- | III<br>reg- | IV<br>aud- |
|---|---|---|---|---|---|
| **ACTIVE** | | | | | |
| Indic. | Pres. | -ō | -eō | -ō | -iō |
|  | Imperf. | -ābam | -ēbam | -ēbam | -iēbam |
|  | Fut. | -ābō | -ēbō | -am | -iam |
| Subj. | Pres. | -em | -eam | -am | -iam |
|  | Imperf. | -ārem | -ērem | -erem | -īrem |
| Imperat. |  | -ā | -ē | -e | -ī |
| Pres. Part. |  | -ans | -ens | -ens | -iens |
| Pres. Infin. |  | -āre | -ēre | -ere | -īre |
| Gerund |  | -andum | -endum | -endum | -iendum |
| **PASSIVE** | | | | | |
| Indic. | Pres. | -or | -eor | -or | -ior |
|  | Imperf. | -ābar | -ēbar | -ēbar | -iēbar |
|  | Fut. | -ābor | -ēbor | -ar | -iar |
| Subj. | Pres. | -er | -ear | -ar | -iar |
|  | Imperf. | -ārer | -ērer | -erer | -īrer |
| Imperat. |  | -āre | -ēre | -ere | -īre |
| Gerundive |  | -andus | -endus | -endus | -iendus |
| Pres. Infin. |  | -ārī | -ērī | -ī | -īrī |
| CHARACTER:— |  | A | E |  | I |

☞ The Imperf. Subj. (1st Pers. Sing.) and the Imperative (2nd Pers. Sing.) may be conveniently found in all conjugations from the Pres. Infin Active:

Impf. Subj. Act. = Pres. Infin. Act. + $m$ (e.g. *laudāre-m*)
    ,,    ,, Pass. = ,,    ,,    ,, + $r$ (e.g. *laudāre-r*)
Imperat. Act. = ,,    ,,    ,, $-re$ (e.g. *laudā*)
    ,,   Pass. = ,,    ,,    ,, (e.g. *laudāre*)

## Table of Endings—*continued*.

### PERFECT ACTIVE TRUNK GROUP

| I | II | III | IV |
|---|----|-----|----|
| laudāv-, | monu-, | rex-, | audīv- |

**ACTIVE**

| | | |
|---|---|---|
| Indic. | { Perf. and Past | -ī |
| | Pluperf. | -eram |
| | Fut. Perf. | -erō |
| Subj. | { Perf. and Past | -erim |
| | Pluperf. | -issem |
| Perf. Infin. | | -isse |

### SUPINE TRUNK GROUP

| I | II | III | IV |
|---|----|-----|----|
| laudāt-, | monit-, | rect-, | audīt- |

**ACTIVE**

| | |
|---|---|
| Fut. Part. | -ūrus |
| Fut. Infin. | -ūrus esse |
| Supines | } -um |
| | } -ū |

**PASSIVE**

| | | |
|---|---|---|
| Perf. Part. | | -us |
| Indic. | { Perf. and Past | -us sum |
| | Pluperf. | -us eram |
| | Fut. Perf. | -us erō |
| Subj. | { Perf. and Past | -us sim |
| | Pluperf. | -us essem |
| Perf. Infin. | | -us esse |
| Fut. Infin. | | -um īrī |

**201** REMARKS ON VERB-ADJECTIVES AND VERB-NOUNS.

There are three **Participles**, declinable both in Singular and Plural; two are active, one passive.

| Active | Passive |
|---|---|
| **Present,** cant-ans, *singing* (for declension see § 100) | **Perfect,** cantāt-us, *sung* (for decl. see § 92). |
| **Future,** cantāt-ūrus, *about to sing* (for decl. see § 92). | |

**202** The **Gerundive** is the adjectival form of the Gerund, and is declinable both in Singular and Plural.

cant-andus, *to-be-sung* (for decl. see § 92).

**203** The **Infinitive** is a verb-noun of neuter gender and indeclinable, and is generally translated by the English Infinitive (*to sing, to be sung*); sometimes by the verb-noun in *-ing* (*singing, being sung*).

There are six forms of the Infinitive, three active and three passive:

| Active | Passive |
|---|---|
| **Present,** cant-āre, *to sing* | **Present,** cant-ārī, *to be sung* |
| **Perfect,** cantāv-isse, *to have sung* | **Perfect,** cantāt-us esse, *to have been sung* |
| **Future,** cantāt-ūrus esse, *to be about to sing* | **Future,** cantāt-um īrī, *to be about to be sung* |

The Future Infinitive Active is compounded of the Future Participle (*cantātūrus*, **which is declinable**) and the Present Infinitive *esse*.

The Perfect Infinitive Passive is compounded of the Perfect Participle Passive (*cantātus*, **which is declinable**)

## REMARKS ON VERB-ADJECTIVES, ETC. 69

and the Present Infinitive *esse*—literally 'to be having-been-sung,' *i.e.* ' to have been sung.'

The Future Infinitive Passive is compounded of the Supine (*cantātum*, **which is indeclinable**) and the Present Infinitive Passive of the verb *eō* 'I go,' and is used where we should say 'to be about to be sung.'

**204** The **Gerund** resembles the Infinitive in being a neuter verb-noun, but is declinable in the Singular, like a neuter noun of the 2nd Decl. (e.g. *bellum*) :—

    Nom., Acc.  cant-andum, *(the) singing*
    Gen.          cant-andī, *of (the) singing*
    Dat., Abl.    cant-andō, *by (the) singing*

**205** The **Supines** are really cases of a verb-noun of the 4th Decl. (and cannot be further declined) :—

    Acc.  cantāt-um, *a-singing, to (the) singing*
    Abl.  cantāt-ū,     *in (the) singing.*

Thus *eō piscātum* means ' I go a-fishing.'

**206**          USE OF PRONOUNS WITH VERBS.

Latin, like English, has pronouns for ' I,' ' thou,' etc., but does not need to express them except for the sake of emphasis : *cantō* = I sing, *ego cantō* = *I* sing ( it is I that sing). In the 3rd person the same form (*cantat*) may mean ' he sings,' ' she sings,' or ' it sings.'

**207**    This is true only of the subject of a Finite verb; the subject of an Infinitive must always be expressed: *e.g.* ' I know that he is alive ' = *scio* eum *vīvere* (I know him to be alive). The fact is that in the finite verb the subject is already expressed, more or less definitely, by the ending : *cantō* = sing-I, *cantās* = sing-you, *cantat* = sing-he, sing-she, or sing-it  Here the addition of a subject-word makes the subject more definite: *mulier cantat*, the woman sings ; *puer cantat*, the boy sings.

## Remarks on the Subjunctive Mood.

**208** The name 'Subjunctive' [*subjungere*, to subjoin] does not tell us much as to the use of the mood, for it is found not only in 'subjoined' clauses, but also in clauses that are not subjoined; again, in many subjoined clauses the Indicative is used. The English Subjunctive will not always serve as a translation of the Latin Subjunctive, the use of which must be studied in the Syntax.

Note the following important uses:

(*ut*) *cantet*, (in order that) he may sing, *or* (so that) he sings.
(*ut*) *cantāret*, (in order that) he might sing, *or* (so that) he was singing.
*cantāret* (*sī posset*), he would sing (if he were able).
*cantāvisset* (*sī potuisset*), he would have sung (if he had been able).

The Subjunctive has four tenses: the Present, Imperfect, Perfect, and Pluperfect; but no Future or Future Perfect.

**209** Note, however, that the Present Subjunctive itself often refers to the future (*veniat*, may he come! *ut veniat*, in order that he may come, etc.). In form the Present Subjunctive is partly the same as the Future Indicative in two conjugations (*regam, audiam*), and the Perfect Subjunctive is almost entirely the same as the Future Perfect Indicative in all four conjugations (*laudār-eris, -erit*, etc.). The Future Participle with *sim* is sometimes used instead of a Future Subj.

### Trunk and Stem.

**210** Behind the three trunks there generally lies a single ground-form, called the **verb-stem**, from which all forms of the verb were historically derived. In the 1st, 2nd, and 4th Conj., this is not the same as the Present trunk, but ends in a vowel:—

|  | Verb Stem. | Present Trunk. |
|---|---|---|
| 1st Conj. | laudā- | laud- |
| 2nd Conj. | monē-, dēlē- | mon-, dēl- |
| 4th Conj. | audī- | aud- |

These vowels are common to nearly all forms of the verb (though they do not retain their quantity throughout), e.g. *laudā-s, laudā-t, laudā-rem, laudā-vi, laudā-tum; dēlē-s, dēlē-t, dēlē-rem, dēlē-am, dēlēv-ī, dēlē-tum; audī-s, audī-t, audī-rem, audī-at, audī-vī, audī-tum*.

The verb-stem, then, is that part of the verb from which the various persons, tenses, moods, and voices were really **formed by the addition of inflections** or by other changes. A trunk is that part of the verb from which a group of forms may be most conveniently **found by the addition of endings**, and which *conveys the meaning* of the verb (limited in various ways). But historically we must trace back all forms to the *stem + inflections*: *laud-ō* to *laudā-ō, laud-ēmus* to *laudā-ī-mus* (ī is inflection of mood), *mon-ēbat* to *monē-bā-t* (*bā* is inflection of Imperfect tense, originally a Past tense of stem *fu-*, 'to become'), *aud-iēbat* to *audī-ēbā-t* (*ēbā* is probably an inflection of tense, formed on the analogy of the 2nd Conj.), *nōv-istī* to *nō-vi-stī* (*vi* is inflection of Perfect). Compare § 186.

## Verbs of 3rd Conjugation in -*iō*. 71

**211** The following verbs of the 3rd Conjugation take the endings of the 4th Conjugation in certain forms belonging to the Present trunk:—

| | | |
|---|---|---|
| capiō, *I take* | fugiō, *I flee* | quatiō, *I shake* |
| cupiō, *I desire* | jaciō, *I throw* | sapiō, *I am sensible* |
| faciō, *I make* | pariō, *I bring forth* | con-spiciō, *I behold* |
| fodiō, *I dig* | rapiō, *I snatch* | il-liciō, *I entice* |

and other compounds of *spic-*, *lic-*.

*Gradior, morior, patior* are conjugated like *capior* (§ 222).

**212**

| ACTIVE | | PASSIVE | |
|---|---|---|---|
| *INDIC.* | *SUBJ.* | *INDIC.* | *SUBJ.* |
| **Present** | | | |
| cap-iō | cap-iam | cap-ior | cap-iar |
| cap-is | cap-iās | cap-eris | cap-iāris |
| cap-it | cap-iat | cap-itur | cap-iātur |
| cap-imus | cap-iāmus | cap-imur | cap-iāmur |
| cap-itis | cap-iātis | cap-iminī | cap-iāminī |
| cap-iunt | cap-iant | cap-iuntur | cap-iantur |
| **Imperfect** | | | |
| cap-iēbam | cap-erem* | cap-iēbar | cap-erer* |
| cap-iēbās | cap-erēs | cap-iēbāris | cap-erēris |
| cap-iēbat | cap-eret | cap-iēbātur | cap-erētur |
| cap-iēbāmus | cap-erēmus | cap-iēbāmur | cap-erēmur |
| cap-iēbātis | cap-erētis | cap-iēbāminī | cap-erēminī |
| cap-iēbant | cap-erent | cap-iēbantur | cap-erentur |
| **Future** | | | |
| cap-iam | | cap-iar | |
| cap-iēs | | cap-iēris | |
| cap-iet | * Remember the rule given in § 198 ☞ | cap-iētur | |
| cap-iēmus | | cap-iēmur | |
| cap-iētis | | cap-iēminī | |
| cap-ient | | cap-ientur | |

| IMPERATIVE | | IMPERATIVE | |
|---|---|---|---|
| S. cap-e,*-itō | P. cap-ite,-itōte | S. cap-ere,*-itor | P. cap-iminī |
| cap-itō | cap-iuntō | cap-itor | cap-iuntor |

| | |
|---|---|
| Pres. Part. cap-iens | Gerundive cap-iendus |
| Pres. Infin. cap-ere | Pres. Infin. cap-ī |
| Gerund cap-iendum | |

## Remarks on the Verb SUM (§§ 188, 189).

**213** Compare the endings of the 3rd Pers. Plur. in the Future Indic., Perfect Indic., Perfect Subj., Fut. Perf. Indic. The *vowel* is *u* or *i*, according as the accent falls on the syllable preceding, or one syllable further back (for the rule of accent see § 7):—

Fut. Indic.  Perf. Indic.  Perf. Subj.  Fut. Perf. Indic.
erúnt       fuérunt       fúerint      fúerint

The same law holds in the four regular conjugations: but compare § 215.

**214** The following are sometimes used as by-forms of the verb *sum*:—

Imperf. Subj. *forem, fores, foret; forent* (especially in principal clauses of conditional sentences).

Fut. Infin. *fore.*

☞ *Sum* is the only verb in Latin that has an uncompounded Fut. Infin.

**215** The Compounds of *sum*, i.e. *ad-sum, de-sum, in-sum, inter-sum, ob-sum, prae-sum, sub-sum, super-sum*, etc., are conjugated like *sum;* but *pro-sum*, 'I am useful,' retains the *d* in which the prefix originally ended (*prod-*), when the following part begins with an *e*, e.g. *prod-est, prod-eram*, but *pro-sum, pro-fui* (for *prod-sum, prod-fui*). Note the 3rd Plur. Fut. Indic. Act. *prod-erunt* (so, too, in other compounds): cf. § 213. *Ab-sum* has a Pres. Part. *ab-sens* (cf. the adjective *prae-sens*, 'present'). The Perf. of *ab-sum* is *ā-fui*, that of *ad-sum* is *af-fui*.

**216** For *possum*, which is also a compound of *sum* (= *pot-sum;* cf. *pot-es, pot-est*, etc.), see §§ 232, 234, 239, 240.

## By-forms of the Regular Verb.

**217** 1. The forms derived from Perfect trunks in *-āv-, -ēv-, -īv-*, sometimes lose a syllable by contraction, *e.g.*—

laudāv-isti becomes laudasti  |  nōv-eram becomes nōram
dēlēv-issem    „    dēlessem  |  nōv-isse    „    nosse
audīv-isse     „    audisse   |

**218** 2. In the 4th Conj. *v* is sometimes dropped, and the *i* shortened; e.g. *audīv-erat* becomes *audi-erat*.

**219** 3. The ending *-ērunt* (3rd Plur.) often becomes *-ēre;* e.g. *laudāv-ēre, monu-ēre*, etc.

**220** 4. In the 2nd Sing. Pass. *-ris* often becomes *-re,* e.g. *laud-ābere* for *laud-āberis;* but rarely in the Pres. Indic., where ambiguity would thereby arise (*laud-āre* for *laud-āris*).

## Deponent Verbs.

**221** Deponent verbs are verbs of passive form, but active meaning. Note, however, that—

1. The Gerundive may have a passive meaning (as in other verbs): *hortandus,* '(fit) to-be-exhorted.'
2. The Present and Future Participles and the Future Infinitive are active in form, as well as in meaning.
3. The Gerund and Supine are formed as in the Active.

Deponents have thus three participles with active meaning (Present, Perfect, and Future: cf. § 201).

| PARTICIPLES | INFINITIVES |
|---|---|
| Pres. hort-ans, *exhorting* | hort-ārī, *to exhort* |
| Perf. hortāt-us, *having exhorted* | hortāt-us esse, *to have exhorted* |
| Fut. hortāt-ūrus, *about to exhort* | hortāt-ūrus esse, *to be about to exhort* |
| SUPINES | GERUND |
| hortāt-um, *to exhort* | hort-andum, *(the) exhorting* |
| hortāt-ū, *in (the) exhorting* | GERUNDIVE |
|  | hort-andus, *(fit) to-be-exhorted* |

**222** Deponents are conjugated like *laud-or, mon-eor, reg-or,* or *aud-ior.* Three follow *cap-ior,* i.e. *mor-ior,* I die, *pat-ior,* I suffer, *grad-ior,* I step. Thus *mor-ior,* I die, *mor-eris,* thou diest, *mor-itur,* he dies; *mor-ere* (Imperat.), die; *mor-ī,* to die; *mor-iens,* dying.

**223** *Or-ior,* I rise, is peculiar; it belongs to the 4th Conj. (Infin. *or-īrī*), but in the Pres. Indic. is conjugated like *capior* (thus *or-eris, or-itur*). The Imperf. Subj. is either *or-īrer* or *or-erer.* (For the Fut. Part. see § 227.) Similarly *pot-ior,* I get possession of, forms *pot-itur,* or *pot-ītur,* etc ; *pot-erētur,* or *pot-īrētur.*

**224** The regular deponent verbs of the 1st Conjugation are conjugated according to the following model:—

# FIRST CONJUGATION—DEPONENT VERB

## hort-: Character A.

| | INDICATIVE | SUBJUNCTIVE |
|---|---|---|
| **Present** | hort-**or**, *I exhort (am exhorting)* | hort-**er** |
| | hort-**āris**, *thou exhortest (art exhorting)* | hort-**ēris** |
| | hort-**ātur**, *he exhorts (is exhorting)* | hort-**ētur** |
| | hort-**āmur**, *we exhort (are exhorting)* | hort-**ēmur** |
| | hort-**āminī**, *you exhort (are exhorting)* | hort-**ēminī** |
| | hort-**antur**, *they exhort (are exhorting)* | hort-**entur** |
| **Imperfect** | hort-**ābar**, *I was exhorting* | hort-**ārer** |
| | hort-**ābāris**, *thou wast exhorting* | hort-**ārēris** |
| | hort-**ābātur**, *he was exhorting* | hort-**ārētur** |
| | hort-**ābāmur**, *we were exhorting* | hort-**ārēmur** |
| | hort-**ābāminī**, *you were exhorting* | hort-**ārēminī** |
| | hort-**ābantur**, *they were exhorting* | hort-**ārentur** |
| **Future** | hort-**ābor**, *I shall exhort* | |
| | hort-**āberis**, *thou wilt exhort* | |
| | hort-**ābitur**, *he will exhort* | |
| | hort-**ābimur**, *we shall exhort* | |
| | hort-**ābiminī**, *you will exhort* | |
| | hort-**ābuntur**, *they will exhort* | |

### IMPERATIVE

| *Unemphatic* | | *Emphatic* | |
|---|---|---|---|
| hort-**āre**, *exhort (thou)* | | hort-**ātor**, *thou shalt exhort* | |
| | | hort-**ātor**, *he shall exhort* | |
| hort-**āminī**, *exhort (ye)* | | | |
| | | hort-**antor**, *they shall exhort* | |

| **Verb-Adjs.** | Pres. Part. | hort-**ans**, *exhorting* |
| | Gerundive | hort-**andus**, *(fit) to-be-exhorted* |

| **Verb-Nouns** | Pres. Infin. | hort-**ārī**, *to exhort, to be exhorting* |
| | Gerund | hort-**andum**, *(the) exhorting* |

# FIRST CONJUGATION—DEPONENT VERB.

## hortāt-

| | INDICATIVE | SUBJUNCTIVE |
|---|---|---|
| **Perfect and Past** | hortāt-us* sum, *I have exhorted (I exhorted)*<br>hortāt-us es, *thou hast exhorted (didst exhort)*<br>hortāt-us est, *he has exhorted (he exhorted)*<br>hortāt-ī sumus, *we have exhorted (exhorted)*<br>hortāt-ī estis, *you have exhorted (exhorted)*<br>hortāt-ī sunt, *they have exhorted (exhorted)* | hortāt-us* sim<br>hortāt-us sis<br>hortāt-us sit<br>hortāt-ī sīmus<br>hortāt-ī sītis<br>hortāt-ī sint |
| **Pluperfect** | hortāt-us* eram, *I had exhorted*<br>hortāt-us erās, *thou hadst exhorted*<br>hortāt-us erat, *he had exhorted*<br>hortāt-ī erāmus, *we had exhorted*<br>hortāt-ī erātis, *you had exhorted*<br>hortāt-ī erant, *they had exhorted* | hortāt-us* essem<br>hortāt-us esses<br>hortāt-us esset<br>hortāt-ī essēmus<br>hortāt-ī essētis<br>hortāt-ī essent |
| **Future Perfect** | hortāt-us* erō, *I shall have exhorted*<br>hortāt-us eris, *thou wilt have exhorted*<br>hortāt-us erit, *he will have exhorted*<br>hortāt-ī erimus, *we shall have exhorted*<br>hortāt-ī eritis, *you will have exhorted*<br>hortāt-ī erunt, *they will have exhorted* | |

* Declined in all three genders (Nominative Case):
    Sing. hortāt-us, -a, -um.   Plur. hortāt-ī, -ae, -a.

| | | |
|---|---|---|
| **VERB. ADJS.** | Perf. Part. hortāt-us, *having exhorted*<br>Fut. Part. hortāt-ūrus, *about to exhort* | |
| **VERB. NOUNS** | Perf. Infin. hortāt-us esse, *to have exhorted*<br>Fut. Infin. hortāt-ūrus esse, *to be about to exhort*<br>Supines { hortāt-um, *to exhort*<br>{ hortāt-ū, *in (the) exhorting* | |

## Peculiarities in the Four Conjugations.

**226**  1. The verbs *dīc-ō* I say, *dūc-ō* I lead, *fac-iō* I make, *fer-ō* I bear, form shortened Imperatives : *dīc, dūc, fac, fer*.

**227**  2. In nine verbs the Fut. Part. is formed otherwise than from the Supine trunk :—

>ori-, mori-, nasci-tūrus
>rui-, frui-, pari-tūrus
>sonā-, secā-, juvā-tūrus
>[but ad-jūtūrus]

*orior*, I arise (Perf. Part. *ort-us*)
*morior*, I die (Perf. Part. *mortu-us*)
*nascor*, I am born (Perf. Part. *nāt-us*)
*ruō*, I fall (Sup. trunk *rut-*)

*fruor*, I enjoy (Perf. Part. *fruc-tus* or *fruit-us*)
*pariō*, I bring forth (Sup. trunk *part-*)
*sonō*, I sound (Sup. trunk *sonit-*)
*secō*, I cut (Sup. trunk *sect-*)
*juvō*, I aid (Sup. trunk *jūt-*)

**228**  3. In the verb *dare* 'to give' the *a* is short by nature in all forms, except *dā* (Imperat.) and *dās* (2nd Sing. Pres. Ind. Act.).

**229**  4. The Perfect Participles *cēnātus, pōtus,* and *pransus* (from *cēnō* I dine, *pōtō* I drink, *prandeō* I breakfast) have an active meaning.

**230**  5. The Perf. Participles of several deponent verbs have a passive as well as an active meaning, e.g. *comitātus*, 'accompanied' and 'having accompanied,' *oblītus*, 'forgotten' and 'having forgotten.'

**231**  6. The following archaic forms are found (chiefly in the poets):—
   (a) A Gerund and Gerundive in *-und-* (for *-end-*), e.g. *oriundum, oriundus* from *orior*; *repetundae* from *repetō*.
   (b) A Present Infinitive Passive in *-ier* for *-ī*, e.g. *laud-ārier = laud-ārī, accing-ier = accing-ī*.
   (c) A Subjunctive in *-sim* (*-assim, -essim*) and a Future Indic. in *-sō* (*-assō, -essō*), e.g. *faxint = faciant, ausim = audeam, levassim = levem, habessit = habeat; faxō = faciam, levassō = levābō, prohibessō = prohibēbō*.
   (d) A contracted 2nd Pers. Sing. and Plur. Perf. Indic. of 3rd Conj., e.g. *dixti = dixistī, accestis = accessistis*.
   (e) An Imperf. of the 4th Conj. in *-ibam, ibās, ibat*, etc.

## Anomalous Verbs.

**232** The following verbs are conjugated irregularly *in the tenses derived from the Present Trunk* (for conjugation see next page):—

| | | | | |
|---|---|---|---|---|
| possum | posse | potu-ī | —— | *be able* |
| volŏ | velle | volu-ī | —— | *be willing, wish* |
| nōlō | nolle | nōlu-ī | —— | *be unwilling* |
| mālō | malle | mālu-ī | ——. | *prefer* |
| ferō | ferre | tul-ī | lāt-um | *bear* |
| fīō | fierī | fact-us sum | —— | *become, be made* |
| eŏ | īre | īv-ī *or* i-ī * | it-um | *go* |

**233** All these verbs, except *ferō*,† have only one voice: for the passive of *ferō* see § 241.

**234** *Possum* is compounded of *pot-* (*potis*) able, and *sum* I am; *pot-es* thou art able, *pot-eram* I was able. Note *pos-sumus* for *pot-sumus, posse* for *pot-esse*, etc. *Possum* has no Imperative and no Future Participle or Future Infinitive.

**235** *Nōlō* is compounded of *ne* (= *nōn*) *volō*, I am not willing.
*Mālō* is compounded of *mā* (= *magis*) *volō*, I am more willing.

**236** *Fīō*, in the tenses from Pres. trunk, serves as the passive of *faciō*, which does not itself form Pres. trunk tenses: *factus sum* (*eram, erō*) belongs to both verbs.

**237** *Queō, quīre, quīv-ī, quit-um*, 'to be able,' and *nequeō, nequīre, nequīv-ī, nequit-um*, 'to be unable,' are conjugated like *eō*, but have no Imperative, Gerund, or Gerundive, and no Participles in common use.

**238** *Edō, ed-ere, ēd-ī, ēs-um* has, besides the regular forms, the following by-forms (contracted):—

| *Pres. Indic.* | *Imperat.* | *Pres. Infin.* |
|---|---|---|
| S. 2. ēs *for* ed-is | S. 2. ēs *for* ed-e | esse *for* ed-ere |
| 3. est *for* ed-it | 2, 3. estō *for* ed-itō | |
| P. 2. estis *for* ed-itis | P. 2. este *for* ed-ite | |

| *Imperf. Subj.* | *Pres. Indic. Pass.* |
|---|---|
| S. 1. essem *for* ed-erem | S. 3. estur *for* ed-itur |
| 2. essēs *for* ed-erēs, etc. | |

---

\* Especially in Compounds: e.g., *red-i-ī, ab-i-it, ad-i-ērunt, sub-i-erant*.
† *Eō* has a Passive in an impersonal sense (e.g. *itur* 'it is gone' = 'people go;' cf. *irī* in the Fut. Infin. Pass., § 203, p. 69), and also in certain Transitive Compounds: (e.g. *inībātur, subeuntur, subibitur, aditus, adirī*: thus *Consilium inībātur* 'a scheme was being entered upon,' *Nōlunt adīrī* 'They are unwilling to be approached.'

# ANOMALOUS VERBS.

| | INDICATIVE | | | | | |
|---|---|---|---|---|---|---|
| | Singular | | | Plural | | |
| | 1 | 2 | 3 | 1 | 2 | 3 |
| **Present** | pos-sum<br>volŏ<br>nōlō<br>mālō<br>ferō<br>fīō<br>eō | pot-es<br>vīs<br>nōnvīs<br>māvīs<br>fers<br>fīs<br>īs | pot-est<br>vult<br>nōnvult<br>māvult<br>fert<br>fit<br>it | pos-sumus<br>volumus<br>nōlumus<br>mālumus<br>ferimus<br>———<br>īmus | pot-estis<br>vultis<br>nōnvultis<br>māvultis<br>fertis<br>———<br>ītis | pos-sunt<br>volunt<br>nōlunt<br>mālunt<br>ferunt<br>fīunt<br>eunt |
| **Imperfect** | pot-eram<br>vol-<br>nōl-<br>māl- ⎫<br>fer- ⎬ēbam<br>fī- ⎭<br>ī-   bam | -erās<br><br><br>-ēbās<br><br><br>-bās | -erat<br><br><br>-ēbat<br><br><br>-bat | -erāmus<br><br><br>-ēbāmus<br><br><br>-bāmus | -erātis<br><br><br>-ēbātis<br><br><br>-bātis | -erant<br><br><br>-ēbant<br><br><br>-bant |
| **Future** | pot-erō<br>vol-<br>nōl-<br>māl- ⎫<br>fer- ⎬am<br>fī- ⎭<br>ī-   bō | -eris<br><br><br>-ēs<br><br><br>-bis | -erit<br><br><br>-et<br><br><br>-bit | -erimus<br><br><br>-ēmus<br><br><br>-bimus | -eritis<br><br><br>-ētis<br><br><br>-bitis | -erunt<br><br><br>-ent<br><br><br>-bunt |

| | Participle | Infinitive | Gerund |
|---|---|---|---|
| **Verb-Adjective** | ———<br>vol-<br>nōl-<br>māl- ⎫ ens<br>fer- ⎬<br>———<br>ī-*<br>*Trunk eunt- | *Verb-Nouns*<br>posse<br>velle<br>nolle<br>malle<br>ferre<br>fierī<br>īre | ———<br>vol-<br>nol-<br>māl- ⎫ endum<br>fer- ⎬<br>———<br>e-undum |

## ANOMALOUS VERBS.

| | SUBJUNCTIVE | | | | | |
|---|---|---|---|---|---|---|
| | Singular | | | Plural | | |
| | 1 | 2 | 3 | 1 | 2 | 3 |
| **Present** | pos-sim<br>vel-<br>nōl- }-im<br>māl-<br>fer-<br>fī- }-am<br>e- | pos-sīs<br><br>-īs<br><br><br>-ās<br> | pos-sit<br><br>-it<br><br><br>-at<br> | pos-sīmus<br><br>-īmus<br><br><br>-āmus<br> | pos-sītis<br><br>-ītis<br><br><br>-ātis<br> | pos-sint<br><br>-int<br><br><br>-ant<br> |
| **Imperfect** | pos-s-<br>vel-l-<br>nol-l-<br>mal-l- }em<br>fer-r-<br>fī-er-<br>i-r- | -ēs | -et | -ēmus | -ētis | -ent |

| | IMPERATIVE | | | |
|---|---|---|---|---|
| | Singular | | Plural | |
| | 2 | 3 | 2 | 3 |
| | nōl-ī, nōl-ītō | nōl-ītō | nōl-ite, nōl-ītōte | nōl-untō |
| | fer, fer-tō | fer-tō | fer-te, fer-tōte | fer-untō |
| | fī | — | fī-te | |
| | ī, ī-tō | ī-tō | ī-te, ī-tōte | e-untō |

**241**  Passive of ferō.

| INDICATIVE | | | | | |
|---|---|---|---|---|---|
| Singular | | | Plural | | |
| fer-or | fer-ris | fer-tur | fer-imur | fer-iminī | fer-untur |
| fer-ēbar | fer-ēbāris | fer-ēbātur | fer-ēbāmur | fer-ēbāminī | fer-ēbantur |
| fer-ar | fer-ēris | fer-ētur | fer-ēmur | fer-ēminī | fer-entur |

| SUBJUNCTIVE | | | | | |
|---|---|---|---|---|---|
| fer-ar | fer-āris | fer-ātur | fer-āmur | fer-āminī | fer-antur |
| fer-r-er | fer-r-ēris | fer-r-ētur | fer-r-ēmur | fer-r-ēminī | fer-r-entur |

| IMPERATIVE | | | | |
|---|---|---|---|---|
| fer-re, fer-tor | | fer-tor | fer-iminī | fer-untor |

| GERUNDIVE fer-endus | PRES. INFIN. fer-r-ī |
|---|---|

## Defective Verbs.

**242**   Defective Verbs are verbs of which one or more groups of forms are wanting.

**243**   ☞ *Coepī* means 'I have begun' ('I begin'), 'I began.' The meanings 'I was beginning,' 'I shall begin' are expressed by *incipiēbam, incipiam* (from *incipiō*). From the Participles *coeptūrus, coeptus* are formed compound tenses (with *sum, esse,* etc.). *Coeptus sum* is generally transl. by an Active in English and is used chiefly with a Passive Infinitive: e.g. *urbs coepta est aedificārī*, the city began to be built.

**244**   *Meminī* and *ōdī* have always the sense of Presents (cf. *coepī*, § 243): *memin-eram, ōderam* are transl. by Engl. Past tense; *meminerō, ōderō* by Engl. Future.

**245**   Other Perfects with present sense are:—
   *nōvī*, I know (from *nōscō*, I learn).
   *consuēvī*, I am accustomed (from *consuēscō*, I accustom myself).

## DEFECTIVE VERBS.

**246**   1. The Perfects **coepī, meminī, ōdī**.

| Indic. | | | |
|---|---|---|---|
| *Perf.* | coep-ī, *I have begun* | memin-ī, *I remember* | ōd-ī, *I hate* |
| *Pluperf.* | coep-eram, *I had [begun* | memin-eram, *I re- [membered* | ōd-eram, *I hated* |
| *Fut. Perf.* | coep-erō, *I shall [have begun* | memin-erō, *I shall [remember* | ōd-erō, *I shall [hate* |
| **Subj.** | | | |
| *Perf.* | coep-erim | memin-erim | ōd-erim |
| *Pluperf.* | coep-issem | memin-issem | ōd-issem |
| **Imperat.** | | memen-tō, -tōte, *re- [member* | |
| **Infin.** | coep-isse, *to have [begun* | memin-isse, *to re- [member* | ōd-isse, *to hate* |
| **Part.** | Sup. trunk coept- | | Sup. trunk ōs- |
| *Fut.* | coept-ūrus, *about to [begin* | | ōs-ūrus, *about to [hate* |
| *Perf.* | coept-us, *begun* (in Passive sense) | | ōs-us, *hating* |

**247**   2. **inquam**, say I (used parenthetically).

Pres.     inquam, inquis, inquit; inquimus —— inquiunt
Imperf.   —— —— inquiēbat
Fut.      —— inquiēs, inquiet
Perf.     —— inquistī, inquit

The only common form is *inquit*, 'quoth he,' 'said he.'

Imperatives (*inque, inquitō*) are found in Plautus and Terence.

**248**   3. **aiō**, I say (I say yes).

Pres.        aiō, aīs, aït; —— —— aiunt
Imperf.      aiēbam, aiēbas, aiēbat; aiēbāmus, aiēbātis, aiēbant
Pres. Subj.  —— aiās, aiat; —— —— aiant
Pres. Part.  aiens

*Aïsne?* say you so? is shortened to *ain?*

**249**   4. **quaesō**, I entreat (used parenthetically).

(Dīc quaesō, tell me pray) forms 1st Pers. Plur. *quaesumus*.

6

## DEFECTIVE VERBS.—IMPERSONAL VERBS.

**250**   5. **fārī**, to speak (old and poetic Infinitive: Deponent).

PRES. —— fāris, fātur, fāmur, —— fantur
FUT. fābor, —— fābitur
IMPERAT. fāre
PRES. PART. fantem, fantī (no Nominative)
PERF. PART. fātus
PERF. INDIC. fātus sum, etc.
GERUND *in the phrase* fandō audīre, *to learn by hearsay.*

**251**   6. The Imperatives of **avēre, salvēre, valēre,** etc.

avē (avētō), avēte, *hail.*
salvē (salvētō), salvēte, *hail.*
valē, valēte, *farewell* (*Valeō,* 'I am strong,' is conjugated throughout).
age, agite, *come now* (*Agō,* 'I do,' is conjugated throughout).
apage, *begone, avaunt.*
cedŏ, cette (archaic Plural), *hand over, tell me* (origin uncertain).

7. **inīt,** he (she, it) begins.   (No other form extant).

**252**            Impersonal Verbs.

Impersonal verbs are verbs which form only the 3rd Pers. Sing. of each tense (Indic. and Subj.) and the Infinitive.

plu-it (-ere), *it is raining*           advesperasc-it (-ere), *it is getting late*
ning-it (-ere), *it is snowing*          fulgur-at (-āre), *it is lightening*
illucesc-it (-ere), *it is dawning*      ton-at (-āre), *it is thundering.*

pig-et (-ēre, -uit), *it vexes*
pud-et (-ēre, -uit *or* -itum est), *it shames*  ⎫
paenit-et (-ēre, -uit), *it repents*             ⎬ aliquem alicūjus reī.
taed-et (-ēre, pertaesum est), *it wearies*      ⎭

miser-et (-ēre, -itum est), *it distresses* (aliquem alicūjus).

lib-et (-ēre, -uit *or* -itum est), *it pleases*  ⎫ alicū *with Infin.*
lic-et (-ēre, -uit *or* -itum est), *it is lawful* ⎭

oport-et (-ēre, -uit), *it behoves* (aliquem *with Infin.*).

rēfert (rēferre), *it profits* (meā, tuā, etc.).   [From *rēs* and *ferō.*]

dec-et [1] (-ēre, -uit), *it befits*         ⎫ aliquem *with Infin.*
dēdec-et [1] (-ēre, -uit), *it does not befit* ⎭

---

[1] Also personally in 3rd Pers. Plur. *nōn tē citharae decent,* lutes befit thee not (*Horace*).

**253** Some personal verbs are *used impersonally* (in the 3rd Sing. and Infin.) in a special sense:—

accid-it (-ere)  ⎫
conting-it (-ere) ⎬ *it happens*
ēven-it (-īre)   ⎪
fit (fierī)      ⎭

⎧ accidō, *I fall upon*
⎨ contingō, *I fall to the lot of*
⎪ ēveniō, *I come out*
⎩ fīō, *I become*

const-at (-āre), *it is well known* (constō, *I am in accord*).
condūc-it (-ere), *it is conducive* (condūcō, *I lead together*).
conven-it (-īre), *it suits* (conveniō, *I come together*).
expœd-it (-īre), *it is expedient* (expediō, *I set free*).
juv-at (-āre), *it delights* (juvō, *I help*).
inter-est (-esse), *it concerns* (intersum, *I take part in*).

fall-it (-ere)   ⎫
fug-it (-ere)    ⎬ *it escapes notice*
praeter-it (-īre)⎭

⎧ fallō, *I deceive*
⎨ fugiō, *I flee*
⎩ praetereō, *I pass by*

plac-et (-ēre), *it seems good, it is resolved* (placeō, *I please*).
etc.

## Principal Parts of Verbs.

**254** The following lists include all important verbs which *form their Perfect and Supine trunks irregularly* (cf. §§ 232, 242). The typical regular verbs are inserted in **clarendon** type.

The Perfect Active trunk is called

**Weak** when it is formed with a suffix (-*v*, -*u*, -*s*);

**Strong** when it is formed without a suffix. Strong Perfect trunks are sometimes formed by Reduplication, *i.e.* by prefixing a short syllable (*pend-*, Perf. *pepend-*); sometimes by lengthening the vowel (*leg-*, Perf. *lēg-*); sometimes they are the same as the Present trunk.

For Compound verbs see §§ 291-299.

☞ For some of the Supines in the following lists the only authority is the form of the Perfect Participle Passive.

FIRST CONJUGATION.

I. **Weak** Perfect trunks.

**255**      1. Formed with *v*, preceded by *ā*.

| laud-ō | -āre | laudāv-ī | laudāt-um | *praise* |
|--------|------|----------|-----------|----------|
| pōt-ō  | -āre | pōtāv-ī  | pōt-um    | *drink*  |
|        |      |          | (cf. § 229.) |       |

**256**  2. Formed with *u*.

| crep-ō | -āre | crepu-ī | crepit-um | *rattle, creak* |
| cub-ō | -āre | cubu-ī | cubit-um | *lie down* |
| dom-ō | -āre | domu-ī | domit-um | *tame* |
| son-ō | -āre | sonu-ī | sonit-um (§227) *sound* |
| vet-ō | -āre | vetu-ī | vetit-um | *forbid* |
| fric-ō | -āre | fricu-ī | frict-um | *rub* |
| sec-ō | -āre | secu-ī | sect-um (§227) *cut* |
| mic-ō | -āre | micu-ī | ——— | *glitter* |
| ton-ō | -āre | tonu-ī | ——— | *thunder* |

## II. Strong Perfect trunks.

**257**  1. Formed by Reduplication.

| d-ō | -are | ded-ī | dat-um | *give* |
| st-ō | -āre | stet-ī | stat-um | *stand* |

**258**  2. Formed by lengthening the vowel.

| juv-ō | -āre | jūv-ī | jūt-um (§ 227) | *aid* |
| lav-ō | -āre | lāv-ī | laut-um, lōt-um, lavāt-um | *wash* |

## SECOND CONJUGATION.

### I. Weak Perfect trunks.

**259**  1. Formed with *u*.

| mon-eō | -ēre | monu-ī | monit-um | *warn* |
| doc-eō | -ēre | docu-ī | doct-um | *teach* |
| ten-eō | -ēre | tenu-ī | tent-um | *hold* |
| misc-eō | -ēre | miscu-ī | mixt-um | *mix* |
| torr-eō | -ēre | torru-ī | tost-um | *roast* |
| cens-eō | -ēre | censu-ī | cens-um | *value, judge* |

## PRINCIPAL PARTS OF VERBS.

**260**    2. Formed with *v*, preceded by a long vowel (generally *ē*).

| | | | | |
|---|---|---|---|---|
| dēl-eō | -ēre | dēlēv-ī | dēlēt-um | *destroy* |
| fl-eō | -ēre | flēv-ī | flēt-um | *weep* |
| n-eō | -ēre | nēv-ī | nēt-um | *spin* |
| com-pl-eō | -ēre | com-plēv-ī | com-plēt-um | *fill up* |
| ab-ol-eō | -ēre | ab-olēv-ī | ab-olit-um | *abolish* |
| ci-eō | -ēre | cīv-ī | cit-um | *rouse* |

**261**                 3. Formed with *s*.

| | | | | |
|---|---|---|---|---|
| aug-eō | -ēre | aux-ī | auct-um | *increase* |
| frīg-eō | -ēre | frix-ī | —— | *be cold* |
| lūc-eō | -ēre | lux-ī | —— | *shine* |
| lūg-eō | -ēre | lux-ī | —— | *mourn* |
| cō-nīv-eō | -ēre | cō-nix-ī | —— | *wink* |
| indulg-eō | -ēre | induls-ī | indult-um | *be indulgent* |
| torqu-eō | -ēre | tors-ī | tort-um | *twist* |
| man-eō | -ēre | mans-ī | mans-um | *remain* |
| jub-eō | -ēre | juss-ī | juss-um | *command* |
| rīd-eō | -ēre | rīs-ī | rīs-um | *laugh* |
| suād-eō | -ēre | suās-ī | suās-um | *advise* |
| ard-eō | -ēre | ars-ī | ars-um | *be on fire* |
| haer-eō | -ēre | haes-ī | haes-um | *cling* |
| mulc-eō | -ēre | muls-ī | muls-um | *soothe* |
| mulg-eō | -ēre | muls-ī | muls-um | *milk* |
| terg-eō | -ēre | ters-ī | ters-um | *wipe* |
| alg-eō | -ēre | als-ī | —— | *be cold* |
| fulg-eō | -ēre | fuls-ī | —— | *glitter* |
| turg-eō | -ēre | turs-ī | —— | *swell* |
| urg-eō | -ēre | urs-ī | —— | *urge* |

II. **Strong** Perfect trunks.

1. Formed by Reduplication.

**262**

| | | | | |
|---|---|---|---|---|
| pend-eō | -ēre | pepend-ī | pens-um | *hang* |
| mord-eō | -ēre | momord-ī | mors-um | *bite* |
| spond-eō | -ēre | spopond-ī | spons-um | *pledge* |
| tond-eō | -ēre | totond-ī | tons-um | *shear* |

## PRINCIPAL PARTS OF VERBS.

**263**     2. Formed by lengthening the vowel.

| | | | | |
|---|---|---|---|---|
| fov-eō | -ēre | fōv-ī | fōt-um | *cherish, warm* |
| mov-eō | -ēre | mōv-ī | mōt-um | *move* |
| vov-eō | -ēre | vōv-ī | vōt-um | *vow* |
| cav-eō | -ēre | cāv-ī | caut-um | *beware* |
| fav-eō | -ēre | fāv-ī | faut-um | *be favourable* |
| pav-eō | -ēre | pāv-ī | —— | *fear* |
| ferv-eō | -ēre | ferv-ī, ferbu-ī | —— | *boil* |
| sed-eō | -ēre | sēd-ī | sess-um | *sit* |
| vid-eō | -ēre | vīd-ī | vīs-um | *see* |

**264**     3. Perfect trunk = Present trunk.

| | | | | |
|---|---|---|---|---|
| prand-eō | -ēre | prand-ī | prans-um | *breakfast* |
| strīd-eō | -ēre | strīd-ī | —— | *hiss* |

**265**     ☞ A number of regular verbs of this Conjugation have no Supine trunk (Perfect in *uī*).

| | | |
|---|---|---|
| arceō, *ward off* | oleō, *smell* | studeō, *be zealous* |
| calleō, *be skilful* | palleō, *be pale* | stupeō, *be stunned, dazed* |
| egeō, *need* | pateō, *lie open* | timeō, *fear* |
| flōreō, *flourish* | rigeō, *be stiff* | tumeō, *swell* |
| horreō, *shudder* | rubeō, *blush* | vigeō, *thrive* |
| lateō, *lie hidden* | sileō, *be silent* | vireō, *be green* |
| madeō, *be wet* | sorbeō, *swallow* | |
| niteō, *shine* | splendeō, *shine* | |

## THIRD CONJUGATION.

### I. Weak Perfect trunks.

1. Formed with *s*.

**266**     *a.* The vowel of the Present trunk short by nature.

| | | | | |
|---|---|---|---|---|
| **reg-ō** | -ere | **rex-ī** | **rect-um** | *rule* |
| teg-ō | -ere | tex-ī | tect-um | *cover* |
| trah-ō | -ere | trax-ī | tract-um | *drag* |
| veh-ō | -ere | vex-ī | vect-um | *carry* |
| coqu-ō | -ere | cox-ī | coct-um | *cook* |

| | | | | |
|---|---|---|---|---|
| stru-ō | -ere | strux-ī | struct-um | *erect* |
| flu-ō | -ere | flux-ī | flux-um | *flow* |
| dīvid-ō | -ere | dīvīs-ī | dīvīs-um | *divide* |
| prem-ō | -ere | press-ī | press-um | *press* |
| ger-ō | -ere | gess-ī | gest-um | *carry, wear* |

**267** *b.* The vowel of the Present trunk long by nature.

| | | | | |
|---|---|---|---|---|
| scrīb-ō | -ere | scrips-ī | script-um | *write* |
| nūb-ō | -ere | nups-ī | nupt-um | *marry* |
| rēp-ō | -ere | reps-ī | rept-um | *creep* |
| dīc-ō | -ere | dix-ī | dict-um | *say* |
| dūc-ō | -ere | dux-ī | duct-um | *lead* |
| af-flīg-ō | -ere | af-flix-ī | af-flict-um | *dash down* |
| sūg-ō | -ere | sux-ī | suct-um | *suck* |
| vīv-ō | -ere | vix-ī | vict-um | *live* |
| fīg-ō | -ere | fix-ī | fix-um | *fix* |
| claud-ō | -ere | claus-ī | claus-um | *shut* |
| plaud-ō | -ere | plaus-ī | plaus-um | *clap* |
| laed-ō | -ere | laes-ī | laes-um | *wound* |
| lūd-ō | -ere | lūs-ī | lūs-um | *play* |
| rād-ō | -ere | rās-ī | rās-um | *scrape* |
| rōd-ō | -ere | rōs-ī | rōs-um | *gnaw* |
| trūd-ō | -ere | trūs-ī | trūs-um | *thrust* |
| ē-vād-ō | -ere | ē-vās-ī | ē-vās-um | *go out* |
| cēd-ō | -ere | cess-ī | cess-um | *yield* |
| ūr-ō | -ere | uss-ī | ust-um | *burn* |

**268** *c.* The vowel of the Present trunk followed by two consonants

| | | | | |
|---|---|---|---|---|
| carp-ō | -ere | carps-ī | carpt-um | *pluck* |
| sculp-ō | -ere | sculps-ī | sculpt-um | *engrave* |
| serp-ō | -ere | serps-ī | serpt-um | *crawl* |
| plang-ō | -ere | planx-ī | planct-um | *beat the breast* |
| pang-ō | -ere | panx-ī | panct-um | *fix* (cf. § 271) |
| cing-ō | -ere | cinx-ī | cinct-um | *gird* |
| ting-ō | -ere | tinx-ī | tinct-um | *dip* |
| ex-stingu-ō | -ere | ex-stinx-ī | ex-stinct-um | *extinguish* |

## PRINCIPAL PARTS OF VERBS.

| | | | | |
|---|---|---|---|---|
| jung-ō | -ere | junx-ī | junct-um | *join* |
| ung-ō | -ere | unx-ī | unct-um | *anoint* |
| contemn-ō | -ere | contemps-ī | contempt-um | *despise* |
| fing-ō | -ere | finx-ī | fict-um | *form* |
| ping-ō | -ere | pinx-ī | pict-um | *paint* |
| string-ō | -ere | strinx-ī | strict-um | *strip* |
| ning-ō | -ere | ninx-ī | —— | *snow* |
| flect-ō | -ere | flex-ī | flex-um | *bend* |
| pect-ō | -ere | pex-ī | pex-um | *comb* |
| nect-ō | -ere | nex-ī, nexu-ī | nex-um | *bind* |
| plect-ō | ere | plex-ī, plexu-ī | plex-um | *plait* |
| sparg-ō | -ere | spars-ī | spars-um | *scatter* |
| merg-ō | ere | mers-ī | mers-um | *immerse* |
| mitt-ō | -ere | mīs-ī | miss-um | *send* |

2. Formed with *v*, preceded by a long vowel.

| | | | | |
|---|---|---|---|---|
| sin-ō | -ere | sīv-ī | sit-um | *permit* |
| lin-ō | -ere | lēv-ī | lit-um | *smear* |
| ser-ō | -ere | sēv-ī | sat-um | *sow* |
| cresc-ō | -ere | crēv-ī | crēt-um | *grow* |
| quiesc-ō | -ere | quiēv-ī | quiēt-um | *rest* |
| suesc-ō | -ere | suēv-ī | suēt-um | *be accustomed* |
| nosc-ō | -ere | nōv-ī | nōt-um | *get to know* |
| scisc-ō | -ere | scīv-ī | scit-um | *decree* |
| pasc-ō | -ere | pāv-ī | past-um | *feed* (Transitive) |
| pet-ō | -ere | petīv-ī | petīt-um | *aim at, desire* |
| quaer-ō | -ere | quaesīv-ī | quaesīt-um | *seek, enquire* |
| rud-ō | -ere | rudīv-ī | (rudīt-um) | *bray* |
| arcess-ō | -ere | arcessīv-ī | arcessīt-um | *summon* |
| capess-ō | -ere | capessīv-ī | capessīt-um | *catch at* |
| facess-ō | -ere | facessīv-ī | facessīt-um | *do eagerly* |
| lacess-ō | -ere | lacessīv-ī | lacessīt-um | *provoke* |
| ter-ō | -ere | trīv-ī | trīt-um | *rub* |
| cern-ō | -ere | crēv-ī | crēt-um | *distinguish* |
| spern-ō | -ere | sprēv-ī | sprēt-um | *spurn* |
| stern-ō | -ere | strāv-ī | strāt-um | *strew* |

## PRINCIPAL PARTS OF VERBS.

**270**  3. Formed with *u*.

| | | | | |
|---|---|---|---|---|
| frem-ō | -ere | fremu-ī | fremit-um | *mutter* |
| gem-ō | -ere | gemu-ī | gemit-um | *sigh* |
| trem-ō | -ere | tremu-ī | —— | *tremble* |
| vom-ō | -ere | vomu-ī | vomit-um | *vomit* |
| gign-ō | -ere | genu-ī | genit-um | *beget* |
| pōn-ō | -ere | posu-ī | posit-um | *place, put* |
| strep-ō | -ere | strepu-ī | strepit-um | *make a noise* |
| al-ō | -ere | alu-ī | alt-um, alit-um | *rear* |
| col-ō | -ere | colu-ī | cult-um | *till* |
| consul-ō | -ere | consulu-ī | consult-um | *consult* |
| occul-ō | -ere | occulu-ī | occult-um | *hide* |
| ser-ō | -ere | -seru-ī | -sert-um | *twine* |
| tex-ō | -ere | texu-ī | text-um | *weave* |
| met-ō | -ere | [messem fēcī] | mess-um | *reap* |
| compesc-ō | -ere | compescu-ī | —— | *restrain* |
| fur-ō | -ere | furu-ī [insāniv-ī] | —— | *rave* |

II. **Strong** Perfect trunks.

**271**  1. Formed by Reduplication.

| | | | | |
|---|---|---|---|---|
| curr-ō | -ere | cucurr-ī | curs-um | *run* |
| posc-ō | -ere | poposc-ī | —— | *demand* |
| pend-ō | -ere | pepend-ī | pens-um | *weigh* |
| tend-ō | -ere | tetend-ī | tent-um, tens-um | *stretch* |
| fall-ō | -ere | fefell-ī | fals-um | *deceive* |
| parc-ō | -ere | peperc-ī | pars-um | *spare* |
| cad-ō | -ere | cecid-ī | cās-um | *fall* |
| caed-ō | -ere | cecīd-ī | caes-um | *cut (fell)* |
| can-ō | -ere | cecin-ī | cant-um | *sing* |
| pang-ō | -ere | pepig-ī | pact-um | *fix, settle* (cf. § 268) |
| tang-ō | -ere | tetig-ī | tact-um | *touch* |
| pung-ō | -ere | pupug-ī | punct-um | *prick* |
| tund-ō | -ere | tutud-ī | tuns-um, tūs-um | *thump* |
| pell-ō | -ere | pepul-ī | puls-um | *push* |
| sist-ō | -ere | -stit-ī | stat-um | *make to halt* |
| disc-ō | -ere | didic-ī | —— | *learn* |

**272** The following have lost Reduplication of the Perfect trunk :—

| per-cell-ō | -ere | per-cul-ī | per-culs-um | *cast down* |
| find-ō | -ere | fid-ī | fiss-um | *split* |
| scind-ō | -ere | scid-ī | sciss-um | *tear* |
| toll-ō | -ere | sus-tul-ī | sub-lāt-um | *lift (take away)* |

**273**    2. Formed by lengthening the vowel.

| leg-ō | -ere | lēg-ī | lect-um | *read, choose* |
| ag-ō | -ere | ēg-ī | act-um | *drive* |
| frang-ō | -ere | frēg-ī | fract-um | *break* |
| re-linqu-ō | -ere | re-līqu-ī | re-lict-um | *leave* |
| vinc-ō | -ere | vīc-ī | vict-um | *conquer* |
| rump-ō | -ere | rūp-ī | rupt-um | *burst* |
| em-ō | -ere | ēm-ī | empt-um | *buy* |
| ed-ō | -ere | ēd-ī | ēs-um | *eat* |
| fund-ō | -ere | fūd-ī | fūs-um | *pour* |

**274**    3. Perfect Trunk = Present Trunk.

*a.* The Present trunk ending in a consonant.

| vert-ō | -ere | vert-ī | vers-um | *turn* |
| verr-ō | -ere | verr-ī | vers-um | *sweep* |
| vell-ō | -ere | vell-ī | vuls-um | *pluck* |
| vīs-ō | -ere | vīs-ī | (vīs-um) | *visit* |
| cūd-ō | -ere | cūd-ī | cūs-um | *hammer, forge* |
| sīd-ō | -ere | (sīd-ī) sēd-ī | — | *seat oneself* |
| mand-ō | -ere | mand-ī | mans-um | *chew* |
| scand-ō | -ere | scand-ī | scans-um | *climb* |
| ac-cend-ō | -ere | ac-cend-ī | ac-cens-um | *kindle* |
| dē-fend-ō | -ere | dē-fend-ī | dē-fens-um | *ward off (defend)* |
| prehend-ō | -ere | prehend-ī | prehens-um | *seize* |
| pand-ō | -ere | pand-ī | pass-um | *spread out* |
| lamb-ō | -ere | lamb-ī | lambit-um | *lick* |
| bib-ō | -ere | bib-ī | — | *drink* |
| īc-ō | -ere | īc-ī | ict-um | *smite* |

## PRINCIPAL PARTS OF VERBS.

**275**     *b.* The Present trunk ending in *v* or *u*.

| | | | | |
|---|---|---|---|---|
| volv-ō | -ere | volv-ī | volūt-um | *roll* |
| solv-ō | -ere | solv-ī | solūt-um | *loosen* |
| acu-ō | -ere | acu-ī | acūt-um | *sharpen* |
| imbu-ō | -ere | imbu-ī | imbūt-um | *wet slightly* |
| exu-ō | -ere | exu-ī | exūt-um | *take off* |
| indu-ō | -ere | indu-ī | indūt-um | *put on* |
| lu-ō | -ere | lu-ī | lūt-um | *wash* |
| minu-ō | -ere | minu-ī | minūt-um | *lessen* |
| statu-ō | -ere | statu-ī | statūt-um | *set up (resolve)* |
| tribu-ō | -ere | tribu-ī | tribūt-um | *assign* |
| ru-ō | -ere | ru-ī | rut-um (§227) | *fall* |
| argu-ō | -ere | argu-ī | ——— | *accuse* |
| con-gru-ō | -ere | con-gru-ī | ——— | *agree* |
| metu-ō | -ere | metu-ī | ——— | *fear* |
| ab-nu-ō | -ere | ab-nu-ī | ——— | *refuse* |
| plu-it | -ere | plu-it | ——— | *rain* |

### VERBS OF THE THIRD CONJUGATION IN -iō.

**276**     I. **Weak** Perfect trunks.

| | | | | |
|---|---|---|---|---|
| rap-iō | -ere | rapu-ī | rapt-um | *snatch* |
| cup-iō | -ere | cupīv-ī | cupīt-um | *desire* |
| sap-iō | -ere | sapīv-ī | ——— | *be sensible* |
| il-lic-iō | -ere | il-lex-ī | il-lect-um | *lure on, entice* |
| pel-lic-iō | -ere | pel-lex-ī | pel-lect-um | *lure to ruin* |
| con-spic-iō | -ere | con-spex-ī | con-spect-um | *behold* |
| quat-iō | -ere | (-quass-ī) | quass-um | *shake* |

**277**     II. **Strong** Perfect trunks.

| | | | | |
|---|---|---|---|---|
| cap-iō | -ere | cēp-ī | capt-um | *take* |
| fac-iō | -ere | fēc-ī | fact-um | *make* |
| jac-iō | -ere | jēc-ī | jact-um | *throw* |
| fug-iō | -ere | fūg-ī | fugit-um | *flee* |
| fod-iō | -ere | fōd-ī | foss-um | *dig* |
| par-iō | -ere | peper-ī | part-um (§227) | *bring forth* |

## FOURTH CONJUGATION.

### I. Weak Perfect trunks.

**278**  1. Formed with *v*.

| | | | | |
|---|---|---|---|---|
| aud-iō | -īre | audīv-ī | audīt-um | *hear* |
| sepel-iō | -īre | sepelīv-ī | sepult-um | *bury* |

**279**  2. Formed with *u*.

| | | | | |
|---|---|---|---|---|
| sal-iō | -īre | salu-ī | salt-um | *leap* |
| amic-iō | -īre | amicu-ī, amix-ī | amict-um | *wrap* |

**280**  3. Formed with *s*.

| | | | | |
|---|---|---|---|---|
| saep-iō | -īre | saeps-ī | saept-um | *fence round* |
| vinc-iō | -īre | vinx-ī | vinct-um | *bind* |
| sanc-iō | -īre | sanx-ī | sanct-um | *hallow* |
| fulc-iō | -īre | fuls-ī | fult-um | *prop up* |
| farc-iō | -īre | fars-ī | fart-um | *stuff* |
| sarc-iō | -īre | sars-ī | sart-um | *patch* |
| haur-iō | -īre | haus-ī | haust-um | *drain* |
| sent-iō | -īre | sens-ī | sens-um | *feel* |

**281**  4. With Perfect and Supine borrowed from another verb.

| | | | | |
|---|---|---|---|---|
| fer-iō | -īre | [percuss-ī] | [percuss-um] | *strike* |

**282**  II. **Strong** Perfect trunk (formed by lengthening the vowel).

| | | | | |
|---|---|---|---|---|
| ven-iō | -īre | vēn-ī | vent-um | *come* |

## DEPONENT VERBS.

**283**  (The Principal Parts of a deponent are Present Indicative, Present Infinitive, and Perfect Indicative: the Supine trunk is seen in the Perfect Participle.)

### FIRST CONJUGATION.

**284**  More than half of all deponents are of the First Conjugation, and all of these form their Perfects regularly:

| | | | |
|---|---|---|---|
| hort-or | -ārī | hortāt-us sum | *exhort* |

**285**  ### SECOND CONJUGATION.

| | | | |
|---|---|---|---|
| ver-eor | -ērī | verit-us sum | *fear* |
| r-eor | -ērī | rat-us sum | *think* |
| fat-eor | -ērī | fass-us sum | *confess* |

## 286

### THIRD CONJUGATION.

| | | | |
|---|---|---|---|
| fung-or | -ī | **funct-us sum** | *discharge* |
| fru-or | -ī | fruct-us *or* fruit-us sum (§ 227) | *enjoy* |
| quer-or | -ī | quest-us sum | *complain* |
| loqu-or | -ī | locūt-us sum | *speak* |
| sequ-or | -ī | secūt-us sum | *follow* |
| nasc-or | -ī | nāt-us sum (§ 227) | *be born* |
| pasc-or | -ī | past-us sum | *feed* (Intrans.) |
| irasc-or | -ī | [succensu-ī] | *become angry* |
| vesc-or | -ī | [ēd-ī] | *feed* |
| nancisc-or | -ī | nact-us *or* nanct-us sum | *get* |
| pacisc-or | -ī | pact-us sum | *bargain for* |
| ulcisc-or | -ī | ult-us sum | *avenge* |
| oblivisc-or | -ī | oblīt-us sum | *forget* |
| proficisc-or | -ī | profect-us sum | *set out* |
| adipisc-or | -ī | adept-us sum | *obtain* |
| comminisc-or | -ī | comment-us sum | *devise* |
| reminisc-or | -ī | ——— | *remember* |
| dēfetisc-or | -ī | dēfess-us sum | *grow weary* |
| expergisc-or | -ī | experrect-us sum | *wake up* |
| lāb-or | -ī | laps-us sum | *glide* |
| am-plect-or | -ī | am-plex-us sum | *embrace* |
| nīt-or | -ī | nīs-us *or* nix-us sum | *lean* |
| ūt-or | -ī | ūs-us sum | *use* |

## 287

### THIRD CONJUGATION IN -ior.

| | | | |
|---|---|---|---|
| pat-ior | -ī | pass-us sum | *suffer* |
| grad-ior | -ī | gress-us sum | *step* |
| mor-ior | -ī | mortu-us sum (§ 227) | *die* |

## 288

### FOURTH CONJUGATION.

| | | | |
|---|---|---|---|
| **part-ior** | **-īrī** | **partīt-us sum** | *divide* |
| ex-per-ior | -īrī | ex-pert-us sum | *try* |
| or-ior | -īrī | ort-us sum (§ 227) | *rise* |
| ord-ior | -īrī | ors-us sum | *commence* |
| as-sent-ior | -īrī | as-sens-us sum | *agree to* |
| mēt-ior | -īrī | mens-us sum | *measure* |

## SEMI-DEPONENT VERBS.

**289**　　　　　　SECOND CONJUGATION.

| | | | |
|---|---|---|---|
| sol-eō | -ēre | solit-us sum | *be wont* |
| aud-eō | -ēre | aus-us sum | *dare* |
| gaud-eō | -ēre | gāvis-us sum | *rejoice* |

**290**　　　　　　THIRD CONJUGATION.

| | | | |
|---|---|---|---|
| fīd-ō | -ere | fīs-us sum | *trust* |

## Compound Verbs.

**291** I. The Compound follows the uncompounded verb, *e.g.* :—

| | | | | |
|---|---|---|---|---|
| dūc-ō | -ere | dux-ī | duct-um | *lead* |
| indūc-ō | -ere | indux-ī | induct-um | *lead in* |

**292** But Reduplication is dropped, *e.g.* :—

| | | | | |
|---|---|---|---|---|
| curr-ō | -ere | cucurr-ī | curs-um | *run* |
| occurr-ō | -ere | occurr-ī | occurs-um | *run against* |
| spond-eō | -ēre | spopond-ī | spons-um | *promise* |
| respond-eō | -ēre | respond-ī | respons-um | *answer* |

except in Compounds of

dare, stăre, sistere, discere, *and* poscere.

| | | | | |
|---|---|---|---|---|
| *e.g.* disc-ō | -ere | didic-ī | —— | *learn* |
| dēdisc-ō | -ere | dēdidic-ī | —— | *unlearn* |

**293** Note too the Perfects—

repper-ī *for* re-peper-ī (re-per-īre　*find out*) : § 298
reppul-ī *for* re-pepul-ī (re-pell-ere　*thrust back*) : § 271
rettul-ī *for* re-tetul-ī　(re-ferre　*bring back*) : § 232

**294** When the Compound has a weakened vowel in the last syllable of the Present trunk, this vowel is retained in the Perfect and Supine, except when it is a short *i*.

| | | | | |
|---|---|---|---|---|
| claud-ō | -ere | claus-ī | claus-um | *shut* |
| inclūd-ō | -ere | inclūs-ī | inclūs-um | *shut in* |
| scand-ō | -ere | scand-ī | scans-um | *climb* |
| ascend-ō | -ere | ascend-ī | ascens-um | *climb up* |
| quaer-ō | -ere | quaesīv-ī | quaesīt-um | *seek* |
| requīr-ō | -ere | requīsīv-ī | requīsīt-um | *be in want of* |
| caed-ō | -ere | cecīd-ī | caes-um | *cut (fell)* |
| occīd-ō | -ere | occīd-ī | occīs-um | *slay* |
| quat-iō | -ere | (quass-ī) | quass-um | *shake* |
| concut-iō | -ere | concuss-ī | concuss-um | *shake violently* |

## COMPOUND VERBS.

**295.** Compounds with short *i* in the last syllable of the Present trunk rarely retain it in the Perfect, and never in the Supine:—

| | | | | |
|---|---|---|---|---|
| ag-ō | -ere | ēg-ī | act-um | *drive* |
| abig-ō | -ere | abēg-ī | abact-um | *drive away* |
| cōg-ō (*for* co-ig-ō) | -ere | coēg-ī | coact-um | *compel* |
| sed-eō | -ēre | sēd-ī | sess-um | *sit* |
| obsid-eō | -ēre | obsēd-ī | obsess-um | *besiege* |
| possid-eō | -ēre | possēd-ī | possess-um | *possess* |
| prem-ō | -ere | press-ī | press-um | *press* |
| opprim-ō | -ere | oppress-ī | oppress-um | *surprise* |
| regō | -ere | rex-ī | rect-um | *rule* |
| corrig-ō | -ere | correx-ī | correct-um | *correct* |
| perg-ō (*for* perrig-ō) | -ere | perrex-ī | perrect-um | *go on* |
| surg-ō (*for* surrig-ō) | -ere | surrex-ī | surrect-um | *rise up* |
| cap-iō | -ere | cēp-ī | capt-um | *take* |
| recip-iō | -ere | recēp-ī | recept-um | *recover* |
| jac-iō | -cre | jēc-ī | ject-um | *throw* |
| inic-iō (*for* injic-iō) | -ere | injēc-ī | inject-um | *throw in* |
| fac-iō | -ere | fēc-ī | fact-um | *make* |
| confic-iō | -ere | confēc-ī | confect-um | *complete* |
| fat-eor | -ērī | fass-us sum | | } *confess* |
| confit-eor | -ērī | confess-us sum | | |
| cad-ō | -ere | cecid-ī | cās-um | *fall* |
| occid-ō | -ere | occid-ī | occās-um | *set, fall* |
| ten-eō | -ēre | tenu-ī | tent-um | *hold* |
| retin-eō | -ēre | retinu-ī | retent-um | *hold back* |
| rap-iō | -ere | rapu-ī | rapt-um | *snatch* |
| dirip-iō | -ere | diripu-ī | dirept-um | *plunder* |
| sal iō | -īre | salu-ī | salt-um | *leap* |
| dēsil-iō | -īre | dēsilu-ī | dēsult-um | *leap down* |

**296.** Note the vowels in:

| | | | | |
|---|---|---|---|---|
| st-ō | -āre | stet-ī | stat-um | *stand* |
| obst-ō | -āre | obstit-ī | —— | *stand against* |
| adst-ō | -āre | adstit-ī | —— | *stand by* |
| const-ō | -āre | constit-ī | —— | *consist* |
| sist-ō | -ere | stit-ī | stat-um | *place* |
| obsist-ō | -ere | obstit-ī | obstit-um | *place against* |
| statu-ō | -ere | statu-ī | statūt-um | *set up* |
| constitu-ō | -ere | constitu-ī | constitūt-um | *resolve* |
| ser-ō | -ere | sēv-ī | sat-um | *sow, plant* |
| conser-ō | -ere | consēv-ī | consit-um | *cover with plants* |
| nosc-ō | -ere | nōv-ī | nōt-um | *learn* |
| cognosc-ō | -ere | cognōv-ī | cognit-um | } *recognise* |
| agnosc-ō | -ere | agnōv-ī | agnit-um | |

**297** II. The following verbs when compounded mostly form a new Perfect :—

☞ The forms in [ ] come straight from the uncompounded verb.

| | | | | |
|---|---|---|---|---|
| can-ō | -ere | cecin-ī | cant-um | *sing* |
| concin-ō | -ere | concinu-ī | —— | *sing together* |
| pung-ō | -ere | pupug-ī | punct-um | *prick* |
| compung-ō | -ere | compunx-ī | compunct-um | *prick deep* |
| pang-ō | -ere | panx-ī | panct-um | *fix* (§ 268) |
| | | pepig-ī | pact-um | *bargain* (§271) |
| comping-ō | -ere | compēg-ī | compact-um | *fix together* |
| par-iō | -ere | peper-ī | part-um | *bring forth* |
| aper-iō | -īre | aperu-ī | apert-um | *open* |
| oper-iō | -īre | operu-ī | opert-um | *cover* |
| ⎡comper-iō | -īre | comper-ī | compert-um | *learn*  ⎤ |
| ⎣reper-iō | -īre | repper-ī | repert-um | *find out* ⎦ |
| em-ō | -ere | ēm-ī | empt-um | *take (buy)* |
| cōm-ō (*for* cŏim-ō) | -ere | comps-ī | compt-um | *adorn* |
| dēm-ō | -ere | demps-ī | dempt-um | *take off* |
| prōm-ō | -ere | promps-ī | prompt-um | *take out* |
| sūm-ō | -ere | sumps-ī | sumpt-um | *take up* |
| [adim-ō | -ere | adēm-ī | adempt-um | *take away*] |
| leg-ō | -ere | lēg-ī | lect-um | *choose (read)* |
| intelleg-ō | -ere | intellex-ī | intellect-um | *understand* |
| negleg-ō | -ere | neglex-ī | neglect-um | *neglect* |
| dīlig-ō | -ere | dilex-ī | dīlect-um | *love* |
| ⎡dēlig-ō | -ere | dēlēg-ī | dēlect-um | *choose out*⎤ |
| ⎣collig-ō | -ere | collēg-ī | collect-um | *collect*     ⎦ |
| il-lic-iō ⎫ | -ere | il-lex-ī | il-lect-um | *lure on, entice* |
| pel-lic-iō ⎬ cf. §211 | -ere | pel-lex-ī | pel-lect-um | *lure to ruin* |
| ē-lic-iō ⎭ | -ere | ē-licu-ī | ē-licit-um | *lure out* |

**298** III. The following verbs when compounded mostly form a new Infinitive :—

| | | | | |
|---|---|---|---|---|
| dō | dare | ded-ī | dat-um | *give, put* |
| abdō | abdere | abdid-ī | abdit-um | *put away* |
| addō | addere | addid-ī | addit-um | *put to, add* |
| condō | condere | condid-ī | condit-um | *put together, found* |
| crēdō | crēdere | crēdid-ī | crēdit-um | *believe* |
| ēdō | ēdere | ēdid-ī | ēdit-um | *give out* |
| indō | indere | indid-ī | indit-um | *put upon* |
| perdō | perdere | perdid-ī | perdit-um | *destroy, lose* |
| prōdō | prōdere | prōdid-ī | prōdit-um | *betray* |
| reddō | reddere | reddid-ī | reddit-um | *give back* |
| subdō | subdere | subdid-ī | subdit-um | *put beneath* |
| trādō | trādere | trādid-ī | trādit-um | *hand down* |
| vendō | vendere | vendid-ī | vendit-um | *sell* |
| [circumdō | circumdare | circumded-ī | circumdat-um | *put round*] |
| cub-ō | -āre | cubu-ī | cubit-um | *lie* |
| accumb-ō | -ere | accubu-ī | accubit-um | *lie at table* |
| incumb-ō | -ere | incubu-ī | incubit-um | *lie upon* |

ALPHABETICAL LIST OF PRINCIPAL PARTS. 97

| | | | | |
|---|---|---|---|---|
| ab-ol-eō | -ēre | ab-olēv-ī | ab-olit-um | *abolish* |
| ad-olesc-ō | -ere | ad-olēv-ī | ad-ult-um | *grow up* |
| obs-olesc-ō | -ere | obs-olēv-ī | obs-olēt-um | *become obsolete* |
| ci-eō | -ēre | civ-ī | cit-um | *rouse* |
| conc-iō | -ĭre | conciv-ī | concit-um | *call together* |
| | | | (concĭt-us, -a, -um) | |
| exc-iō | -ĭre | exciv-ī | excit-um | *call forth,* |
| | | | (excĭtus, -a, -um) | *excite* |
| dīc-ō | -ere | dix-ī | dict-um | *say* |
| indic-ō | -āre | indicāv-ī | indicāt-um | *indicate* |
| dēdic-ō | -āre | dēdicāv-ī | dēdicāt-um | *dedicate* |
| [indĭc-ō | -ere | indix-ī | indict-um | *announce*] |
| dūc-ō | -ere | dux-ī | duct-um | *lead* |
| ēduc-ō | -āre | ēducāv-ī | ēducāt-um | *educate* |
| [ēdūc-ō | -ere | ēdux-ī | ēduct-um | *lead out*] |
| af-flīg-ō | -ere | af-flix-ī | af-flict-um | *dash upon* |
| prō-flīg-ō | -āre | prō-flīgāv-ī | prō-flīgāt-um | *dash down* |

299 **Alphabetical Index to Principal Parts.**

**A**

| | | | | | Section |
|---|---|---|---|---|---|
| abd-ō | -ere | abdid-ī | abdit-um | *put away* | 298 |
| abig-ō | -ere | abēg-ī | abact-um | *drive away* | 295 |
| abnu-ō | -ere | abnu-ī | —— | *refuse* | 275 |
| abol-eō | -ēre | abolēv-ī | abolit-um | *abolish* | 260 |
| accend-ō | -ere | accend-ī | accens-um | *kindle* | 2ˈ,6 |
| accumb-ō | -ere | accubu-ī | accubit-um | *lie at table* | 298 |
| acu-ō | -ere | acu-ī | acūt-um | *sharpen* | 275 |
| adim-ō | -ere | adēm-ī | adempt-um | *take away* | 297 |
| adipisc-or | -ī | adept-us sum | | *obtain* | 286 |
| add-ō | -ere | addid-ī | addit-um | *put to, ad* | 298 |
| adolesc-ō | -ere | adolēv-ī | adult-um | *grow up* | 298 |
| adst-ō | -āre | adstit-ī | —— | *stand by* | 296 |
| afflīg-ō | -ere | afflix-ī | afflict-um | *dash down* | 267 |
| agnosc-ō | -ere | agnōv-ī | agnit-um | *recognise* | 296 |
| ag-ō | -ere | ēg-ī | act-um | *drive* | 273 |
| alg-eō | -ēre | als-ī | —— | *be cold* | 261 |
| al-ō | -ere | alu-ī | alt-um, alit-um | *rear* | 270 |
| amic-iō | -īre | amicu-ī, amix-ī | amict-um | *wrap* | 279 |
| amplect-or | -ī | amplex-us sum | —— | *embrace* | 286 |
| aper-iō | -īre | aperu-ī | apert-um | *open* | 297 |
| arc-eō | -ēre | arcu-ī | —— | *ward off* | 265 |
| arcess-ō | -ere | arcessiv-ī | arcessīt-um | *summon* | 269 |
| ard-eō | -ēre | ars-ī | ars-um | *be on fire* | 261 |

7

## ALPHABETICAL LIST OF PRINCIPAL PARTS.

| | | | | | Section |
|---|---|---|---|---|---|
| ascend-ō | -ere | ascend-ī | ascens-um | *climb up* | 294 |
| assent-ior | -īrī | assens-us sum | | *agree to* | 288 |
| argu-ō | -ere | argu-ī | —— | *accuse* | 275 |
| aud-eō | -ēre | aus-us sum | | *dare* | 289 |
| **aud-iō** | **-īre** | **audīv-ī** | **audīt-um** | *hear* | 278 |
| aug-eō | -ēre | aux-ī | auct-um | *increase* | 261 |

### B

| | | | | | |
|---|---|---|---|---|---|
| bib-ō | -ere | bib-ī | —— | *drink* | 274 |

### C

| | | | | | |
|---|---|---|---|---|---|
| cad-ō | -ere | cecid-ī | cās-um | *fall* | 271 |
| caed-ō | -ere | cecīd-ī | caes-um | *cut, fell* | 271 |
| call-eō | -ēre | callu-ī | —— | *be skilful* | 265 |
| can-ō | -ere | cecin-ī | cant-um | *sing* | 271 |
| capess-ō | -ere | capessīv-ī | capessīt-um | *catch at* | 269 |
| cap-iō | -ere | cēp-ī | capt-um | *take* | 277 |
| carp-ō | -ere | carps-ī | carpt-um | *pluck* | 268 |
| cav-eō | -ēre | cāv-ī | caut-um | *beware* | 263 |
| cēd-ō | -ere | cess-ī | cess-um | *yield* | 267 |
| cens-eō | -ēre | censu-ī | cens-um | *value, judge* | 259 |
| cern-ō | -ere | crēv-ī | crēt-um | *distinguish* | 269 |
| ci-eō | -ēre | cīv-ī | cit-um | *rouse* | 260 |
| cing-ō | -ere | cinx-ī | cinct-um | *gird* | 268 |
| circumd-ō | -are | circumded-ī | circumdat-um | *put round* | 298 |
| claud-ō | -ere | claus-ī | claus-um | *shut* | 267 |
| cognosc-ō | -ere | cognōv-ī | cognit-um | *recognise* | 296 |
| cŏg-ō | -ere | coēg-ī | coact-um | *compel* | 295 |
| collig-ō | -ere | collēg-ī | collect-um | *collect* | 297 |
| col-ō | -ere | colu-ī | cult-um | *till* | 270 |
| comminisc-or | -ī | comment-us sum | | *devise* | 286 |
| cŏm-ō | -ere | comps-ī | compt-um | *adorn* | 297 |
| comper-iō | -īre | comper-ī | compert-um | *learn* | 297 |
| compesc-ō | -ere | compescu-ī | —— | *restrain* | 270 |
| comping-ō | -ere | compēg-ī | compact-um | *fix together* | 297 |
| compl-eō | -ēre | complēv-ī | complēt-um | *fill up* | 260 |
| compung-ō | -ere | compunx-ī | compunct-um | *prick deep* | 297 |
| concin-ō | -ere | concinu-ī | —— | *sing together* | 297 |
| conc-iō | -īre | concīv-ī | concīt-um | *call together* | 298 |
| | | (concĭt-us, -a, -um) | | | |
| concut-iō | -ere | concuss-ī | concuss-um | *shake violently* | 294 |

# ALPHABETICAL LIST OF PRINCIPAL PARTS.

|   |   |   |   |   | Section |
|---|---|---|---|---|---|
| cond-ō | -ere | condid-ī | condit-um | *put together* | 298 |
| confic-iō | -ere | confēc-ī | confect-um | *complete* | 295 |
| confit-eor | -ērī | confess-us sum | | *confess* | 295 |
| congru-ō | -ere | congru-ī | —— | *agree* | 275 |
| cōnīv-eō | -ēre | cōnix-ī | —— | *wink* | 261 |
| conser-ō | -ere | consēv-ī | consit-um | *cover with plants* | 296 |
| conspic-iō | -ere | conspex-ī | conspect-um | *behold* | 276 |
| constitu-ō | -ere | constitu-ī | constitūt-um | *resolve* | 296 |
| const-ō | -āre | constit-ī | —— | *consist* | 296 |
| consul-ō | -ere | consulu-ī | consult-um | *consult* | 270 |
| contemn-ō | -ere | contemps-ī | contempt-um | *despise* | 268 |
| coqu-ō | -ere | cox-ī | coct-um | *cook* | 266 |
| corrig-ō | -ere | correx-ī | correct-um | *correct* | 295 |
| crēd-ō | -ere | crēdid-ī | crēdit-um | *believe* | 298 |
| crep-ō | -āre | crepu-ī | crepit-um | *rattle, creak* | 256 |
| cresc-ō | -ere | crēv-ī | crēt-um | *grow* | 269 |
| cub-ō | -āre | cubu-ī | cubit-um | *lie down* | 256 |
| cūd-ō | -ere | cūd-ī | cūs-um | *hammer, forge* | 274 |
| cup-iō | -ere | cupīv-ī | cupīt-um | *desire* | 276 |
| curr-ō | -ere | cucurr-ī | curs-um | *run* | 271 |

## D

| dēdic-ō | -āre | dēdicāv-ī | dēdicāt-um | *dedicate* | 298 |
|---|---|---|---|---|---|
| dēfend-ō | -ere | dēfend-ī | dēfens-um | *ward off, defend* | 274 |
| dēfetisc-or | -ī | dēfess-us sum | | *grow weary* | 286 |
| dēl-eō | -ēre | dēlēv-ī | dēlēt-um | *destroy* | 260 |
| dēlig-ō | -ere | dēlēg-ī | dēlect-um | *choose out* | 297 |
| dēm-ō | -ere | demps-ī | dempt-um | *take off* | 297 |
| dēsil-iō | -īre | dēsilu-ī | dēsult-um | *leap down* | 295 |
| dīc-ō | -ere | dix-ī | dict-um | *say* | 267 |
| dīlig-ō | -ere | dīlex-ī | dīlect-um | *love* | 297 |
| dīrip-iō | -ere | dīripu-ī | dīrept-um | *snatch* | 295 |
| disc-ō | -ere | didic-ī | —— | *learn* | 271 |
| dīvid-ō | -ere | dīvīs-ī | dīvīs-um | *divide* | 266 |
| d-ō | -are | ded-ī | dat-um | *give* | 257 |
| doc-eō | -ēre | docu-ī | doct-um | *teach* | 259 |
| dom-ō | -āre | domu-ī | domit-um | *tame* | 256 |
| dūc-ō | -ere | dux-ī | duct-um | *lead* | 267 |

## E

| | | | | | Section |
|---|---|---|---|---|---|
| ed-ō | -ere | ĕd-ī | ēs-um | eat | 273 |
| ĕd-ō | -ere | ĕdid-ī | ĕdit-um | give out | 298 |
| ēduc-ō | -āre | ēducāv-ī | ēducāt-um | educate | 298 |
| ēdūc-ō | -ere | ēdux-ī | ēduct-um | lead out | 298 |
| eg-eō | -ēre | egu-ī | —— | need | 265 |
| ēlic-iō | -ere | ēlicu-ī | ēlicit-um | lure out | 297 |
| em-ō | -ere | ēm-ī | empt-um | buy | 273 |
| ēvād-ō | -ere | ēvās-ī | ēvās-um | go out | 267 |
| exc-iō | -īre | excīv-ī | excītum | call forth | 298 |

(excit-us, -a, -um)

| | | | | | |
|---|---|---|---|---|---|
| expergisc-or | -ī | experrect-us sum | | wake up | 286 |
| exper-ior | -īrī | expert-us sum | | try | 288 |
| exstingu-ō | -ere | exstinx-ī | exstinct-um | extinguish | 268 |
| exu-ō | -ere | exu-ī | exūt-um | take off | 275 |

## F

| | | | | | |
|---|---|---|---|---|---|
| facess-ō | -ere | facessīv-ī | facessīt-um | do eagerly | 269 |
| fac-iō | -ere | fēc-ī | fact-um | make | 277 |
| fall-ō | -ere | fefell-ī | fals-um | deceive | 271 |
| farc-iō | -īre | fars-ī | fart-um | stuff | 280 |
| fat-eor | -ērī | fass-us sum | | confess | 285 |
| fav-eō | -ēre | fāv-ī | faut-um | be favorable | 263 |
| fer-iō | -īre | [percuss-ī] | [percuss-um] | strike | 281 |
| ferv-eō | -ēre | ferv-ī, ferbu-ī | —— | boil | 263 |
| fīd-ō | -ere | fīs-us sum | | trust | 290 |
| fīg-ō | -ere | fix-ī | fix-um | fix | 267 |
| find-ō | -ere | fid-ī | fiss-um | split | 272 |
| fing-ō | -ere | finx-ī | fict-um | form | 268 |
| flect-ō | -ere | flex-ī | flex-um | bend | 268 |
| fl-eō | -ēre | flēv-ī | flēt-um | weep | 260 |
| flŏr-eō | -ēre | flŏru-ī | —— | flourish | 265 |
| flu-ō | -ere | flux-ī | flux-um | flow | 266 |
| fod-iō | -ere | fōd-ī | foss-um | dig | 277 |
| fov-eō | -ēre | fōv-ī | fōt-um | cherish, warm | 263 |
| frang-ō | -ere | frēg-ī | fract-um | break | 273 |
| frem-ō | -ere | fremu-ī | fremit-um | mutter | 270 |
| fric-ō | -āre | fricu-ī | frict-um | rub | 256 |
| frīg-eō | -ēre | frix-ī | —— | be cold | 261 |
| fru-or | -ī | fruct-us or | | enjoy | 286 |

fruit-us sum (§ 227)

| | | | | | |
|---|---|---|---|---|---|
| fug-iō | -ere | fūg-ī | fugit-um | flee | 277 |

# ALPHABETICAL LIST OF PRINCIPAL PARTS. 101

|  |  |  |  |  | Section |
|---|---|---|---|---|---|
| fulc-iō | -ĭre | fuls-ī | fult-um | *prop up* | 280 |
| fulg-eō | -ēre | fuls-ī | ——— | *glitter* | 261 |
| fund-ō | -ere | fūd-ī | fūs-um | *pour* | 273 |
| **fung or** | -ĭ | **funct-us sum** |  | *discharge* | 286 |
| fur-ō | -ere | furu-ī[insānīv-ī] ——— | | *rave* | 270 |

### G

| gaud-eō | -ēre | gāvīs-us sum |  | *rejoice* | 289 |
|---|---|---|---|---|---|
| gem-ō | -ere | gemu-ī | gemit-um | *sigh* | 270 |
| ger-ō | -ere | gess-ī | gest-um | *carry, wear* | 266 |
| gign-ō | -ere | genu-ī | genit-um | *beget* | 270 |
| grad-ior | -ī | gress-us sum |  | *step* | 287 |

### H

| haer-eō | -ēre | haes-ī | haes-um | *cling* | 261 |
|---|---|---|---|---|---|
| haur-iō | -īre | haus-ī | haust-um | *drain* | 280 |
| horr-eō | -ēre | horru-ī | ——— | *shudder* | 265 |
| **hort-or** | -ārī | **hortāt-us sum** |  | *exhort* | 284 |

### I

| īc-ō | -ere | īc-ī | ict-um | *smite* | 274 |
|---|---|---|---|---|---|
| illic-iō | -ere | illex-ī | illect-um | *lure on, entice* | 276 |
| imbu-ō | -ere | imbu-ī | imbūt-um | *wet slightly* | 275 |
| inclūd-ō | -ere | inclūs-ī | inclūs-um | *shut in* | 294 |
| incumb-ō | -ere | incubu-ī | incubit-um | *lie upon* | 298 |
| indic-ō | -āre | indicāv-ī | indicāt-um | *indicate* | 298 |
| indīc-ō | ere | indix-ī | indict-um | *announce* | 298 |
| ind-ō | -ere | indid-ī | indit-um | *put upon* | 298 |
| indulg-eō | -ēre | induls-ī | indult-um | *be indulgent* | 261 |
| indu-ō | -ere | indu-ī | indūt-um | *put on* | 275 |
| injic-iō | -ere | injēc-ī | inject-um | *throw in* | 295 |
| intelleg-ō | -ere | intellex-ī | intellect-um | *understand* | 297 |
| īrasc-or | -ī | [succensu-ī] |  | *become angry* | 286 |

### J

| jac-iō | -ere | jēc-ī | jact-um | *throw* | 277 |
|---|---|---|---|---|---|
| jub-eō | -ēre | juss-ī | juss-um | *command* | 261 |
| jung-ō | -ere | junx-ī | junct-um | *join* | 268 |
| juv-ō | -āre | jūv-ī | jūt-um (§ 227) | *aid* | 258 |

## L

| | | | | | Section |
|---|---|---|---|---|---|
| lāb-or | -ī | laps-us sum | | *glide* | 286 |
| lacess-ō | -ere | lacessīv-ī | lacessīt-um | *provoke* | 269 |
| laed-ō | -ere | laes-ī | laes-um | *wound* | 267 |
| lamb-ō | -ere | lamb-ī | lambit-um | *lick* | 274 |
| lat-eō | -ēre | latu-ī | —— | *lie hidden* | 265 |
| **laud-ō** | **-āre** | **laudāv-ī** | **laudāt-um** | *praise* | 255 |
| lav-ō | -āre | lāv-ī | {laut-um, lōt-um, lavāt-um} | *wash* | 258 |
| leg-ō | -ere | lēg-ī | lect-um | *read, choose* | 273 |
| lin-ō | -ere | lēv-ī | lit-um | *smear* | 269 |
| loqu-or | -ī | locūt-us sum | | *speak* | 286 |
| lūc-eō | -ēre | lux-ī | —— | *shine* | 261 |
| lūd-ō | -ere | lūs-ī | lūs-um | *play* | 267 |
| lūg-eō | -ēre | lux-ī | —— | *mourn* | 261 |
| lu-ō | -ere | lu-ī | lūt-um | *wash* | 275 |

## M

| | | | | | |
|---|---|---|---|---|---|
| mad-eō | -ēre | madu-ī | —— | *be wet* | 265 |
| mand-ō | -ere | mand-ī | mans-um | *chew* | 274 |
| man-eō | -ēre | mans-ī | mans-um | *remain* | 261 |
| merg-ō | -ere | mers-ī | mers-um | *immerse* | 268 |
| mēt-ior | -īrī | mens-us sum | | *measure* | 288 |
| met-ō | -ere | [messem fēcī] | mess-um | *reap* | 270 |
| metu-ō | -ere | metu-ī | —— | *fear* | 275 |
| mic-ō | -āre | micu-ī | —— | *glitter* | 256 |
| minu-ō | -ere | minu-ī | minūt-um | *lessen* | 275 |
| misc-eō | -ēre | miscu-ī | mixt-um | *mix* | 259 |
| mitt-ō | -ere | mīs-ī | miss-um | *send* | 268 |
| **mon-eō** | **-ēre** | **monu-ī** | **monit-um** | *warn* | 259 |
| mord-eō | -ēre | momord-ī | mors-um | *bite* | 262 |
| mor-ior | -ī | mortu-us sum (§ 227) | | *die* | 287 |
| mov-eō | -ēre | mōv-ī | mōt-um | *move* | 263 |
| mulc-eō | -ēre | muls-ī | muls-um | *soothe* | 261 |
| mulg-eō | -ēre | muls-ī | muls-um | *milk* | 261 |

## N

| | | | | | |
|---|---|---|---|---|---|
| nancisc-or | -ī | nact-us *or* nanct-us sum | | *get* | 286 |
| nasc-or | -ī | nāt-us sum (§ 227) | | *be born* | 286 |
| nect-ō | -ere | nex-ī, nexu-ī | nex-um | *bind* | 268 |

# ALPHABETICAL LIST OF PRINCIPAL PARTS.

| | | | | | Section |
|---|---|---|---|---|---|
| negleg-ō | -ere | neglex-ī | neglect-um | *neglect* | 297 |
| n-eō | -ēre | nēv-ī | nēt-um | *spin* | 260 |
| ning-ō | -ere | ninx-ī | —— | *snow* | 268 |
| nit-eō | -ēre | nitu-ī | —— | *shine* | 265 |
| nit-or | -ī | nīs-us *or* nīx-us sum | —— | *lean* | 286 |
| nosc-ō | -ere | nōv-ī | nōt-um | *get to know* | 269 |
| nūb-ō | -ere | nups-ī | nupt-um | *marry* | 267 |

## O

| | | | | | |
|---|---|---|---|---|---|
| oblīvisc-or | -ī | oblīt-us sum | | *forget* | 286 |
| obsid-eō | -ēre | obsēd-ī | obsess-um | *besiege* | 295 |
| obsist-ō | -ere | obstit-ī | obstit-um | *place against* | 296 |
| obsolesc-ō | -ere | obsolēv-ī | obsolēt-um | *become obsolete* | 298 |
| obst-ō | -āre | obstit-ī | —— | *stand against* | 296 |
| occid-ō | -ere | occid-ī | occās-um | *set, fall* | 295 |
| occīd-ō | -ere | occīd-ī | occīs-um | *slay* | 294 |
| occul-ō | -ere | occulu-ī | occult-um | *hide* | 270 |
| ol-eō | -ēre | olu-ī | —— | *smell* | 265 |
| oper-iō | -īre | operu-ī | opert-um | *cover* | 297 |
| opprim-ō | -ere | oppress-ī | oppress-um | *surprise* | 295 |
| ord-ior | -īrī | ors-us sum | | *commence* | 288 |
| or-ior | īrī | ort-us sum (§ 227) | | *rise* | 288 |

## P

| | | | | | |
|---|---|---|---|---|---|
| pacisc-or | -ī | pact-us sum | | *bargain for* | 286 |
| pall-eō | -ēre | pallu-ī | —— | *be pale* | 265 |
| pand-ō | -ere | pand-ī | pass-um | *spread out* | 274 |
| pang-ō | -ere | panx-ī | panct-um | *fix* | 268 |
| pang-ō | -ere | pepig-ī | pact-um | *fix, settle* | 271 |
| parc-ō | -ere | peperc-ī | pars-um | *spare* | 271 |
| par-iō | -ere | peper-ī | part-um(§ 227) | *bring forth* | 277 |
| **part-ior** | **-īrī** | **partīt-us sum** | | *divide* | 288 |
| pasc-ō | -ere | pāv-ī | past-um | *feed* (Trans.) | 269 |
| pasc-or | -ī | past-us sum | | *feed* (Intrans.) | 286 |
| pat-eō | -ēre | patu-ī | —— | *lie open* | 265 |
| pat-ior | -ī | pass-us sum | | *suffer* | 287 |
| pav-eō | -ēre | pāv-ī | —— | *fear* | 263 |
| pect-ō | -ere | pex-ī | pex-um | *comb* | 268 |
| pellic-iō | -ere | pellex-ī | pellect-um | *lure to ruin* | 297 |
| pell-ō | -ere | pepul-ī | puls-um | *push* | 271 |

| | | | | | Section |
|---|---|---|---|---|---|
| pend-eō | -ēre | pepend-ī | pens-um | *hang* | 262 |
| pend-ō | -ere | pepend-ī | pens-um | *weigh* | 271 |
| percell-ō | -ere | percul-ī | perculs-um | *cast down* | 272 |
| perd-ō | -ere | perdid-ī | perdit-um | *destroy, lose* | 298 |
| perg-ō | -ere | perrex-ī | perrect-um | *go on* | 295 |
| pet-ō | -ere | petiv-ī | petit-um | *aim at, desire* | 269 |
| ping-ō | -ere | pinx-ī | pict-um | *paint* | 268 |
| plang-ō | -ere | planx-ī | planct-um | *beat the breast* | 268 |
| plaud-ō | -ere | plaus-ī | plaus-um | *clap* | 267 |
| plect-ō | -ere | plex-ī, plexu-ī | plex-um | *plait* | 268 |
| plu-it | -ere | plu-it | —— | *rain* | 275 |
| pōn-ō | -ere | posu-ī | posit-um | *place, put* | 270 |
| posc-ō | -ere | poposc-ī | —— | *demand* | 271 |
| possid-eō | -ēre | possēd-ī | possess-um | *possess* | 295 |
| pōt-ō | -āre | pōtāv-ī | pōt-um (§229) | *drink* | 255 |
| prand-eō | -ēre | prand-ī | prans-um | *breakfast* | 264 |
| prehend-ō | -ere | prehend-ī | prehens-um | *seize* | 274 |
| prem-ō | -ere | press-ī | press-um | *press* | 266 |
| prōd-ō | -ere | prōdid-ī | prōdit-um | *betray* | 298 |
| proficisc-or | -ī | profect-us sum | | *set out* | 286 |
| prōflig-ō | -āre | prōflīgāv-ī | prōflīgāt-um | *dash down* | 298 |
| prōm-ō | -ere | promps-ī | prompt-um | *take out* | 297 |
| pung-ō | -ere | pupug-ī | punct-um | *prick* | 271 |

**Q**

| | | | | | |
|---|---|---|---|---|---|
| quaer-ō | -ere | quaesīv-ī | quaesīt-um | *seek, enquire* | 269 |
| quat-iō | -ere | (·quass-ī) | quass-um | *shake* | 276 |
| quer-or | -ī | quest-us sum | | *complain* | 286 |
| quiesc-ō | -ere | quiēv-ī | quiēt-um | *rest* | 269 |

**R**

| | | | | | |
|---|---|---|---|---|---|
| rād-ō | -ere | rās-ī | rās-um | *scrape* | 267 |
| rap-iō | -ere | rapu-ī | rapt-um | *snatch* | 276 |
| recip-iō | -ere | recēp-ī | recept-um | *recover* | 295 |
| redd-ō | -ere | reddid-ī | reddit-um | *give back* | 298 |
| refer-ō | -re | rettul-ī | relāt-um | *bring back* | 294, 232 |
| **reg-ō** | **-ere** | **rex-ī** | **rect-um** | *rule* | 266 |
| relinqu-ō | -ere | relīqu-ī | relict-um | *leave* | 273 |
| reminisc-or | -ī | —— | | *remember* | 286 |
| r-eor | -ērī | rat-us sum | | *think* | 285 |
| repell-ō | -ere | reppul-ī | repuls-um | *thrust back* | 249, 271 |

# ALPHABETICAL LIST OF PRINCIPAL PARTS.

|  |  |  |  |  | Section |
|---|---|---|---|---|---|
| reper-iō | -ire | repper-ī | repert-um | *find* | 293, 297 |
| rēp-ō | -ere | reps-ī | rept-um | *creep* | 267 |
| requīr-ō | -ere | requīsīv-ī | requīsit-um | *be in want of* | 294 |
| respond-eō | -ēre | respond-ī | respons-um | *answer* | 292 |
| retin-eō | -ēre | retinu-ī | retent-um | *hold back* | 295 |
| rīd-eō | -ēre | rīs-ī | rīs-um | *laugh* | 261 |
| rig-eō | -ēre | rigu-ī | —— | *be stiff* | 265 |
| rōd-ō | -ere | rōs-ī | rōs-um | *gnaw* | 267 |
| rub-eō | -ēre | rubu-ī | —— | *blush* | 265 |
| rud-ō | -ere | rudīv-ī | (rudit-um) | *bray* | 269 |
| rump-ō | -ere | rūp-ī | rupt-um | *burst* | 273 |
| ru-ō | -ere | ru-ī | rut-um (§ 227) | *fall* | 275 |

## S

|  |  |  |  |  |  |
|---|---|---|---|---|---|
| saep-iō | -ire | saeps-ī | saept-um | *fence round* | 280 |
| sal-iō | -ire | salu-ī | salt-um | *leap* | 279 |
| sanc-iō | -ire | sanx-ī | sanct-um | *hallow* | 280 |
| sap-iō | -ere | sapīv-ī | —— | *be sensible* | 276 |
| sarc-iō | -ire | sars-ī | sart-um | *patch* | 280 |
| scand-ō | -ere | scand-ī | scans-um | *climb* | 274 |
| scind-ō | -ere | scid-ī | sciss-um | *tear* | 272 |
| scisc-ō | -ere | scīv-ī | scīt-um | *decree* | 269 |
| scrīb-ō | -ere | scrīps-ī | scrīpt-um | *write* | 267 |
| sculp-ō | -ere | sculps-ī | sculpt-um | *engrave* | 268 |
| sec-ō | -āre | secu-ī | sect-um (§ 227) | *cut* | 256 |
| sed-eō | -ēre | sēd-ī | sess-um | *sit* | 263 |
| sent-iō | -īre | sens-ī | sens-um | *feel* | 280 |
| sepel-iō | -īre | sepelīv-ī | sepult-um | *bury* | 278 |
| sequ-or | -ī | secūt-us sum |  | *follow* | 286 |
| ser-ō | -ere | sēv-ī | sat-um | *sow* | 269 |
| ser-ō | -ere | -seru-ī | sert-um | *twine* | 270 |
| serp-ō | -ere | serps-ī | serpt-um | *crawl* | 268 |
| sīd-ō | -ere | (sīd-ī) sēd-ī | —— | *seat oneself* | 274 |
| sil-eō | -ēre | silu-ī | —— | *be silent* | 265 |
| sin-ō | -ere | sīv-ī | sit-um | *permit* | 269 |
| sist-ō | -ere | -stit-ī | stat-um | *make to halt* | 271 |
| sol-eō | -ēre | solit-us sum |  | *be wont* | 289 |
| solv-ō | -ere | solv-ī | solūt-um | *loosen* | 275 |
| son-ō | -āre | sonu-ī | sonit-um (§ 227) | *sound* | 256 |
| sorb-eō | -ēre | sorbu-ī | —— | *swallow* | 265 |
| sparg-ō | -ere | spars-ī | spars-um | *scatter* | 268 |

| | | | | | | Section |
|---|---|---|---|---|---|---|
| spern-ō | -ere | sprēv-ī | sprēt-um | | *spurn* | 269 |
| splend-eō | -ēre | splendu-ī | —— | | *shine* | 265 |
| spond-eō | -ēre | spopond-ī | spons-um | | *pledge* | 262 |
| statu-ō | -ere | statu-ī | statūt-um | | *set up, resolve* | 275 |
| stern-ō | -ere | strāv-ī | strāt-um | | *strew* | 269 |
| st-ō | -āre | stet-ī | stat-um | | *stand* | 257 |
| strep-ō | -ere | strepu-ī | strepit-um | | *make a noise* | 270 |
| strid-eō | -ēre | strīd-ī | —— | | *hiss* | 264 |
| string-ō | -ere | strinx-ī | strict-um | | *strip* | 268 |
| stru-ō | -ere | strux-ī | struct-um | | *erect* | 266 |
| stud-eō | -ēre | studu-ī | —— | | *be zealous* | 265 |
| stup-eō | -ēre | stupu-ī | —— | | *be stunned, dazed* | 265 |
| suād-eō | -ēre | suās-ī | suās-um | | *advise* | 261 |
| subd-ō | -ere | subdid-ī | subdit-um | | *put beneath* | 298 |
| suesc-ō | -ere | suēv-ī | suēt-um | | *be accustomed* | 269 |
| sūg-ō | -ere | sux-ī | suct-um | | *suck* | 267 |
| sūm-ō | -ere | sumps-ī | sumpt-um | | *take up* | 297 |
| surg-ō | -ere | surrex-ī | surrect-um | | *rise up* | 295 |

**T**

| | | | | | | |
|---|---|---|---|---|---|---|
| tang-ō | -ere | tetig-ī | tact-um | | *touch* | 271 |
| teg-ō | -ere | tex-ī | tect-um | | *cover* | 266 |
| tend-ō | -ere | tetend-ī | tent-um, tens-um | | *stretch* | 271 |
| ten-eō | -ēre | tenu-ī | tent-um | | *hold* | 259 |
| terg-eō | -ēre | ters-ī | ters-um | | *wipe* | 261 |
| ter-ō | -ere | trīv-ī | trīt-um | | *rub* | 269 |
| tex-ō | -ere | texu-ī | text-um | | *weave* | 270 |
| tim-eō | -ēre | timu-ī | —— | | *fear* | 265 |
| ting-ō | -ere | tinx-ī | tinct-um | | *dip* | 268 |
| toll-ō | -ere | sustul-ī | sublāt-um | | *lift, take away* | 272 |
| tond-eō | -ēre | totond-ī | tons-um | | *shear* | 262 |
| ton-ō | -āre | tonu-ī | —— | | *thunder* | 256 |
| torqu-eō | -ēre | tors-ī | tort-um | | *twist* | 261 |
| torr-eō | -ēre | torru-ī | tost-um | | *roast* | 259 |
| trād-ō | -ere | trādid-ī | trādit-um | | *hand down* | 298 |
| trah-ō | -ere | trax-ī | tract-um | | *drag* | 266 |
| trem-ō | -ere | tremu-ī | —— | | *tremble* | 270 |
| tribu-ō | -ere | tribu-ī | tribūt-um | | *assign* | 275 |
| trūd-ō | -ere | trūs-ī | trūs-um | | *thrust* | 267 |

|   |   |   |   |   | Section |
|---|---|---|---|---|---|
| tum-eō | -ēre | tumu-ī | — | *swell* | 265 |
| tund-ō | -ere | tutud ī | tuns-um, tūs-um | *thump* | 271 |
| turg-eō | -ēre | turs-ī | — | *swell* | 261 |

## U

| ulcisc-or | -ī | ult-us sum | | *avenge* | 286 |
|---|---|---|---|---|---|
| ung-ō | -ere | unx-ī | unct-um | *anoint* | 268 |
| urg-eō | -ēre | urs-ī | — | *urge* | 261 |
| ūr-ō | -ere | uss-ī | ust-um | *burn* | 267 |
| ūt-or | -ī | ūs-us sum | | *use* | 286 |

## V

| veh-ō | -ere | vex-ī | vect-um | *carry* | 266 |
|---|---|---|---|---|---|
| vell-ō | -ere | vell-ī | vuls-um | *pluck* | 274 |
| vend-ō | -ere | vendid-ī | vendit-um | *sell* | 298 |
| ven-iō | -īre | vēn-ī | vent-um | *come* | 282 |
| **ver-eor** | **-ērī** | **verit-us sum** | — | *fear* | 285 |
| verr-ō | -ere | verr-ī | vers-um | *sweep* | 274 |
| vert-ō | -ere | vert-ī | vers-um | *turn* | 274 |
| vesc-or | -ī | [ēd-ī] | | *feed* | 286 |
| vet-ō | -āre | vetu-ī | vetit-um | *forbid* | 256 |
| vid-eō | -ēre | vīd-ī | vīs-um | *see* | 263 |
| vig-eō | -ēre | vigu-ī | — | *thrive* | 265 |
| vinc-iō | -īre | vinx-ī | vinct-um | *bind* | 280 |
| vinc-ō | -ere | vīc-ī | vict-um | *conquer* | 273 |
| vir-eō | -ēre | viru-ī | — | *be green* | 265 |
| vīs-ō | -ere | vīs-ī | (vīs-um) | *visit* | 274 |
| vīv-ō | -ere | vix-ī | vict-um | *live* | 267 |
| volv-ō | -ere | volv-ī | volūt-um | *roll* | 275 |
| vom-ō | -ere | vomu-ī | vomit-um | *vomit* | 270 |
| vov-eō | -ēre | vōv-ī | vōt-um | *vow* | 263 |

## PREPOSITIONS, CONJUNCTIONS, AND INTERJECTIONS.

The use of Prepositions, Conjunctions and Interjections is treated in Syntax: cf. Accidence § 9.

The following rules are however given in this place for the sake of convenience :—

## Prepositions.

**300 RULE 1.** Put the Ablative with *dē*,
Cum and *cōram*, *ab* and *ē*,
Sine, tenus, *prō* and *prae*.
☞ For *ab* use *ā* before a consonant.
„ „ „ *abs* before the word *tē* 'thee.'
For *ē* use *ex* before a vowel or *h*
(optionally, before any letter).
} with Abl.

*Palam* 'openly' and *clam* 'secretly' are always Adverbs in classical prose, except in one passage of Cæsar.

**RULE 2.** *In* and *sub* take the
Accusative when they denote *motion towards* (in answer to the question 'whither?')
e.g. *in urbem īre*, to go **into** the city.
*sub mūrōs proficiscī*, to march **up to** the walls.
*sub jugum mittere*, to send **under** the yoke.
Ablative when they denote *rest at* (in answer to the question 'where?')
e.g. *in urbe esse*, to be **in** the city.
*sub mūrīs stāre*, to stand **under** the walls.

**RULE 3.** All other Prepositions take the Accusative in classical prose.

EXCEPTION.—*Super* when it means 'concerning' [rare] takes the Abl.: e.g. *super hāc rē*, 'concerning this.'

☞ *Super* 'above' and *subter* 'beneath' sometimes take the Abl. (for Acc.) in the poets, but without distinction of meaning.

---

APPENDIX.

## Pronunciation of Latin.

Various methods of pronouncing Latin are now current in the British Isles. The pronunciation which has been generally prevalent in England dates from the seventeenth century, when English sounds went through a period of rapid transition, and the pronunciation of Latin suffered a corresponding change. Milton protested against the fashion of giving to Latin vowels and consonants their English sounds.

## PRONUNCIATION OF LATIN.

The following tables* show how Latin was probably pronounced by the Romans: but it must be remembered that
(1) Few sounds are *exactly* reproduced in two different languages.
(2) Some points in the pronunciation of Latin are still doubtful.
For purposes of convenience and comparison phoneticians employ symbols of their own, each representing a single sound. Such an alphabet is given below (in the right-hand column).

### SIMPLE VOWEL SOUNDS.

| | | English. | Latin. | French. | German. | Phonetic Symbol. |
|---|---|---|---|---|---|---|
| 1 | A-sounds | f*a*ther | long in m*ā*ter<br>short in p*a*ter | p*â*te<br>p*a*s | Vater<br>Mann | a |
| 2 | E-sounds | i. (close) f*a*te[1]<br>ii. (open) f*e*d | always long: m*ē*<br>always short: t*e*net | b*é*b*é*<br>n*e*t | Rebe<br>bes | e<br>æ |
| 3 | I-sounds | mach*i*ne<br>*i*n, p*i*t | long in *ī*mus<br>short in reg*i*mus | g*î*te | mir | i |
| 4 | O-sounds | i. (close) n*o*[2]<br>ii. (open) n*o*t | always long: cant*ō*<br>always short: m*o*do | r*ô*le<br>b*o*l | so<br>oft | o<br>ɔ |
| 5 | U-sounds | r*u*de<br>p*u*t | long in t*ū*<br>short in cons*u*l | go*û*te<br>go*u*tte | Ufer<br>um | u |

[1] Many English sounds which are commonly regarded as simple vowel sounds are in reality diphthongal in character. Thus, the 'a' in Engl. 'fate' is not a pure vowel, but ends in a faint ee (i) sound.

[2] The 'o' in Engl. 'no' is not a pure vowel, but ends in a faint oo (u) sound.

OBS. 1. The 'Greek letter' *y* (Introduction, § 1) was probably sounded like French u (in p*u*).

OBS. 2. It is not customary to distinguish the natural quantity of vowels

---

* Adapted for use in schools from the recent scheme of the Cambridge Philological Society and the earlier Syllabus of Professors Palmer and Munro.

which are long by position (§ 3). But the Romans no doubt said rēx (§ 4) not rĕx, scrīptus not scrĭptus (from trunks rēg-, scrīb-), and so on. In more difficult cases we may infer the natural quantity from the testimony of grammarians (e.g. mēnsa, cēnsor, cōnsul, īgnis, benīgnus, līgnum, cūncti, but cĭngere, pĭngere, pŭngere : fōns but fŏntis, mēns but mĕntem, etc.), or from a comparison of cognate languages (e.g. French droit, toit, from dīrēctum, tēctum ; but lit 'bed' from lĕctus : cf. Greek λέχος, Spanish tiempo from tĕmpus, -miente from mĕntem, etc.)

### DIPHTHONGS.

Diphthongs are produced by running two different vowel sounds together so as to make a single syllable (cf. Introduction, § 1). The Latin diphthongs were 'falling' ('decrescendo') like English dipthongs, not 'rising' ('crescendo') like French diphthongs. The following modern equivalents are only approximately correct, but may be regarded as sufficiently near for practical purposes.

|                  | Latin Examples.     | Approximate Modern Equivalents.                         |
|------------------|---------------------|---------------------------------------------------------|
| ae = a͡-e        | mensae, taedae      | Engl. there = Long open e; Germ. Bär.[1]                |
| au = a͡-u        | laudō               | Engl. house; or more exactly Germ. Haus.                |
| ei = e͡-i (rare) | hei                 | Engl. grey.                                             |
| eu = e͡-u (rare) | heu, seu, neuter    | [Engl. pay (y)ou.][2]                                   |
| oe = o͡-e        | foedus              | Engl. fate = Long close e.[3]                           |
| ui = u͡-i (rare) | cui, huic           | French oui 'yes' [Engl. cooing].[3]                     |

[1] So Munro. It is probable that in *root syllables* Latin ae was half way between ai (Eng. 'aye') and the long open e : but in *endings* the pronunciation of ae must have undergone rapid change and become a long open e, at any rate in the everyday speech of the people, and it would not be far wrong to use this sound in root syllables also.

[2] These modern equivalents must be so pronounced as to make one syllable.

[3] It is probable that in the classical period Lat. oe sounded somewhat like the vowel sound in *boy*. But here, as in the case of ae, a somewhat later pronunciation is a convenient compromise : the diphthong is comparatively rare (coepī, poena, moenia, foedus, coetus, proelia).

## SIMPLE CONSONANT SOUNDS.

| | English. | Latin. | French. | German. | Phonetic Symbol. |
|---|---|---|---|---|---|
| Labial | *b*ay<br>*p*ay | *b*ellum<br>*p*ellō | *b*as<br>*p*as | Weil<br>Paar | b<br>p |
| Labio-dental | *f*ine | *f*ingō | *f*aux | fett | f |
| Dental | *d*o<br>*t*o<br>*z*eal<br>*s*eal | *d*ō<br>*t*onō, ēdi*t*iō<br>*Z*ephyrus, ga*z*a¹<br>*s*ūs, ro*s*a | *d*os<br>*t*a<br>*z*èle<br>*s*a | da<br>Tag<br>Weise<br>Haus | d<br>t<br>z<br>s |
| Palatal | *y*ou | *j*ugum, *j*aciō | trava*il* | Jahr | y |
| Guttural | *g*ood<br><br>*c*ould | *g*audeō, *g*enus<br>re*g*it<br>*c*anō, *c*ecinī<br>*c*ondi*c*iō, s*c*it<br>*k*alendae | *g*are<br><br>*c*ar | gut<br><br>können | g<br><br>k |
| Lingual | *l*ow<br>*r*ow | *l*avō, consu*l*<br>*R*ōma, datu*r*² | *l*a<br>*r*at | Land<br>Rand | l<br>r |
| Nasal | *m*y<br>*n*igh<br><br>si*ng* | *m*ox, *m*ensa*m*³<br>*n*ox, Ae*n*ēa*n*<br>i*n*cipit, co*n*gerō<br>i*n*quam | *m*is<br>*n*i | mein<br>nein<br><br>singen | m<br>n<br><br>ŋ |
| Rough Breathing | *h*ouse | *h*ōra, co*h*ors | | Haus | h |

¹ Only in loan-words: cf. Introduction, § 1.
² Trilled, as in French and Scottish.
³ Final *m* was (1) lightly sounded before a consonant (*e.g.* mensa*m* tenet). (2) almost absorbed before a vowel or *h* (*e.g.* filia*m* amābat, filia*m* habēbat: each of these pairs of words counts in verse as five syllables).

OBS. 1. The exact pronunciation of Latin v is, perhaps, not yet finally settled. Most authorities regard it as = Engl. w (in *way*); others as resembling, though not exactly identical with, Engl. v (in *v*ain). Seelmann holds that the letter went through three stages: 1. = Engl. w (till 4th or 5th century A.D.); 2. = Germ. w. (a 'bilabial fricative,' *i.e.* a v pronounced with both lips); 3. = Engl. v (a 'labio-dental fricative'). The pronunciation as = Engl. w may be considered optional.

### DOUBLE CONSONANTS.

PH, TH, CH.—The combinations ph, th, ch were pronounced like the corresponding Voiceless Mutes (see classification of consonants, below), but with aspiration, like initial p, t, k, in Irish brogue; *not* like p*h*ilosop*h*er, *t*hen, loo*h* (Scottish). For practical purposes Latin ph, th, ch, may be pronounced like initial p, t, k, in English (*Ph*oebus = *P*oebus, nymp*h*a = nymp*a*, *th*eātrum = *t*eatrum, Cart*h*āgō = Cartāgō, *Ch*eirōn = *K*eiron, Bac*ch*us = Bac*k*us).

X is a double consonant, representing two sounds (ks): *e.g.*, du*x* = duc-*s*, au*xi* = auc-*si*, for au*g*-*si* : cf. auc-tor for aug-tor.

On QU, GU, see Introduction, § 1.

### CLASSIFICATION OF CONSONANTS.

In the above table of Simple Consonant Sounds consonants are arranged according to the place of articulation (lips, teeth, etc.). They may also be classified as :

1. **Voiced**, *i.e.* formed with vibration of the vocal chords.
2. **Voiceless**, *i.e.* formed without vibration of the vocal chords.

Or again as :

1. **Shut**, *i.e.* formed by a stream of air breaking through a closure of the mouth.
2. **Open**, *i.e.* formed by a stream of air rubbing against a narrow passage of the mouth.
3. **Liquid**, *i.e.* formed by gently pressing a stream of air as it passes through the mouth or nose.

|  | Shut ('Mute') | Open ('Spirant') | Liquid |
|---|---|---|---|
| Voiced | b  d  g | v  z  y | l  r  m  n  ŋ |
| Voiceless | p  t  k | f  s  h |  |

*PARALLEL GRAMMAR SERIES*

A
# LATIN GRAMMAR
## FOR SCHOOLS

BASED ON THE PRINCIPLES AND REQUIREMENTS
OF THE
GRAMMATICAL SOCIETY

BY

E. A. SONNENSCHEIN, M.A. (Oxon.)

PROFESSOR OF CLASSICS
IN THE
MASON COLLEGE, BIRMINGHAM

### PART II.—SYNTAX

*Subtilitas naturæ subtilitatem sensus et intellectus multis partibus superat.*—BACON

STEREOTYPED　　　　　EDITION

LONDON
SWAN SONNENSCHEIN & CO.
PATERNOSTER SQUARE
—
1892

# PARALLEL GRAMMAR SERIES.

The following are the distinguishing features of this Series:

### 1.—Uniformity of Classification and Terminology.

The same grammatical phenomenon is classified alike and named alike wherever found. Slightly different phenomena are described by slightly different but not inconsistent names. A pupil using these Grammars will therefore not be distracted by discordant grammatical views or puzzled by divergent formulæ where a single formula would suffice.

The order of the various Grammars being identical, mastery of one involves mastery of the principles and methods of the others.

These important results are attained **without any revolution in terminology.** It has been found that the existing stock of names, if used economically, is sufficient or very nearly sufficient.

Syntax is based on Analysis of Sentences; and the principle of **Comenius,** "Per exempla," as distinct from "Per præcepta," is followed: *i.e.,* rules are based upon a preceding set of selected examples, from which they may be inductively inferred.

### 2.—Uniformity of Scope.

The Series is designed to meet the needs of High Schools and Grammar Schools. Each Grammar is therefore of sufficient scope to cover the whole school course. Experience has shown the importance of utilising the local memory, but this advantage is sacrificed if the pupil passes from book to book and from one arrangement of the page to another.

On the other hand, this series is designed to supplement and not to supplant the teacher. Exposition and discussion are therefore confined to narrow limits. The object of the promoters has been to present in as brief space as possible a conspectus of the main features of the languages.

### 3.—Uniformity of Size and Type.

All the Grammars are printed in three sizes of type—Small Pica, Long Primer, and Brevier—corresponding to three stages of learning. A line down the margin gives additional prominence to the elementary matter. Great care has been bestowed upon making the pages as pictorial as possible, in order thereby to aid the local memory.

It is hoped that these volumes may fairly claim the title of a **Series of Parallel Grammars.** No labour has been spared in making them uniform, not merely externally, but also in principle and method.

SWAN SONNENSCHEIN & CO., PATERNOSTER SQUARE, LONDON.

# PREFACE.

IN the arrangement of the syntax two objects have been borne in mind : (i) a treatment based on the analysis of sentences ; (ii) a clear conspectus of the uses of forms (cases, tenses, moods, etc.) Part I. (pp. 117-163) starts with the *sentence*, and shows how Latin expresses certain *meanings*, and to what extent it leaves the lines of demarcation between meanings confused : here the different volumes of this series (Latin, Greek, French, and German) are parallel in the strictest sense of the word, and the paragraphs correspond. Part II. (p. 164 to the end of the book) classifies the uses of *forms*, sometimes giving a mere summary of matters already treated on the method of sentences in Part I., sometimes containing such new matter as is more conveniently treated under this head. Cross-references indicate how the two parts of syntax supplement one another. Part II. is not necessarily more advanced; though in practice it has been found a good plan to make Part I. the centre of instruction.

The four pages of introduction (pp. 113—116) set forth the precise sense in which terms of syntax are used in the Parallel Grammar Series, and are intended chiefly for reference.

While brevity and simplicity have been studied, the treatment has been made full enough to serve as a basis for teaching Latin Composition.

I desire to acknowledge obligations not only to the writers mentioned in my Preface to Accidence, but also to the grammars of Roby, Kennedy, and Lattmann, and to the papers recently published by Professor W. G. Hale, of Cornell University, on the sequence of tenses and *cum*-constructions. To Professor Hale and to P. Giles, Esq., Fellow of Caius College, Cambridge, I am indebted for some valuable suggestions, which have been incorporated in the present (stereotyped) edition.

The principal rules have been rendered prominent by means of a marginal line.

The Table of Contents will be found on p. 220.

E. A. S.

MASON COLLEGE, BIRMINGHAM,
    *November 1st*, 1889.

# PARALLEL GRAMMAR SERIES.

The following are the distinguishing features of this Series:

## 1.—Uniformity of Classification and Terminology.

The same grammatical phenomenon is classified alike and named alike wherever found. Slightly different phenomena are described by slightly different but not inconsistent names. A pupil using these Grammars will therefore not be distracted by discordant grammatical views or puzzled by divergent formulæ where a single formula would suffice.

The order of the various Grammars being identical, mastery of one involves mastery of the principles and methods of the others.

These important results are attained **without any revolution in terminology.** It has been found that the existing stock of names, if used economically, is sufficient or very nearly sufficient.

Syntax is based on Analysis of Sentences; and the principle of Comenius, "Per exempla," as distinct from "Per præcepta," is followed: *i.e.*, rules are based upon a preceding set of selected examples, from which they may be inductively inferred.

## 2.—Uniformity of Scope.

The Series is designed to meet the needs of High Schools and Grammar Schools. Each Grammar is therefore of sufficient scope to cover the whole school course. Experience has shown the importance of utilising the local memory, but this advantage is sacrificed if the pupil passes from book to book and from one arrangement of the page to another.

On the other hand, this series is designed to supplement and not to supplant the teacher. Exposition and discussion are therefore confined to narrow limits. The object of the promoters has been to present in as brief space as possible a conspectus of the main features of the languages.

## 3.—Uniformity of Size and Type.

All the Grammars are printed in three sizes of type—Small Pica, Long Primer, and Brevier—corresponding to three stages of learning. A line down the margin gives additional prominence to the elementary matter. Great care has been bestowed upon making the pages as pictorial as possible, in order thereby to aid the local memory.

It is hoped that these volumes may fairly claim the title of a **Series of Parallel Grammars.** No labour has been spared in making them uniform, not merely externally, but also in principle and method.

---

SWAN SONNENSCHEIN & CO., PATERNOSTER SQUARE, LONDON.

# PREFACE.

IN the arrangement of the syntax two objects have been borne in mind: (i) a treatment based on the analysis of sentences; (ii) a clear conspectus of the uses of forms (cases, tenses, moods, etc.) Part I. (pp. 117-163) starts with the *sentence*, and shows how Latin expresses certain *meanings*, and to what extent it leaves the lines of demarcation between meanings confused: here the different volumes of this series (Latin, Greek, French, and German) are parallel in the strictest sense of the word, and the paragraphs correspond. Part II. (p. 164 to the end of the book) classifies the uses of *forms*, sometimes giving a mere summary of matters already treated on the method of sentences in Part I., sometimes containing such new matter as is more conveniently treated under this head. Cross-references indicate how the two parts of syntax supplement one another. Part II. is not necessarily more advanced; though in practice it has been found a good plan to make Part I. the centre of instruction.

The four pages of introduction (pp. 113—116) set forth the precise sense in which terms of syntax are used in the Parallel Grammar Series, and are intended chiefly for reference.

While brevity and simplicity have been studied, the treatment has been made full enough to serve as a basis for teaching Latin Composition.

I desire to acknowledge obligations not only to the writers mentioned in my Preface to Accidence, but also to the grammars of Roby, Kennedy, and Lattmann, and to the papers recently published by Professor W. G. Hale, of Cornell University, on the sequence of tenses and *cum*-constructions. To Professor Hale and to P. Giles, Esq., Fellow of Caius College, Cambridge, I am indebted for some valuable suggestions, which have been incorporated in the present (stereotyped) edition.

The principal rules have been rendered prominent by means of a marginal line.

The Table of Contents will be found on p. 220.

E. A. S.

MASON COLLEGE, BIRMINGHAM,
*November 1st*, 1889.

# CONTENTS OF SYNTAX.

|  | PAGE |
|---|---|
| **Introductory Analysis** . . . . . | 113—116 |
| **Syntax—Part I.** . . . . . . | 117—210 |
|    The Subject . . . . . . | 117 |
|    The Predicate . . . . . . | 118—129 |
|       Second Form of the Predicate . . | 119—121 |
|       Third Form of the Predicate . . | 122—126 |
|       Fourth Form of the Predicate . . | 127—129 |
|       Fifth Form of the Predicate . . | 129 |
|    Attributes . . . . . . . | 130 |
|    Adjuncts . . . . . . . | 130 |
|    Kinds of Sentences . . . . . | 131—134 |
|    The Complex Sentence . . . . | 135—163 |
|       Adverb Clauses . . . . . | 135—147 |
|       Adjective Clauses . . . . | 147—149 |
|       Noun Clauses . . . . . | 150—159 |
|       Reported Speech . . . . | 160—163 |
| **Syntax—Part II.** . . . . . . | 164—210 |
|    Use of the Cases . . . . . | 164—180 |
|    Use of Prepositions . . . . . | 180—182 |
|    Use of Voices . . . . . . | 182 |
|    Use of Moods and Tenses . . . | 183—196 |
|    Use of Verb-nouns and Verb-adjectives . | 196—201 |
|    Use of Pronouns, etc. . . . . | 202—205 |
|    Use of Conjunctions . . . . . | 205—207 |
|    Use of Interjections . . . . . | 207 |
|    Order of Words . . . . . | 208—210 |
| **Prosody and Metre** . . . . . | 210—214 |
| **Calendar, Weights, Money, Abbreviations** . | 215—216 |
| **Index** . . . . . . . . | 217—219 |

## INTRODUCTION TO SYNTAX.

Syntax is the part of grammar which treats of the *construction of sentences*.

For the classification of sentences, see § 338.

## *ANALYSIS OF SENTENCES.*
### Forms of the Predicate.

| | | Subject. | Predicate. | | |
|---|---|---|---|---|---|
| | | | *Verb (alone).* | | |
| 301 | I. | Avēs<br>Birds | canunt<br>sing | | |
| | | | *Verb.* | *Predicate Adjective or Noun.* | |
| 302 | II. | Croesus<br>Croesus | erat<br>was | dīves *or* rex<br>rich *or* a king | |
| | | | *Verb.* | *Object.* | |
| 303 | III. | Rōmulus<br>Romulus | condidit<br>founded | Rōmam<br>Rome | |
| | | | *Verb.* | *Two Objects.* | |
| 304 | IV. | Aristotelēs<br>Aristotle | docuit<br>taught | Alexandrum<br>Alexander | sapientiam<br>philosophy |
| | | | *Verb.* | *Object.* | *Pred. Adj. or Noun.* |
| 305 | V. | Hominēs<br>People | vocant<br>call | eum<br>him | fēlīcem *or* poētam<br>happy *or* a poet |

8

## Attributes.

**306** A Noun (whether standing in the Subject or in the Predicate) may be qualified by an Adjective (or Adjective-equivalent: § 310); *e.g. cārī* amīcī, *dear* friends. Such a qualifying part of the sentence is called an **Attribute**.

## Adjuncts.

**307** A Verb, an Adjective (whether standing as Predicate Adjective or as Attribute), or an Adverb, may be qualified by an Adverb (or Adverb-equivalent: § 311); *e.g.*—

Pugnāte *fortiter*. Fight *bravely*.
*Satis* beātus est. He is *quite* happy.
*Valdē* dīligenter. *Very* diligently.

Such a qualifying part of the sentence is called an **Adjunct**.

## Equivalents.

**308** The Noun, the Adjective, and the Adverb may be replaced by other parts of speech doing the same work in the sentence. A word doing the work of a different part of speech, or a group of words doing the work of a single part of speech, is called an **Equivalent**.

A group of words forming an Equivalent and not having Subject and Predicate of its own is called a **Phrase**.

A group of words forming an Equivalent, and having Subject and Predicate of its own is called a **Subordinate Clause** (cf. § 312).

### NOUN-EQUIVALENTS.

**309** A Noun-equivalent may be:—

(1) A Pronoun, *e.g.*—

*Tū* fortūnātus es; *ego* miser sum. *You* are fortunate; *I* am wretched.
*Ego* sum. It is *I*.

(2) A Verb-noun,[1] *e.g.*—

*Legere* difficile est. *To read* (*Reading*) is difficult.

(3) An Adjective, *e.g.*—

*Dīvitēs* et *pauperēs* eum amant. *Rich* and *poor* love him.
*Bonī*. *The good*. *Doctī*. *The learned*.
*Sapiens*. *A wise man*. *Bonum*. *The good*.
*Pulchrum*. *The noble*. *Bona*. *Goods*.

---

[1] The Verb-noun and Verb-adjective participate in all the constructions of the verb to which they belong.

(4) A Clause (in a Complex Sentence, § 312), *e.g.*—
Tē mihī injūriam fēcisse manifestum est. *That you have wronged me* is clear.

## ADJECTIVE-EQUIVALENTS.

**310.** An Adjective-equivalent may be :—
(1) A Verb-adjective (see note on p. 114), *e.g.*—
Flūmen *currens*. A *running* stream.
(2) A Noun in Apposition, *i.e.* a Noun forming another name for the same thing, *e.g.*—
Victōria *Rēgina*. *Queen* Victoria (= *Royal* Victoria).
(3) A Noun in an oblique case, *e.g.*—
Conjūrātiō *Catilīnae*. The conspiracy *of Catiline* (= The *Catilinarian* conspiracy).
Decemvirī *lēgibus scrībendīs*. A commission of ten *for drawing up laws*.
Senex *albīs capillīs*. A *white-haired* old man.
Bonō animō es. Be *of good cheer*. (Equivalent of a Predicate Adjective.)
(4) A Clause (in a Complex Sentence, § 312), *e.g.*—
Domus *quam ēmī*. The house *which I have bought*.

## ADVERB-EQUIVALENTS.

**311.** An Adverb-equivalent may be :—
(1) A phrase formed with a Preposition, *e.g.*—
*In silvīs* vēnātur. He hunts *in the woods*.
*Prō mē* dixit. He spoke *for me*.
(2) A Noun (or Pronoun) in an oblique case, *e.g.*—
*Domum* eō. I am going *home*.
*Decem mīlia passuum* profectī sunt. They marched *ten miles*.
*Multōs annōs* vīvet. He will live *many years*.
*Proximā nocte* mortuus est. He died *last night*.
(3) A Clause (in a Complex Sentence, § 312), *e.g.*—
*Quum vēneris*, dīcam. *When you come*, I will tell you.

## The Simple and the Complex Sentence.

**312** (1) Haec est domus mea. This is my house.

(2) Haec est domus quam aedificāvī. This is the house which I have built.

A sentence like (1), which contains only one group of words having a Subject and Predicate, is called **Simple** [Lat. *simplex* = onefold].

A sentence like (2), which contains

(*a*) A Principal group, having Subject and Predicate of its own :
(*b*) A Subordinate group, having Subject and Predicate of its own,

is called **Complex**, and each of the groups is called a **Clause** (cf. § 308).

| *Principal Clause.* | *Subordinate Clause.* |
|---|---|
| Haec est domus | quam aedificāvī. |

## Kinds of Subordinate Clause.

**313** Subordinate Clauses may be classified according to the part of speech to which they are akin, as :—

1. **Noun Clauses,** *i.e.* Clauses playing the part of a Noun.
2. **Adjective Clauses,** *i.e.* Clauses playing the part of an Adjective.
3. **Adverb Clauses,** *i.e.* Clauses playing the part of an Adverb.

## Co-ordination.

**314** Two or more sentences, clauses, phrases, or single words, linked together by one of the Conjunctions

| et (atque, āc, -que), *and* | neque (nēve), *nor* |
| sed (at, autem, vērō), *but* | nam (namque, enim, etenim), *for* |
| aut (vel, an, -ve), *or* | |

are called **Co-ordinate**.

**314\*** A clause introduced by the Relative *quī*, 'who,' or by such a conjunction as *quum*, 'when,' *quamquam*, 'although,' may be equivalent to a Co-ordinate Sentence : in such cases *quī* = *et is* or *sed is* or *nam is; quum* = *et tum; quamquam* = *et tamen, atquī,* 'and yet '; *e.g.*—

*Themistoclēs ā patre exhērēdātus est:* **quae** *contumēlia nōn frēgit eum,* ***sed*** *ērexit.* Themistocles was disinherited by his father : **but this disgrace** did not crush him, but spurred him on.

## The Two Parts of Syntax.

**315** Syntax has to answer two questions:—
1. How are meanings expressed in *sentences* and *parts of sentences*?
The answer is given in Part I. of Syntax (§§ 316—371).
2. How are *words* and *their forms* used?
The answer is given in Part II. of Syntax (§§ 372—603).

## SYNTAX.—PART I.

☞ Those constructions which are peculiar to the Complex Sentence will be treated *after* those which are common to the Simple and the Complex Sentence.

### *THE SUBJECT.*
#### Case of the Subject.

**316** *Puer cantat.* The boy is singing.
*Tū fortūnātus es.* You are prosperous.
*Ego miser sum.* I am wretched.
*Dīcat aliquis.* Some one may say.
*Doctī dissentiunt.* The learned disagree.
*Hostis cēdere.* The enemy began to retreat. (Historical Infinitive, § 339*.)
*Pater meus, quī apud mē est, aegrōtat.* My father, who is with me, is ill.

RULE: The Subject, if a declinable word, stands in the Nominative.

#### Subject not expressed by a separate word.

**316ª** *Crēdō.* I believe.
*Abī.* Go away.
*Pluit.* It is raining. (Impersonal verb: § 252).
*Dīcunt. (Ferunt. Trādunt. Narrant.)* Men say. (The story runs.)
*Videās.* One may see (lit.: 'you,' *i.e.* 'anyone': cf. § 340 ☞).
*Crēderēs.* One might have believed.

RULE: The Subject is often not expressed by a separate word, when it is sufficiently indicated in the verb-ending (§ 206).

☞ The Passive of Intransitive verbs may be used in the 3rd Pers. Sing., without any subject expressed, to denote that an action takes place (**Impersonal Passive Construction**); *e.g.* *Sīc ītur ad astra.* 'Tis thus men rise to the stars (*ītur:* 'there is a going'). *Pugnātum est ācriter.* The battle raged fiercely ('there was fighting').

## THE PREDICATE.
### Agreement of the Verb with the Subject.

**317** *Puer cant-at.* The boy sing-s.  *Puerī cant-ant.* The boys sing.
*Tū doc-ēs.* Thou teach est.  *Nōs doc-ēmus.* We teach.

RULE: The finite Verb (§ 178) agrees with its Subject in number and person.

**Constructiō ad sensum.** (Construction according to sense.)

**318** A Singular noun of multitude may take a Plural verb: *e.g.*—
*Magna multitūdō convēnit* or *convēnērunt.* A great number of persons has *or* have assembled.

### Compound Subject.

**319** ☞ A Compound Subject is a Subject made up of two or more nouns (or noun-equivalents) linked together by one of the conjunctions *et, atque, āc, -que,* or united in thought without a conjunction.

#### 1. Number of Verb.

**320** *Pater et māter ējus vīvunt.* His father and mother are alive.
*Sapientia, temperantia, fortitūdō nōn sine voluptāte sunt.* Wisdom, temperance, courage are not without pleasure.

RULE: When the Subject is compound, the Verb is Plural.

#### 2. Person of Verb.

**321** *Ego et fīlius meus valēmus.* My son and I are well.
*Tū et fīlia tua valētis.* You and your daughter are well.

RULE: If the words composing the subject are of different persons, then the Plural Verb is of the 1st Person rather than the 2nd or 3rd, and of the 2nd Person rather than the 3rd.

☞ Reason:—

I + my son = we (1st Pers. Plur.): hence *valēmus* (1st Pers. Plur.)

You + your daughter = you (2nd Pers. Plur.): hence *valetis* (2nd Pers. Plur.)

**322** OBS. The Verb may agree with the part of Subject which stands *nearest* to it, especially if the nouns composing the Subject denote sexless things: *e.g.*—

*Mens et ratiō et consilium in senibus est.* Mind and reason and wisdom are found in old men.

**Constructiō ad sensum.**

**322\*** If the words that compose the subject are so closely connected as to form *one idea*, the verb may be Singular : *e.g.*—
*Senātus populusque dēcrēvit.* The Senate and People passed a resolution.

**Cum.**

**322†** *Cum* may serve as an equivalent of *et* : e.g.—
*Dux cum aliquot prinoipibus capiuntur.* The general and several chiefs are taken.

**Aut, vel, neque.**

**323** The conjunctions *aut, vel, neque* do not link words so as to form a Compound Subject : *e.g.*—
*Probārem hōc si Sōcratēs aut Antisthenēs diceret.* I should agree to this if Socrates or Antisthenes said so.

But the Verb may be Plural : *e.g.*—
*Si quid Sōcratēs aut Aristippus contrā consuētūdinem civilem fēcērunt.* If Socrates or Aristippus acted in aught contrary to the social law. (Rare with *aut . . . aut : neque . . . neque.*)

☞ When the Subjects are Personal Pronouns, the Verb is generally Plural : *e.g.*—
*Haec neque ego neque tū fēcimus.* This neither you nor I have done.

## SECOND FORM OF THE PREDICATE.

(PREDICATE = VERB + PREDICATE ADJECTIVE OR NOUN, § 302.)

**324** The same kind of verbs may stand in a Predicate of the Second Form as in English :—

1. *Sum.* I am. e.g. *Sum* **beātus.** I am **happy.**

   ☞ *Est, sunt* (3rd Pers.) are often not expressed : e.g.
   *Omnia praeclāra rāra.* All that is excellent is rare. (χαλεπὰ τὰ καλά.)

   *Fīō.* I become, I am made.
       e.g. *Fīs* **senex.** You are becoming **old.**
   *Maneō.* I remain. e.g. *Manet* **īdem.** He remains **the same.**
   *Videor.* I seem. e.g. *Vidētur* **sapiens.** He seems **wise.**

2. The Passives (cf. § 334)—
   *Creor, ēligor.* I am chosen.
       e.g. *Creātur* **consul.** He is chosen **consul.**
   *Appellor, vocor, nōminor, dīcor.* I am called.
       e.g. *Vocātur* **magn** . He is called **great.**
   *Putor, habeor, existimor, jūdicor.* I am thought.
       e.g. *Putāris* **sapiens.** You are thought **wise.**

☞ On *Vidētur esse sapiens* (*Putātur scire*), see § 368a ☞.

**Obs. 1.** The use of the Predicate Adjective or Noun is not confined to Predicates containing one of these verbs: we may say :—

*Fortis* Etrūria crēvit. Etruria grew strong.

*Filius salvus* rediit. The son has returned safe (*i.e.* The son has returned and is safe).

*Nix cāna* cadit. Snow falls white.

*Hannibal in patriam senex* revertit. H. returned home an old man (*i.e.* H. was an old man when he returned home).

☞ The above sentences are ambiguous in Latin: thus

*Nix cāna cadit* might mean 'The white snow is falling.'

In English the position of the adjective tells us whether it is used as an attribute or predicatively.

**Obs. 2.** The Latin Predicate Adjective may be sometimes translated by an English Adverb: e.g.

*Invītus* (*Imprūdens*) *fēcit*. He did it unwillingly (unwittingly).

## Agreement of the Predicate Adjective and Noun.

### Predicate Adjective.

**325** *Mōs est antīqu-us.* The custom is ancient.

*Urbēs sunt antīqu-ae.* The cities are ancient.

*Templum est antīqu-um.* The temple is ancient.

RULE: The Predicate Adjective agrees in gender, number, and case with the word to which it refers (here the Subject).

### Predicate Noun.

*Mōs est lex.* A custom is a law.

*Urbs est caput Ītaliae.* The city (*i.e.* Rome) is the capital of Italy.

*Templum est arx.* The temple is a stronghold.

RULE: The Predicate Noun agrees in case with the word to which it refers (here the Subject).

**Obs.** *Sōl est rex coeli.* The sun is the king of the sky. *Lūna est rēgina coeli.* The moon is the queen of the sky.

*Ūsus est magister optimus.* Experience is the best teacher (instructor).

*Nātūra est magistra optima.* Nature is the best teacher (instructress).

*Athēnae erant inventrīcēs artium.* Athens was the mother (inventress) of arts and sciences. [Note the Plural.]

☞ For the Predicate Genitive and Dative see §§ 389, 420.

# AGREEMENT OF PREDICATE ADJECTIVE AND NOUN.

**Peculiarities.**

**I.**

*Triste lupus stabulis.* A wolf is a bane to sheepfolds. (*Virg.*)
*Varium et mūtābile semper ₁ fēmina.* A woman is always a fickle and changeable thing. (*Virg.*)

RULE: The neuter adjective may be used as a noun-equivalent (§ 309.)

**II.**

*Hōc opus, hic labor est.* This is the task, this the toil.
*Hae sunt imāginēs meae, haec nōbilitās.* These are my ancestral busts, this my title.
*Quae est causa tristitiae tuae?* What is the cause of your sadness?
*Thēbae, quod caput Boeōtiae est.* Thebes, which is the head of Boeotia.
*Animal plēnum ratiōnis, quem hominem vocāmus.* An animal endowed with reason, which we call man. (Fifth Form of the Predicate, § 334.)

RULE: If the Subject is a demonstrative, interrogative, or relative pronoun, it is generally made to agree in gender, number, and case with the Predicate Noun.

## 325* Agreement of Predicate Adjective with Compound Subject.

### 1. When the Compound Subject denotes Persons.

*Pater et māter ējus mortu-ī sunt.* His father and mother are dead.

RULE: When the Verb is Plural (§ 320) and the nouns composing the Subject denote persons of different sexes, the Predicate Adjective is masculine.

☞ Reason:—

'Father and mother' = Two human beings (*duo hominēs:* Masc. § 64).

### 2. When the Compound Subject denotes Sexless Things.

*Injustitia et intemperantia sunt fugiend-a.* Injustice and intemperance are to be shunned (things to be shunned).
*Mors et somnus sunt simil-ia.* Death and sleep are alike.

RULE: When the Verb is Plural (§ 320) and the nouns composing the Subject denote sexless things, the Predicate Adjective is, as a rule, neuter.

325† OBS. The Predicate Adjective may however agree with the part of the Subject which stands nearest to it: *e.g. Bracchia eorum et umerī ab aquā līber-ī erant.* Their arms and shoulders were free of the water (§ 322).

## THIRD FORM OF THE PREDICATE.
(Predicate = Verb + Object, § 303).
### Verbs taking the Accusative.

**326** *Puer turbinem verberat.* The boy is whipping the top.

Rule: The Object, if a declinable word, generally stands in the Accusative.

☞ For Verbs of Motion which, when compounded with Prepositions, become capable of taking an Accusative, see § 377.

**326\*** An Object which is of kindred meaning to the verb is called **cognate**. A Cognate Object is generally qualified by an Attribute :
*Risum amārum risit.* He laughed a bitter laugh.
*Vitam exsulis vivit.* He is living the life of an exile.

But cognate object + attribute are sometimes expressed by a single word, not of kindred meaning with the verb :
(a) A neuter adjective :
*Dulce ridet.* She has a sweet laugh (*dulce = dulcem risum*) or laughs sweetly.
*Acerba tuētur.* He has a fierce look. (Cf. Eng. 'to look daggers.')
(b) A neuter pronoun :
*Hōc laetor.* I rejoice at this (I rejoice with this joy : $hōc = hanc$ *laetitiam*).
*Illud tē hortor.* I exhort you as follows.
(c) A noun :
*Olet unguenta.* He smells of ointments (*unguenta = odōrem unguentōrum*).

**326†** English Verbs constructed with a fixed Preposition.

Caution : Many Latin verbs which take an Accusative correspond to English verbs which are constructed with a fixed Preposition :
*Arma virumque canō.* I sing-of arms and a hero.
*Fātum suum queritur.* He complains-of his fate.
*Salūtem dēspērāmus.* We despair-of deliverance.
*Miror neglegentiam tuam.* I wonder-at your carelessness.
*Risī tē hodiē multum.* I have laughed-at you a great deal to-day.
*Tyrrhēnum nāvigat aequor.* He is sailing-over the Tuscan sea.
*Quem fugis?* From whom art thou fleeing?
*Maneō tē.* I am waiting-for you.

Such verbs are not, as a rule, used in the Passive ; but note—
*Rideor.* I am laughed-at.
*Errātis agris.* The country having been wandered-through (§ 361).
[Passive of *errāre agrōs*, 'to wander-through the country.']

## Passive Construction.

**327** | *Brūtus Caesarem occīdit.* | *Caesar ā Brūtō occīsus est.*
Brutus slew Caesar. | Caesar was slain by Brutus.

*Lupa Rōmulum nūtrīvit.* | *Rōmulus ā lupā nūtrītus est.*
A she-wolf fed Romulus. | Romulus was fed by a she-wolf.

*Labor firmat puerōs.* | *Puerī labōre firmantur.*
Toil strengthens boys. | Boys are strengthened by toil.

*Īra eum commōvit.* | *Commōtus est īrā.*
Wrath stirred him. | He was stirred by anger.

RULE: In the Passive construction of verbs taking the Accusative
what was the Object in the Active becomes the Subject (Nominative);
what was the Subject in the Active stands in the Ablative
with *ā* or *ab*, if it denotes a living creature (Agent);
without a preposition, if it denotes something not living.

☞ For the Dative of the Agent see § 413.

## Verbs taking the Genitive.

**327\*** | *Vīvōrum* **meminī**, *neque* **oblīvīscor** *mortuōrum.* I remember the living and do not forget the dead.

**Misereor** *tuī.* I pity you. (= *Miseret mē tuī*, § 447.)

RULE: With *pity, remember, forget,*
A Genitive mostly is set.

☞ *Miseror,* 'I pity' (1st Conjug.) generally takes the Accusative.

### Accusative for Genitive.

*Mementō illum diem* or *illīus diēī*
*Reminīscere illīus diēī*
*Recordāre illum diem*
*Nē oblītus sīs illum diem* or *illīus diēī*
} Remember that day.

RULE: With verbs of *remembering* and *forgetting*, the Object, if a thing (not person), often stands in the Accusative.

#### Passive Construction.

The Passive of *oblīviscī* is supplied by *in oblīviōnem alicuī venīre.*
      ,,    *meminisse*     ,,    *in mentem alicuī venīre.*
*e.g. Mihī in mentem venit tuī.* I think of you. (You are remembered by me.)

## Verbs taking the Dative (Cui-Verbs).

**328** A. Corresponding to English verbs which take an Object:—

**Imperō** *alicui*. I command a person.
**Pāreō (Oboediō, Obsequor, Obtemperō**, § 418; **Serviō)** *alicui*.
 I obey a person.
**Studeō** *alicui*. I am devoted to a person.
 [*Studeō litterīs*. I study (pursue) literature.]
**Nūbō** *virō*. I marry a husband.
**Noceō** *alicui*. I hurt a person. **Faveō** *alicui*. I favour a person.
**Parcō** *alicui*. I spare a person. [*Parcō labōrī*. I spare trouble.]
**Placeō (Displiceō)** *alicui*. I please (displease) a person.
**Invideō** *alicui*. I envy a person.
**Confīdō (Diffīdō)** *alicui*. I trust (distrust) a person.
 [*Confīdō aliquā rē*. I put confidence in a thing.]
**Ignōscō** *alicui*. I forgive a person.
**Resistō (Repugnō)** *alicui*. I resist a person.
**Indulgeō** *alicui*. I indulge (am indulgent to) a person.
 [*Indulgeō īrae (animō)*. I give way to anger (passion).]
**Suādeō (Persuādeō)** *alicui*. I advise (persuade) a person.
**Crēdō** *alicui*. I believe a person.
 [*Crēdō ista (Acc.)*. I believe that statement of yours.]

RULE:  A Dative put—remember pray—
 With *imperāre* and *obey*,
 *Studēre, nūbere, nocēre,*
 *Favēre, parcere, placēre;*
 To these add *envy, trust, forgive,*
 *Resist, indulge, persuade, believe.*

Other verbs of this kind are:

| | |
|---|---|
| *Blandior*. I flatter. | *Minor*. I threaten. |
| *Grātulor*. I congratulate. | *Opitulor (Auxilior)*. I assist. |
| *Medeor*. I heal. | *Supplicō*. I entreat. |

B. Corresponding to English verbs which are constructed with a fixed Preposition:—

**Īrāscor (Suscēnseō)** *alicui*. I am angry with a person.
**Vacō** *philosophiae*. I have leisure for philosophy.

☞ For Verbs which, when compounded with Prepositions or Adverbs, become capable of taking a Dative, see § 418.

## Notes on Cui-Verbs.

**328\*** 1. These verbs were in origin intransitive (*pārēre*, to be obedient; *favēre*, to be well inclined; *nocēre*, to be harmful), the Dative being originally adverbial, *i.e.* denoting 'to' or 'for' (*pāreō tibī*, I am obedient to you).

2. CAUTION: The following verbs of similar meaning to those enumerated in § 328 take an Accusative:

*Jubēre aliquem.*  To command a person.
*Hortārī aliquem.*  To exhort a person.
*Vetāre (Prohibēre) aliquem.*  To forbid (restrain) a person.
*Dūcere uxōrem.*  To marry a wife.
*Laedere aliquem.*  To hurt (injure) a person.
*Offendere aliquem.*  To offend (injure) a person.
*Dēlectāre aliquem.*  To delight (please) a person.
*Adūlārī aliquem.*  To flatter a person.
*Cūrāre (Medicāre, Sānāre) aliquem.*  To heal a person.
*Juvāre (Adjuvāre) aliquem.*  To assist a person.

3. Several verbs take either a Dative or an Accusative, according to the sense: *e.g.*

{ *Cavēre alicui.*  To be watchful on behalf of a person.
{ *Cavēre aliquem.*  To be on one's guard against a person.
{ *Consulere alicui.*  To consult the interests of a person.
{ *Consulere aliquem.*  To ask a person's advice.
{ *Moderārī (Temperāre) reī.*  To restrain a thing.
{ *Moderārī (Temperāre) rem.*  To guide a thing.
{ *Temperāre vīnum.*  To mix wine.

## Passive Construction of Cui-Verbs.

**329**
*Imperātur mihī.*  I am commanded.
*Imperātum est tibī.*  You were commanded.
*Imperābitur eī.*  He will be commanded.

RULE: The Passive of verbs that take a Dative is expressed impersonally (*i.e.* in the 3rd Pers. Sing., without a Nominative).

The Perfect Passive of *parcō* is supplied by *mihī temperātum est* ('I have been spared').
The Perfect Passive of *invideō* is supplied by *invidiae fuī* ('I have been envied'). Cf. § 420. Obs. 2.

## Verbs taking the Ablative.

**329.** A. Corresponding to English verbs which take an Object :—

*Praestat victōriā* **ūtī** *quam* **fruī**. It is better to use a victory than to enjoy it.

*Officiō suō* **fungī** *cupit*. He wishes to do (perform) his duty.

*Voluptāte virtūs saepe* **carēre**, *numquam* **indigēre** *potest*. Virtue may often lack (be without), but can never need, pleasure.

RULE: With *use, perform, lack, need, enjoy,*
An Ablative you must employ.

B. Corresponding to English verbs which are constructed with a fixed Preposition :—

**Potior** *urbe*. I get (have) possession of the city. ☞ Also with Gen. (*rērum potīrī*, to get possession of supreme power).

**Vescor** *lacte et pāne*. I live on milk and bread.

## Verbs taking the Infinitive.

**330.** *Nōn possum scrībere.* I cannot write.
*Discis saltāre.* You are learning to dance.

RULE: The following verbs, like the corresponding English verbs, take an Infinitive in a Predicate of the Third Form :

**Possum.** I can. **Nequeō.** I am unable, I cannot.

**Volō, nōlō, mālō.** I will, I am unwilling, I prefer.

**Cupiō.** I desire. **Studeō.** I am eager. **Audeō.** I venture.

**Dēbeō.** I ought.

**Cūnctor, moror, dubitō, vereor.** I delay, I hesitate.

**Cōnor.** I attempt.

**Incipiō, īnstituō, coepī.** I begin.

**Pergō, persevērō.** I continue.

**Dēsinō, dēsistō, intermittō.** I cease.

**Festīnō, mātūrō, properō.** I hasten.

**Cōgitō, in animō habeō.** I intend.

**Statuō, cōnstituō, dēcernō.** I resolve.

**Soleō, cōnsuēvī.** I am wont.

**Assuēscō, cōnsuēscō.** I accustom myself.

**Discō.** I learn. **Sciō.** I know [*nāre*, how to swim].

CAUTION: Beware of confusing the English Infinitive of Purpose with the Object Infinitive: 'I came to see' is *Vēnī ut vidērem* (§ 350).—For 'I hope (promise, pretend) to . . .' see § 368a.

☞ *Cupiō esse justus.* I desire to be just.
*Nōlō fierī cōnsul.* I am unwilling to be made consul.

RULE: A Predicate Adjective or Noun depending on an Infinitive agrees in gender, number, and case with the word to which it refers. (Cf. § 333 ☞.)

## FOURTH FORM OF THE PREDICATE.
(PREDICATE = VERB + TWO OBJECTS, § 304.)

### Verbs taking two Accusatives.[1]

#### 1. Verbs of teaching and concealing.

330 *Doceō tē linguam Latīnam.* I am teaching you the Latin language.
*Nōn tē cēlāvī hunc sermōnem.* I have not concealed this talk from you (kept you in the dark about this talk).

RULE: **Doceō** and **cēlō** take two Accusatives, one of the person, the other of the thing.

#### Special Constructions.

OBS. But note:—
*Doceō tē tībiīs* (Abl.). I am teaching you the flute (*fidibus*, the lyre).
*Docēbō tē dē hāc rē.* I will keep you informed about this.
*Cēlāvistī mē dē hāc rē.* You have kept me in ignorance about this.

#### Passive Construction.

The passive construction is supplied by:—
*Discis ā mē linguam Latīnam.* You are learning Latin from me.
*Ērudīris hāc arte ā mē.* You are being instructed in this art by me.
*Doctus litterīs Graecīs.* Learned in Greek literature.
*Certior fīēs dē hāc rē.* You shall be informed about this matter.
*Cēlātus es dē hāc rē.* You have been kept in the dark about this.

☞ 1. Such a construction as *doctus iter melius* 'taught a better course,' is poetical.
2. *Cēlāris haec* (Acc. of Neuter Demonstr. Pron.), 'You are being kept in the dark about these things' is good prose Latin. (Cf. § 330 \*\*.)

---

[1] For Compounds of *trans*, see § 377.

### 2. Verbs of asking.

**330\*\***

*Ōrō auxilium.* I entreat (beg for) aid.
*Ōrō tē.* I entreat you.
*Interrogō tē.* I question you.
*Hōc tē ōrō.* This I beg of you.
*Illud tē interrogō.* I ask you the following question.

RULE: Verbs of 'asking' take, as a rule, *one* Accusative (of the person *or* of the thing): or *two* Accusatives when the thing asked is expressed by a neuter pronoun or adjective (e.g. *multa*).

OBS: 'I ask help of you' is *Ōrō tē* **ut adjuvēs** (§369 a), or *Petō* (*Poscō, Postulō, Flāgitō*) **abs tē** *auxilium*.

'I ask you your opinion' is *Interrogō te* **quid sentiās** (§ 370), or *Quaerō* **ex** (**abs**) **tē quid sentiās**.

Note however the following unusual, official or poetical constructions:
*Caesar Aeduōs frūmentum flāgitāvit.* Caesar demanded corn of the Aeduans.
*Cōnsul senātōrem sententiam rogat.* The consul asks the senator his opinion.
*Interrogātus (Rogātus) sententiam.* Having been asked his opinion.
*Ōtium dīvōs rogat.* He entreats the Gods for peace.
*Poscēris exta bovis.* You are asked for the entrails of an ox.

## Verbs taking an Accusative and a Dative.

**331**

*Dō tibī ānulum.* I give you a ring, *or* I give a ring to you.
*Adēmit cīvibus lībertātem.* He took from his fellow-citizens freedom of speech.
*Erranti viam monstrēmus.* Let us show the road to the wanderer.
*Dīcam tibī omnia.* I will tell you all.

RULE: Verbs of 'giving,' 'taking,' 'showing,' 'telling,' etc., take an Accusative (**Direct Object**), and a Dative (**Indirect Object**).

OBS.: *Dōnō* also takes an Accusative and an Ablative: *e.g.*
*Dōnō tē ānulō.* I present you with a ring.

☞ For Verbs which, when compounded with Prepositions, become capable of taking an Acc. and a Dat., see § 418.

### Passive Construction.

**332**

The Passive construction is possible in Latin only when the Direct Object becomes the Subject: *e.g.*

*Via mihī monstrāta est.* The way was shown me, *or* I was shown the way

## Verbs taking a Case and an Infinitive.

**333**  *Docet mē saltāre.* He teaches me to dance.
*Jubēsne mē cantāre?* Do you bid me sing?
*Sine mē loquī.* Permit me to speak. (Let me speak.)

RULE: The following Verbs, like the corresponding verbs in English, take an Accusative and an Infinitive:

| | |
|---|---|
| **Doceō.** I teach. | **Vetō.** I forbid. |
| **Jubeō.** I command. | **Sinō, patior.** I permit. |

☞ *Jubeō tē esse jus*tum. I bid you to be just (§ 330 ☜).
Compare Complex Sentence, § 369c.

## FIFTH FORM OF THE PREDICATE.

(PREDICATE = VERB + OBJECT + PRED. ADJ. OR NOUN, § 305.)

**334**  The same kind of verbs may stand in a Predicate of the Fifth Form as in English—

*Faciō, reddō.* I make. e.g. *Bovēs* **aquam turbidam** *fēcērunt.* The oxen have made the water muddy.

*Creō, ēligō.* I choose, elect. e.g. *Populus* **tē consulem** *creāvit.* The nation has elected you consul.

*Appellō, vocō, nōminō, dīcō.* I call. e.g. *Hominēs* **eum magnum** *appellant.* People call him great.

*Putŏ, existimō, jūdicō.* I think. e.g. *Putŏ* **tē sapientem.** I think you wise.

*Habeō, dō, sūmō.* I have, I give, I take. e.g. *Sumpsērunt* **eum imperātōrem.** They took him as general.

*Praebeō, praestō.* I show (with Reflexive Pronoun). e.g. *Praebuit* **sē fortem.** He showed himself brave.

Obs. 1. The passive sense 'I am made' is generally expressed by *fīō* (§ 324), not by *reddor*.

Obs. 2. The Participle is often used as a Predicate Adjective; with verbs of 'perceiving' the Infinitive may be used in the same sense, e.g.:

*Vīdī eum morientem (morī).* I saw him dying (die).

*Audiō gallum canentem (canere).* I hear the cock crowing (crow).

**335**  For the agreement of the Predicate Adjective and Noun (here with the Object) see § 325. For the Predicate Dative see § 420.

## ATTRIBUTES (§ 306).

☞ §§ 336 and 337 deal with Adjectives and with Nouns in Apposition (cf. § 310, 2). For other Attributes see Use of Genitive, §§ 387—400; Ablative, § 434; Dative, § 415; Accusative, § 385; Prepositions, § 455.

### Agreement of Attributes.
#### Adjective as Attribute.

**336**

I.

*Vir bon-us.* A good man.
*Mulierēs bon-ae.* Good women.
*Bon-um consilium.* Good counsel.
*Hunc virum.* This man (Acc.).
*Qu-ārum mulierum?* Of which women.
*Librum su-um āmīsit.* He (She) has lost his (her) book.
*Candens sīdus.* A shining constellation. [Verb-adjective.]
*Castra mūnīt-a.* A fortified camp. [Verb-adjective.]

RULE: The Adjective agrees in gender, number, and case with the word which it qualifies (cf. §§ 325, 335).

II.

*Omn-ēs terrae et maria.*
*Terrae et maria omn-ia.*  } All lands and seas.
*Omn-ēs terrae et omn-ia maria.*

RULE: If an Adjective qualifies two or more words of different genders, it agrees with the one that stands nearest (or else is repeated with each).

#### Noun as Attribute.

**337** *Ager Aeduōrum,* **gentis** *validae.* The country of the Aedui, a powerful tribe.
**Themistoclēs** *vēnī ad tē.* I, Themistocles, am come to you.
*Athēnae,* **inventrīcēs** *artium.* Athens, the mother of arts and sciences.

RULE: The Noun in Apposition—§ 310 (2)—agrees in case with the word which it qualifies (cf. §§ 325, 335).

## ADJUNCTS (§ 307).

☞ Adjuncts are either Adverbs or Adverb-equivalents. For Adverb-equivalents, see Use of Accusative, §§ 381 — 384; Genitive, §§ 401—408; Dative, §§ 411—414, 417, 418; Ablative, §§ 422—432; Place, Space and Time, §§ 435-445; Prepositions, §§ 456—460.

## KINDS OF SENTENCES.

**338** Sentences may be classified as follows:—
1. STATEMENTS:
   *She sings.*
   *She would sing, if you asked her.* (**Conditional Statement**; the two clauses form a Complex Sentence: §§ 353—355).
2. COMMANDS, WISHES, CONCESSIONS:
   *Sing.*
   *Let her sing. She shall sing.*
   *God save the Queen.*
   *Be it so.*
   A Negative Command is called a Prohibition: e.g. *Do not sing.*
3. QUESTIONS:
   *Does she sing ?*
4. EXCLAMATIONS:
   *How beautifully she sings !*

### STATEMENTS.

**339** *Cantat.* He (she, it) sings.
*Nōn cantat.* He (she, it) does not sing. (Negative statement.)
RULE: Statements as to a matter of fact are expressed by the Indicative. (The Negative particle is *nōn*.)

### Historical Infinitive.

**339\*** *Nihil consiliō neque imperiō agī : fors omnia regere.* Nothing was proceeding by counsel or command : chance directed all.
RULE: The Infinitive is sometimes used for the Imperfect Indicative in vivid descriptions (Historical Infinitive). For the case of the Subject see § 316.

### Modest Assertions.

**340** *Crēdiderim.* I am inclined to believe.
*Hic quaerat quispiam.* At this point some one may perhaps ask.
*Dīxerit aliquis.* Some one may be inclined to say.
*Crēderēs (Dīcerēs, Putārēs).* One might have believed (said, thought).
RULE: Modest (hesitating *or* cautious) assertions are expressed by the Subjunctive (Negative *nōn*);
  by the Pres. or Perf. Subj., if referring to present time;
  by the Imperf. Subj., if referring to past time.

☞ The subject is, as a rule, either 1st Pers. Sing., or indefinite : the 2nd Pers. Sing. often has indefinite sense ('you' = 'anyone,' German '*man*,' French 'on ').[1]—When the Subjunctive approaches the meaning 'can' it is called the 'Potential Subj.' CAUTION: 'Can' is properly expressed by *possum* with Infin. (§ 330).

---

[1] This indefinite 2nd Pers. Sing. Subjunctive is also found in complex sentences : e.g., *Bonus segnior fit, ubī (sī) neglegās.* The good man becomes slacker, when (if) one neglects him.

### Statements as to what ought to have been done.

**140\***  *Potius diceret* . . . He should rather have said . . . (= *Oportuit eum dicere*, § 453).
*Frūmentum nē ēmissēs.* You ought not to have bought corn. (= *Nōn oportuit tē frūmentum emere*.)
RULE: Statements as to what ought to have been done are sometimes expressed by the Imperfect or Pluperfect Subjunctive (Negative *nē*).

## COMMANDS, WISHES, CONCESSIONS.
### Commands.

**341a**
| | | |
|---|---|---|
| *Cantā.* Sing. | *Cantātō.* | Thou shalt sing. |
| *Cantet.* Let him sing. | *Cantātō.* | He shall sing. |
| *Cantēmus.* Let us sing. | | |
| *Cantāte.* Sing. | *Cantātōte.* | Ye shall sing. |
| *Cantent.* Let them sing. | *Cantantō.* | They shall sing. |

RULE: Commands are expressed
in the 2nd Person by the Imperative;
in the 3rd Person by the Present Subjunctive or Imperative;
in the 1st Person Plural by the Present Subjunctive.

Obs. The 2nd Pers. of the Present Subjunctive is not, as a rule, used to express a command, except when the subject is indefinite (cf. § 340 ☞):
*Quidquid agis, prūdenter agās.* Whatever one does, one should do cautiously.

### Prohibitions.

**341b**
{ *Nē cantāverīs.* Do not sing. *Nē commōtus sīs.* Be not moved.
{ *Nōlī cantāre.* Do not sing (literally 'Be unwilling to sing').
*Nē cantet.* Let him not sing.
*Nē cantēmus.* Let us not sing.
*Nē cantāveritis* (*Nōlīte cantāre*). Do not sing.
*Nē cantent.* Let them not sing.

RULE: Prohibitions are expressed
in the 2nd Person by the Perfect Subjunctive, or by *nōlī*, *nōlīte* with Infinitive (cf. too §369a, obs. 3);
in the other Persons by the Present Subjunctive.
The negative particle is *nē*. ('And . . . not,' 'nor,' is *nēve*, *neū*, cf. § 582).

Obs. 1. The poets sometimes express a prohibition by *nē* with the 2nd Pers. of the Imperative:
*Nē saevī, magna sacerdōs.* Be not wrathful, great priestess.
*Equō nē crēdite, Teucrī.* Trust not to the horse, Trojans.

Obs. 2. *Nē* with the Imperative in *-tō* (2nd and 3rd Pers.) is hardly used except in legal phraseology :—*Hominem mortuum in urbe nē sepelītō, nēve ūritō.* A dead man thou shalt not bury or burn in the city.

Obs. 3. *Nē requirās* (Pres. Subj.). Let no man ask (cf. § 341 a, Obs.).

## Wishes.

**342** *Vīvat!* (*Utinam vīvat!*)  May he live!
*Utinam vīveret!*  Would that he were alive [but he is not]!
*Utinam illīs temporibus vīxisset!*  Would that he had been alive at that time [but he was not]!

RULE: Wishes as to the future are expressed by the Pres. Subj., with or without *utinam*.
Wishes that something were (at the present time) otherwise than it actually is, are expressed by the Imperf. Subj., with *utinam*.
Wishes that something had been (in the past) otherwise than it actually was, are expressed by the Pluperf. Subj., with *utinam*.
The negative particle is *nē*.

☞ With the tenses and mood employed in expressing wishes, cf. those used in Conditional Sentences § 355.

## Concessions.

**343** *Estō.*  Be it so.
*Sit hōc vērum.*  Suppose this to be true.  (This may be true.)
*Fuerīs doctus, fuerīs prūdens: pius nōn fuistī.*  Granted that you were learned, granted that you were prudent; dutiful you were not.  (You may have been learned, etc.)

RULE: Concessions are expressed by the Emphatic Imperative or the Present or Perfect Subjunctive (Negative *nē*).

## Questions.

**344** *Cantatne?*  Is he (she, it) singing?  *or* Does he (she, it) sing?
*Quis cantat?*  Who is singing?

### Deliberative Questions.

**344\*** *Cantemne?* Am I to sing?  *Cantāremne?* Was I to sing?
*Quid faciat?* What is he to do?  *Quid faceret?* What was he to do?

RULE: Deliberative questions (*i.e.* questions as to what is or was to be done) are expressed by the Subjunctive (Negative *nōn*):
by the Present Subj., if referring to present or future time;
by the Imperfect Subj., if referring to past time.

Obs. 'Am I to sing?' may also be expressed by the Pres. Indic.: e.g. *Cantō an nōn cantō?*  Am I to sing or not?

**344†**       **Modes of Introducing Questions.**

All questions (whether as to a matter of fact or deliberative) belong to one of two classes:
  I. Questions which may be answered with 'Yes' or 'No.'
  II. Questions which cannot be answered with 'Yes' or 'No.'

I.

*Cantāvistīne?* Did you sing? [*Cantāvī.* Yes. *Nōn cantāvī.* No.]
*Num cantāvistī?* Did you sing? [*Nōn cantāvī.* No.]
*Nōnne cantāvistī?* Did you not sing? *or* You sang, did you not? [*Cantāvī.* Yes.]

RULE: Questions which may be answered with 'Yes' or 'No' are, as a rule, introduced by the interrogative particles *-ne, num.*

☞ *Num* stands at the beginning of the sentence: *-ne* is attached to the first word in the sentence, which is emphatic: *Tūne cantāvistī?* Did *you* sing? (Was it you that sang?) In a negative question of this class, *nōn* is put at the beginning, and *-ne* is attached to it (*Nōnne*).

'Yes' is generally expressed by simply repeating the verb; 'no' by repeating the verb with *nōn.*

'Yes' may also be rendered by *ita, ita vērō, etiam.*
'No' may also be rendered by *minimē, minimē vērō.*

On the particles *utrum . . . an* see § 584.

II.

*Quis cantāvit?* Who sang?
*Quālis (Quī) erat cantus?* What sort of a song was it?
*Quandō cantābis?* When will you sing?
*Ut valēs?* How do you do?

RULE: Questions which cannot be answered with 'Yes' or 'No' are introduced (as in Eng.) by interrogative pronouns, adjectives, or adverbs, without any interrogative particle.

EXCLAMATIONS.

**345** Many of the above-mentioned forms of speech may become exclamatory (*i.e.* may be used to express emotion), *e.g.*—

*Quam pulchrē cantāvit!* How beautifully he (she, it) sang!
*Quibus gaudiīs exsultābis!* With what joys will you exult!
*Quae erit laetitia!* What a joy it will be!
*Quam pulcher!* What a fine fellow! (Understand *est,* ' he is.')
*Hā* [*Vae*] *mihī!* Woe is me!
*Salvē!* [*Salvētō!*] Hail!

Compare uses of Interjections (§ 587), Vocative (§ 373), Accusative (§ 386), Accusative with Infinitive (§ 531), *ut* with Subjunctive (§ 532).

# THE COMPLEX SENTENCE (§ 312).

## ADVERB CLAUSES (§ 313).

**346** Adverb Clauses are classified according as they express:—

(*a*) **Time.**
*Introducing words:*
| | |
|---|---|
| quum | when |
| postquam | after |
| antequam | } before |
| priusquam | |
| ubĭ, ut, simulatque | } as soon |
| ubĭ (ut) prīmum | } as |
| dōnec | until |
| quoad | so long as, until |
| dum | while, until |

(*b*) **Place.**
| | |
|---|---|
| ubĭ, quā | where |
| quō | whither |
| unde | whence |

(*c*) **Reason.**
| | |
|---|---|
| quia, quod | because |
| quoniam | } since |
| quum | |
| quandŏquidem | } seeing |
| siquidem | } that |

(*d*) **Purpose.**
| | |
|---|---|
| ut | in order that |
| nē | lest |
| quō | by which (the more) |

(*e*) **Result.**
| | |
|---|---|
| ut | that, so that |

(*f*) **Condition.**
| | |
|---|---|
| sī | if |
| nisi | unless, if not |
| [sīn | but if] |
| [sīve | or if, or] |
| [sīve ... sīve | whether ... or] |
| dum | } provided that |
| dummodo | |

(*g*) **Concession.**
| | |
|---|---|
| etsī | } even if |
| tametsī | |
| quamquam | |
| quamvīs | |
| licet | } although |
| ut | |
| quum | |

(*h*) **Comparison.**
| | |
|---|---|
| ut, sīcut | } as |
| quemadmodum | |
| quō | { in proportion as |
| quam | as, than |
| [quasi | |
| velutsī | } as if, as |
| tamquam | though] |
| tamquam sī | |

## Temporal Clauses. (Clauses of Time.)

**347 Quum.**

*Quum Caesar in Galliam vēnit, duae erant ibī factiōnēs.* When (At the time when) Caesar came to Gaul, there were two parties there. [Clause of Date, defining a *tum*, expressed or implied in the Principal Clause.]

*Quum rediĕris dīcam.* When you return (§ 493) I will speak.

*Quum (Quandōcumque, Utcumque, Quotiēs) pluit, domī maneō.* Whenever it rains, I remain at home.

*Quum domum* **redīret,** *interfectus est.* When (As, While) he was returning home, he was murdered.

*Quum domum* **rediisset,** *interfectus est.* When (After) he had returned home, he was murdered.

*Epaminondās, quum* **vīoisset** *Lacedaemoniōs atque* **vidēret** *sē mori, quaesīvit salvusne esset clipeus.* Epaminondas, having defeated the Spartans, and seeing that he was dying, asked whether his shield was safe.

**Antequam, priusquam, dōneo, quoad, dum.**

*Haec disputāvit paulō antequam (priusquam) mortuus est.* He held this discourse a little while before he died.

*Mīlitēs nōn prius (ante) fīnem sequendī fēcērunt, quam mūrō appropinquārunt.* The soldiers did not cease pursuing until they came near the wall.

*Antequam (Priusquam) sē hostēs ex terrōre* **reciperent,** *ad oppidum contendit.* He hastened to the town before the enemy **should** recover from their fright.

*Dōnec grātus eram tibī.* So long as I found favour in thine eyes.

*Impetum hostium sustinuit quoad (dōnec) cēterī pontem* **interrumperent (interrūpissent)**. . . . until the rest **should** break down (**should** have broken down) the bridge.

*Mātrem, dum vīvēbat, apud sē habēbat.* He kept his mother at his house, while she lived.

*Interfectus est dum inter primōrēs pugnat* (for tense cf. § 496). He was slain whilst fighting in the first ranks.

*Exspectō dum* **dīcat** *(dīcit).* I am waiting till he **speak** (speaks).

*Exspectābam dum* **dīceret.** I was waiting till he **should** speak.

### Postquam, ubi, ut, simulatque.

*Postquam domum rediit, interfectus est.* After he had returned home, he was murdered. (For tense of *rediit*, cf. § 495.)

*Quod ubi (ut, simulatque) audīvit.* . . . As soon as he heard this. . . .

RULES: The general mood in Temporal Clauses is the Indicative,[1] as in English; but—

(1) *Quum* = 'as,' 'while,' 'after' takes the Imperfect or Pluperfect Subjunctive (for Indicative) in narrative. [Narrative Clause of Situation.]

(2) *Antequam, priusquam, dōnec, quoad, dum* take the Subjunctive (Pres., Imperf., or Pluperf.) when the action is marked as merely contemplated or in prospect, and not as a fact.

## Local Clauses. (Clauses of Place.)

*Ubi tyrannus est, ibi nulla est rēspublica.* Where a tyrant is, there is no political life.

*Ubicumque es, mihi quidem cārus es.* Wherever you are, to me at all events you are dear.

RULE: The mood in Local Clauses is the Indicative, as in English.

Obs.: A Local Clause may take the Subjunctive under the same circumstances as an Adjective Clause (cf. § 364).

## Causal Clauses. (Clauses of Reason.)

*Secūri percussus est, proptereā quod dictō nōn pāruerat.* He was beheaded, because he had not obeyed orders.

*Idcircō tacent, quia perīculum metuunt.* They are silent, because they fear danger.

*Quae quum ita sint, domī maneō.* Since this is so (This being so), I remain at home.

*Quae quum ita essent, domī mansī.* Since this was so (This being so), I remained at home.

RULE: The general mood in Causal Clauses is the Indicative,[1] as in English: but *quum* = 'since' (*Quum Causāle*) takes the Subjunctive. Negative *nōn*.

On Adjective Clauses with causal sense, see § 364.

---

[1] For Temporal and other Adverb Clauses in Ōrātiō Oblīqua see § 371.

**349.** **Nōn quod (Nōn quō) 'not that.' Nōn quīn, 'not that ... not.'**

*Pugilēs ingemiscunt, nōn quod* **doleant** *sed quia profundendā vōce omne corpus intenditur.* Boxers utter a groan, not because they feel pain (*Rejected reason*), but because in uttering the sound the whole body is put in tension (*True reason*).

*Nōn quō* **nōlim,** *sed quod nequeō.* Not that I am unwilling, but that I cannot.

*Nōn quīn breviter respondērī* **possit.** . . Not that a brief answer might not be given . . .

RULE: The rejected reason takes the Subjunctive.
The true reason takes the Indicative.

## Final Clauses. (Clauses of Purpose.)

**350.** *Edō ut* **vīvam.** I eat to live (in order that I may live).

*Edō nē* **moriar.** I eat in order not to die (that I may not die).

*Hōc fēcit ut vīs aquae* **minuerētur,** *nēve pontī* **nocēret.** This he did in order that the force of the water might be broken, and not injure the bridge.

*Lēgem brevem esse oportet* **quō** *facil'***ius** *teneātur.* The law ought to be brief, that it may be the more easily understood.

RULES: 1. The Mood in Final Clauses is the Subjunctive (Pres. or Imperf.).
The Pres. Subj. expresses a present or future purpose. } cf. § 516.
The Imperf. Subj. expresses a past purpose.
2. 'In order that . . . not' is *nē*; 'in order that no one' *nē quis* (lit. 'lest anyone,' § 152); 'in order that . . . never' *nē umquam.*
3. 'In order that' with a Comparative is *quō* (= *ut eō*).

Obs. 1. 'And in order that . . . not' is *nēve* (*nēu*): cf. § 582.
Obs. 2. *Ut nē* is used with special emphasis for *nē.*

On Adjective Clauses with final sense, see § 364.

### Equivalents of a Final Clause.

**351.** 'They came to take counsel' may be expressed—
*Vēnērunt ut dēlīberārent* (§ 350).
„ *quī dēlīberārent* (§ 364).
„ *ad dēlīberandum* (§ 534).
„ *dēlīberandī causā* (§ 534).
„ *dēlīberātum* (§ 542).
„ *dēlīberātūrī* (Livy, Tacitus, etc.).

## Consecutive Clauses. (Clauses of Result.)

**352** *Tanta vīs probitātis est, ut eam vel in hoste* **dīligāmus.** So great is the power of honesty, that we love it even in a foe.

*Tam cupidus erat dīcendī, ut in nullō umquam flagrantius studium* **vīderim.** . . . that I have never seen a more burning zeal in anyone.

*Verrēs Siciliam ita perdidit, ut' restituī in antīquum statum nōn jam* **possit.** Verres so ruined Sicily, that it cannot be any more restored to its old condition.

*Imperātōriā formā erat, ut nēmō eum nōn* **admīrārētur.** He was a man of imperial mien, so that everyone admired him.

*Perīre nōn potes ut nōn aliōs quoque* **perdās.** You cannot be ruined without ruining others too.

*Adeō jūdicēs exarsērunt,* The jurors were so enraged,
   *ut Sōcratem* **condemnāverint.** that they condemned Socrates. (ὥστε κατέγνωσαν.)
   *ut Sōcratem* **condemnārent.** as to condemn Socrates.
              (ὥστε καταγνῶναι.)

*Exercitus labōrābat, usque eō ut complūrēs diēs frūmentō mīlitēs* **caruerint,** *et vix extrēmam famem* **sustentārent.** The army was hard pressed, to such an extent that for several days the soldiers had no food, and with difficulty endured (*during all that time*) the extremities of hunger.

RULE: The Mood in Consecutive Clauses is the Subjunctive (Pres., Imperf., Perf.). Negative *nōn:* 'that no one' is *ut nēmō*.

☞ The Imperf. Subj. may mark an action as *continuous* or *habitual,* as distinct from the Perf. Subj. which marks it as simply *occurring.* But more frequently the distinction between these tenses corresponds to that between the Infin. and the Indic. in English. The Imperf. Subj. (= Engl. Infin.) may be used to mark a consequence as merely contemplated or in prospect in the past: the Perf. Subj. (= Engl. Indic.) is used only to express an *actual consequence* in the past.

On Adjective Clauses with consecutive sense, see § 364.

Obs.: *Ita* may be used in the Principal Clause with **limiting sense** (= 'only in so far'): e.g. *Hunc ita vereor ut nōn metuam.* I respect this man without fearing him (= I respect this man but I do not fear him).

## If-clauses. (Clauses of Condition.)

**353** A Complex Sentence containing an Adverb Clause of **condition**, is called a **Conditional Sentence.**

Conditional Sentences fall into two main classes [1]:—

   A. Those in which the If-clause does not imply anything as to the fact, or fulfilment of the condition (*Open Condition*), and the Principal Clause does not speak of what *would be* or *would have been*:

     *e.g.* If you are right, I am wrong. (Implying nothing as to whether you are actually right or not.)

   B. Those in which the If-clause implies a negative (*Rejected Condition*), and the Principal Clause speaks of what *would be* or *would have been*:

     *e.g.* If wishes were horses, beggars would ride. (Implying: "but wishes are *not* horses.")

### A.

**354** *Sī haec facit, peccat.* If he does (is doing) this, he sins (is sinning).
*Sī haec fēcit, peccāvit.* If he did this, he sinned.
*Sī haec fēcerit, pūniētur.* If he does (= shall have done: § 493) this, he will be punished.
*Sī haec fēcit, stultus est.* If he did (has done) this, he is a fool.
*Sī prūdens est, veniet.* If he is wise, he will come.
*Sī scīs, dīc.* If you know, speak.
*Refellitō, sī poteris.* Refute it, if you can (=shall be able: § 493).
*Moriar, sī sciō!* May I die, if I know!

RULE: When the Principal Clause does not speak of what *would be* or *would have been*, the If-clause takes the Indicative (☞ Note on § 347).

Note that in Class A the Principal Clause is free, *i.e.* may contain an Indicative, an Imperative, or a Subjunctive of Command or Wish.

   Obs. 1. GENERAL CONDITIONS, *i.e.* Conditions in which 'if' = 'if ever,' are usually expressed by an Indicative; occasionally by a Subjunctive.[2]

   *Sī quaesieram, respondēbat.* If on any occasion I asked, he used to answer. (For tense of *quaesieram* see § 494.)

---

[1] For a third and less important class (C), see § 501.
[2] Especially in the indefinite 2nd Pers. Sing. ('you'='anyone'): cf. note on p. 131.

## B.

**355** (a) *Sī haec faceret, peccāret.* If he **were doing** this, he **would be sinning**.

(b) *Sī haec fēcisset, peccāvisset.* If he **had done** this, he **would have sinned**.

(c) *Sī haec faciat (fēcerit), peccet (peccāverit).* If he **were to do** this, he **would sin**.

RULE: When the Principal Clause speaks of what *would be* or *would have been*, both Clauses take the Subjunctive:—

    (a) the Imperf. Subj., if referring to present time.
    (b) the Pluperf. Subj., if referring to past time.
    (c) the Pres. or Perf. Subj., if referring to future time.

(a) *Sī faceret* implies 'he **is** not doing so.'
(b) *Sī fēcisset* implies 'he **did** not do so.'
(c) *Sī faciat (fēcerit)* implies 'I do not say that he **will** do so.'

☞ The English Past (Subj.) is ambiguous, and may refer to present or future time: e.g.—

If he knew (=were aware: verb denoting a state) he would tell. *Sī scīret dīceret.*

If he came (=were to come: verb denoting an act) I should tell him. *Sī veniat dīcam.*

Obs. 1. The two Clauses need not refer to the same time: *e.g. Ego nisi peperissem, Rōma nōn oppugnārētur.* Had I not borne a son, Rome would not (now) be under siege.—LIVY.

Obs. 2. The Imperf. Subj. more commonly referred to past time in early Latin, *e.g.* in Plautus; and this usage survived in classical Latin, though it was comparatively rare: e.g. *At tum sī dīcerem, nōn audīrer.* But had I spoken (been speaking) then, I should not have been listened to.—CICERO.

Obs. 3. The Pres. Subj. occasionally refers to present time, especially in the poets: *sī sim,* 'if I were' = *sī essem.*

☞ For Adjective Clauses equivalent to If-clauses see § 364.

**356** EXCEPTION. Instead of the Subj. in the **Principal Clause** of Class B, an Indicative is found:—

(a) In expressions meaning 'can,' 'must,' 'ought' (chiefly past tenses): e.g.—

| | |
|---|---|
| *Sī haec facerēs,* | If you were doing this, |
|   *culpārī poterās.* |   you might be blamed. |
|   *culpārī dēbēbās.* |   you ought to be blamed. |
|   *culpandus erās.* |   " " " |
|   *aequum erat tē culpārī.* |   " " " |

*Sī haec fēcissēs,*     If you had done this,
    *culpārī potuistī (poterās).*   you might have been blamed.[1]
    *culpārī dēbuistī (dēbēbās).*   you ought to have been blamed.[1]

But the Subj. may also be used : *culpārī possēs* or *potuissēs*.

(*b*) With the Future Participle (chiefly past tenses) :—

*Sī haec fēcissēs, peccātūrus fuistī* (= *peccāvissēs*).

(*c*) When a Principal Clause has to be supplied in thought (Anacolūthon) : e.g.—

*Numerōs meminī, sī verba tenērem.* I remember the tune (*Supply :* and would sing it), if only I knew the words.

*Pons Sublicius iter paene hostibus dedit, nī ūnus vir fuisset.* The Sublician Bridge almost provided a road for the enemy (*Supply :* and would have actually done so), had it not been for one man.

### Modes of introducing If-clauses.

**357** 'If . . . not,' 'unless' is generally expressed by *nisi*. *Sī nōn* is used when a single word is negatived, or in opposition to *at* (often without a verb expressed): e.g. *Multōs tulit Rōmānōrum cīvitās, sī nōn sapientēs, at certē summā laude dignōs.*

'Whether . . . or,' introducing alternative clauses of condition (= 'if . . . or if'), is expressed by *sīve . . . sīve (seu . . . seu)*: e.g. *Sīve fēcit, sīve nōn fēcit, pūniētur.*

'But if,' linking a clause of condition to a preceding clause, is expressed by *sīn, sīn autem, quodsī.* 'But if . . . not' is *sīn minus, sīn aliter.*

'If perchance' is *sī forte.* 'If only' is *sī modo.*

For *sī*, 'in the hope that,' see § 370 Obs. 1.

### Condition disguised or suppressed.

**357\*** *Nōn mihī, nisi admonitō, vēnisset in mentem.* It would not have struck me, had I not been reminded (= *nisi admonitus essem*).

*Quid hunc paucōrum annōrum accessiō jurāre potuisset?* What good would the addition of a few years have been to him?

*Longum est ad omnia respondēre.* It would be tedious (cf. § 356a) if I were to reply to every point.

---

[1] Note the peculiarity of the English Perfect Infinitive ('to have been blamed'), and cf. § 453.

CONCESSIVE CLAUSES. 143

Dependent Form of { (a) **sī haec facerēt, peccāret.**
{ (b) **sī haec fēcisset, peccāvisset.**

**357†** 1. Dependent on a verb of 'saying,' 'thinking,' etc. (§ 368a).

(a) *Scio (Sciēbam) eum, si faceret, peccātūrum esse.*
(b) *Scio (Sciēbam) eum, si fecisset, peccātūrum fuisse.*

RULE: The If-clause remains unchanged. The Principal Clause takes the Future Participle with *esse* or *fuisse* (cf. § 491).

Obs. 1. Expressions meaning 'can,' 'must,' 'ought' (§ 356) in the Principal Clause take (a) Pres. Infin.: e.g. *Scio (Sciēbam) eum, si vellet, venire posse*, 'might come'; (b) Perf. Infin. *Scio (Sciēbam) eum, si voluisset, venire potuisse*, 'might have come.'

Obs. 2. When the Principal Clause is Passive it cannot be expressed except by a periphrasis (rarely used): e.g.—

(a) *Scio (Sciēbam), si faceret, futūrum esse ut pūnīrētur.*
(b) *Scio (Sciēbam), si fecisset, futūrum fuisse ut pūnīrētur.*

2. Dependent on a construction which itself requires the Subjunctive (e.g. *Nōn dubitō quīn, Ita sē rēs habet ut, Quaerō num*).

(a) *Nōn dubitō (dubitābam) quīn, si faceret, peccāret.*
(b) *Nōn dubitō (dubitābam) quīn, si fecisset, peccātūrus fuerit.*
*Nōn dubitō (dubitābam) quīn eum, si fecisset, paenituisset.*
*Nōn dubitō (dubitābam) quīn, si fecisset, pūnītus esset.*

RULE: The If-clause remains unchanged. In the Principal Clause the Imperf. Subj. remains unchanged; the Pluperf. Subj. is changed wherever possible (*i.e.* where the Verb is Active Voice and has a Future Participle) into the Future Participle with *fuerit* (cf. § 491), otherwise it remains unchanged.

Obs. Expressions meaning 'can,' 'must,' 'ought' (§ 356) in the Principal Clause take (a) Imperf. Subj.: e.g. *Nōn dubitō (dubitābam) quīn, si vellet, venire posset*, 'might come'; (b) Perf. Subj.: e.g. *Nōn dubitō (dubitābam) quīn, si voluisset, venire potuerit*, 'might have come.'

## Concessive Clauses.

**358** *Quamquam dīves es, nōn es beātus.* Although you are rich ⎫
*Quamvis dīves sīs, nōn es beātus.* However rich you may be ⎬ you are not happy.
*Quum dīves sīs, nōn es beātus.* Although you are rich ⎭

*Ut dēsint vīrēs, tamen est laudanda voluntās.* Though power be wanting, yet the will is praiseworthy.

RULE: *Quamquam* takes the Indicative. (☞ Note on § 347.)
*Quamvis, licet, ut,* and *quum* 'although' (*Quum Concessivum*) take the Subjunctive in prose.
*Etsi, etiamsi* (like *si*) take either the Indic. or Subj.
*Tametsi* almost always takes the Indicative.

## Comparative Clauses.

**359** | **Ut, sīcut, quemadmodum, quam; quālis, quantus, quot, etc.**

*Sīc est, ut dīxī (Est sicut dīxī)*  It is as I said.
*Ita vīvam, ut tē amō.*  So may I live as I love you.
*Tālis (Īdem) est quālis (quī) semper fuit.*  He is such (the same) as he always has been.
*Tantum scīmus quantum memoriā tenēmus.*  We know as much as we remember.
*Tot erant quot sunt maris flūctūs.*  They were as many as the waves of the sea.
*Tam placidus erit quam agnus.*  He will be as quiet as a lamb. [2]
*Vēnit quam celerrimē (quam celerrimē potuit).*  He came as quickly as he could. [2]
*Vīcīnus tuus pulchriōrem habet domum, quam tū habēs.*  Your neighbour has a finer house than you have.
*Vīcīnus tuus pulchriōrem habet domum quam tua est.*  Your neighbour has a finer house than yours is.
*Patria mihī cārior est quam vīta.*  My country is dearer to me than my life (*i.e.* than my life is). [2]
*Patriam magis amō quam vītam.*  I love country more than life (*i.e.* than I love life). [2]
*Rēs aliter cecidit āc putātum est.*  The matter turned out otherwise than was expected. [3]
**Quō** *quisque est doctior, eō modestior est.* ⎫  The more learned a man
**Ut** *quisque est doctissimus, ita modestis-* ⎬  is, the more modest
   *simus est.* ⎭   he is. [4]

RULES: 1. The mood in Comparative Clauses is the Indicative, as in English. (☞ Note on § 347.)

2. The verb of the Comparative Clause is often omitted (Contracted Comp. Cl.): the case of the word following *quam* is then determined by mentally supplying the verb.

Obs. When a Contracted Comp. Cl. is subordinate to an Acc. with Infin., its Subject is attracted into the Acc.: e.g. *Scītō patriam mihī cāriōrem esse quam vītam.*

3. With Adjectives and Adverbs that denote likeness or difference (*pār, pariter; similis, similiter; aequē, perinde; alius, aliter; contrārius, contrā, secus*), 'as' or 'than' is *atque, āc.*

4. 'The more ... the more' is *quō ... eō,* or *ut ... ita.*

**360** **Quam ut, quasi, velut sī, tamquam sī,** etc.

*Hūmānior est quam ut (quam qui) injūriārum memor* **sit.** He is too highminded to remember wrongs.
*Nihil magis optō quam ut* **valeās.** I pray for nothing more than that you should be well.
*Morī mālō quam haec* **faciam.** I prefer death to doing this.
*Quid ego hīs testibus ūtor, quasi rēs dubia* **sit?** Why do I call these witnesses as if (as though) the matter were doubtful?
*Id fēcī quasi* **dīvīnārem.** This I did, as though I foresaw.

RULE: An *ut* or *sī* clause subordinate to a Contracted Comparative Clause takes the Subjunctive.

The tense of the Subj. with *quasi, velut sī,* etc., is
Pres. or Perf.
Imperf. or Pluperf. } according to Rule of Sequence (§ 522).

Contrast Conditional Sentences (*sī esset* 'if it were') : § 355.

### ABLATIVE OF COMPARISON.

**360\*** *Patria mihī* **vītā** *cārior est.* My country is dearer to me than my life.
*Caesar mīlitum vītam* **suā salūte** *habēbat cāriōrem.* Caesar held the life of the soldiers dearer than his own welfare.
*Ītalia est patria mea,* **quā** *nihil magis amō.* Italy is my country; than which I love nothing more.
*Nōn diūtius* **ūnō annō** *remanēbant in locō.* They did not stay where they were longer than one year.

RULES: 1. An Ablative may do duty for *quam* 'than' with a Nominative or Accusative in a Contracted Comparative Clause.
2. For *quam* with the Nom. or Acc. of a **Relative Pronoun** this Abl. is **always** used.

☞ Otherwise avoid the Abl. (for *quam* with the Acc.) when ambiguity would arise: *e.g.* in *Brūtum magis amō* **quam Cassium.** Here the Abl. might suggest *quam Cassius* (*amat*).

Obs. Note the phrases—
*exspectātiōne (opīniōne) celerius,* more quickly than had been expected.
*spē mājor,* greater than had been hoped.

### Quam omitted.

**360†** *Plūs duo mīlia mīlitum periērunt.* More-than-2000 soldiers perished.
*Spatium minus decem annōrum.* A space of less-than-ten years.

RULE: *Quam* may be omitted (without influencing the construction) between *plūs, amplius, minus, longius,* and a word of number or measure.

## Ablative Absolute.

**361.** **Trōjā stante** *Graecī multōs labōrēs perferēbant.* While Troy was standing (Troy standing), the Greeks endured much suffering.

**Trōjā captā** *Graecī domum rediērunt.* After Troy had been taken (Troy taken), the Greeks returned home.

RULE: In the construction called the Ablative Absolute:—

No Conjunction is employed;
For the Subject we have an Ablative;
For the Predicate we have a Participle (agreeing with the Subject).

CAUTIONS: 1. Avoid the Abl. Abs. in translating an English sentence in which the Subject of the Subordinate Clause denotes the same person or thing as some part (*e.g.*, the Subject or Object) of the Principal Clause: *e.g.*—

(*a*) 'As I was reading, I fell asleep.'
(*b*) 'After the town had been captured, the enemy destroyed it.'

Use Simple Sentences: (*a*) *Legens obdormīvī;* (*b*) *Urbem captam dīruērunt hostēs.*

2. Owing to Latin having no Pres. Part. Pass. or Perf. Part. Act., 'While this was being done, the enemy kept watch' must be translated—

*Dum haec geruntur,*
or *Quum haec gererentur,* } *hostēs vigilābant.*

'Caesar, having praised his soldiers, returned' must be translated—

*Caesar quum mīlitēs collaudāvisset,*
or *Caesar mīlitibus collaudātīs* (Pass. constr.) } *rediit.*

#### Origin of the Construction.

**361\*.** The Ablative Absolute originated in an Ablative denoting Cause (§ 424) or Time (§ 439):

*Bellum commōvit cōgente Cleopatrā.* He stirred up a war by reason of (at the time of) Cleopatra compelling (Cleopatra's compulsion).

Compare such phrases as *ante urbem conditam,* 'before the city built,' 'before the building of the city' (§ 548). But it has come to be a general **equivalent** of an Adverb Clause.

## Ways of translating the Ablative Absolute.

**361†** The Ablative Absolute (*Serviō regnante*) may be equivalent to a
Temporal Clause : 'While Servius is (was) king.'
Causal Clause : 'Because Servius is (was) king.'
Conditional Clause : 'If Servius is (was, were, etc.) king.'
Concessive Clause : 'Though Servius is (was) king.'
Co-ordinate Sentence : *Hīs dictīs abiit*, 'He said this and departed.'

### PECULIARITIES.

#### Noun or Adjective for Participle (Predicate).

**361‡** *Hannibale duce* Under the leadership of Hannibal.
(Hannibal being leader.)
*Cicerōne et Antōniō consulibus* In the consulship of Cicero and Antonius.

*nōbīs puerīs* in our boyhood
*mē invītō* against my will
*salvīs lēgibus* without breaking the laws

But *Puerī nōlēbāmus discere* ' In our boyhood we were unwilling to learn ' : cf. Caution 1 (p. 146).

#### Participle without Subject.

Such phrases as the following are found in historians :—
*audītō, cognitō, compertō, nuntiātō*, 'news having been brought.'

## ADJECTIVE CLAUSES (§ 313).

**362** An Adjective Clause is introduced by a Relative Pronoun or Relative Adjective, referring to a Noun or Noun-equivalent, called the Antecedent, in the Principal Clause.

OBS. 1. A Conjunction may be equivalent to a Relative : e.g.
*Nōvī locum* ubī *nātus est*. I know the place where he was born.
*Hōc est tempus* quum *hominēs dormiunt*. This is the time when people sleep.

OBS. 2. For *quī* = *et is, sed is, nam is*, see § 314*.

## Agreement of the Relative.

**369**

*Via* **quae** *hūc dūcit longa est.* The road which (that) leads hither is long.

*Via* **quam** *cēpī longa est.* The road which (that) I took is long.

*Via* **cūjus** *ad fīnem pervēnī longa est.* The road to the end of which I have travelled is long.

*Via* **cuī** *nōmen Flāmīniae datum est longa est.* The road to which the name 'Flaminian Road' (§ 412) has been given is long.

*Erant itinera duo* **quibus itineribus** *exīre possent.* There were two roads by which they had a chance of escaping.

*Tanta erat vīs procellae* **quantam** *numquam anteā vīderam.* The fury of the storm was such as I had never seen before.

*In hōc bellō,* **quāle bellum** *nulla gens barbara gessit, praeclārē vīcimus.* In this war, the like of which no foreign nation has ever waged, we have been gloriously victorious.

**Ego,** *quī tē* **confīrmō,** *ipse mē nōn possum.* I, who am trying to reassure you, cannot reassure myself.

*Ō* **fortūnāte adulescens** *quī tuae virtūtis Homērum praecōnem* **invēnerīs!** O happy young man to have found in Homer a herald of thy worth!

RULE: The Relative agrees in Gender, Number and Person[1] with its Antecedent. The **Case** of the Relative depends on the part which it plays (as Subject, Object, etc.) in its own Clause.

OBS. 1. If the Relative refers to the Principal Clause as a whole, it stands in the Neuter Singular (often with *id*); if to several words, in the Plural (cf. § 320):

*Arātus,* **id quod** (or **quod**) *sapientis virī fuit, omnibus cōnsuluit.* Aratus, as befitted a wise man, considered the interests of all.
*Laudastī patrem et mātrem,* **quī** (cf. § 325*) *mortuī sunt.*

---

[1] Note the peculiarity in *Nōn* **is** *sum quī mortem* **timeam.** 'I am not a person that fears death.' *Nōn* **is** *es quī mortem* **timeās.** 'You are not a person that fears death,' etc.

## MOODS IN RELATIVE CLAUSES.

Obs. 2. In Latin, as in English, the **Antecedent**, if a Pronoun, is often omitted (cf. § 370, Caution 1):
*Quod dīcis falsum est.* What ( = That which) you say is false.
*Quīcumque hōc dīcit errat.* Whoever says this is wrong.
But 'I judged from what I saw' is *Ex iīs quae vidēbam jūdicāvī.*

Obs. 3. But the relative is never omitted in Latin, as it sometimes is in English:
*Nōvī hominem* **quem** *quaeris.* I know the person you are seeking.

Obs. 4. The Antecedent is occasionally attracted into the case of the Relative:
**Urbem quam** *statuō vestra est.* The city which I am founding is yours.
( = *Urbs quam statuō* or *Quam urbem statuō.* Cf. § 569.)
☞ For *Thēbae quod caput Bocōtiae est,* see § 325, Peculiarity II., p. 121.

## Moods in Relative Clauses.

364| *Quicquid id est, timeō Danaōs et dōna ferentēs.* In any case (Whatever it is), I fear the Greeks, even when offering gifts.
*Mīsit lēgātōs quī pācem* **peterent.** He sent ambassadors to sue (who **should** sue) for peace.
*Quis inveniētur quī haec* **crēdat?** Who will be found to believe this?
*Dignus es cuī fidēs* **habeātur.** You are worthy to be trusted.
*Et quod* **spectārem** *nīl nisi pontus erat.* And there was nothing for me to look upon but the sea.
*Nec quod* **spērāret** *habēbat.* And he had nothing to hope for.
*Mē caecum quī haec nōn* **vīderim!** Blind that I was, not to have seen this!
*Quī hōc* **dīcat** *erret.* He who should say this would err.
*Egomet quī leviter Graecās litterās* **attigissem,** *tamen complūrēs ibī diēs sum commorātus.* Though I had taken only a slight interest in Greek, I nevertheless spent several days there (*i.e.* at Athens).

Rule: The general mood in Relative Clauses is the Indicative,[1] as in English (see further examples in § 363); but the Subjunctive is used in Relative Clauses equivalent to Final, Consecutive, Causal, or Concessive Clauses, or to If-clauses which take a Subjunctive.

On the use of the Subjunctive in 'Characterising Clauses' see § 504 (*Sunt quī putent*). On Relative Clauses in Ōrātiō Oblīqua, see § 371.

---

[1] Especially with *quīcumque, quisquis* ('General Relatives': § 162).

## NOUN CLAUSES (§ 313).

**365** Noun Clauses are of two kinds :—

A. Those which express *that* something *is* or *should be*. (Dependent Statements, Dependent Commands): *e.g.*—

| Princ. Cl. Dependent Noun Cl. | Corresponding Indep. Sentence. |
|---|---|
| *Dīcō tē esse inīquum.* | *Inīquus es.* |
| I say that you are unfair. | You are unfair. (STATEMENT.) |
| *Imperō ut aequus sīs.* | *Aequus estō.* |
| I command that you be fair. | Be fair. (COMMAND.) |

B. Those which are introduced by an interrogative or exclamatory word (Dependent Questions, Dependent Exclamations): e.g.—

| | |
|---|---|
| *Quaerō num aequum sit.* | *Num aequum est ?* |
| I ask whether it is fair. | Is it fair? (QUESTION.) |
| *Vidē quam inīquus sīs.* | *Quam inīquus es !* |
| See how unfair you are. | How unfair you are! (EXCLAM.) |

**366** Noun Clauses may play the part of

1. Subject: e.g. *Manifestum est tē inīquum esse.* It is clear that you are unfair. (That you are unfair is clear.)
2. Object: e.g. *Dīcō tē inīquum esse.* I say that you are unfair.
3. Noun in Apposition (Attribute): e.g. *Spēs est tē nōn fore inīquum.* There is hope that you will not be unfair.
4. Adjunct: e.g. *Gaudeō tē nōn esse inīquum.* I rejoice that you are not unfair. (Cf. *Gaudeō hāc rē*, § 424).

## Dependent Statements and Commands.

**367** Dependent Statements and Commands assume the following forms in Latin :—

1. The **Accusative** with the **Infinitive**: e.g.—

| | |
|---|---|
| *Dīcō tē esse inīquum.* | *Jubeō tē esse aequum.* |
| I declare thee to be unfair. | I command thee to be fair. |

In this construction (Latin and English) :—
 No Conjunction is employed ;
 For the Subject we have an Accusative ;
 For the Finite Verb we have an Infinitive ;
 The Predicate Adjective or Noun stands in the Accusative.

The Accusative with the Infinitive as an equivalent of a Noun Clause has its origin in a Simple Sentence :—

# DEPENDENT STATEMENTS AND COMMANDS. 151

*Dīcō tē esse inīquum.* { (1) I declare thee to be unfair.
{ (2) I declare that thou art unfair.

*Jubeō tē esse aequum.* { (1) I command thee to be fair.
{ (2) I command that thou be fair.

For the tenses of the Infinitive see § 533.

2. **Quod** with a (Nominative and) **Finite Verb**: e.g.—

*Hūc accēdit quod inīquus es.* There is the additional fact that you are unfair.

*Hāc rē hominēs bestiīs praestant, quod loquī possunt.* Herein are men superior to brutes that they can speak.

*Peropportūnē accidit quod adsum.* It is a fortunate circumstance that I am here.

*Grātum mihī fēcistī quod ades.* You have done me a service in that you are here.

*Gaudeō (Queror) quod nōn adest.* I rejoice (complain) that he is not here.

*Praetereō quod eam sibī domum dēlēgit.* I pass by the fact that he chose for himself that house.

These Noun Clauses are on the whole little used in classical Latin; in the large majority of cases where English uses 'that,' some other construction is preferred in Latin.

3. **Ut, ut ... nōn** with a (Nominative and) **Subjunctive**: e.g.—

*Fierī potest ut inīquus sīs.* It is possible that you are unfair.

4. **Ut, nē, quōminus** with a (Nominative and) **Subjunctive**: e.g.—

*Imperō tibī ut aequus sīs.* I command you to be fair.

*Imperō tibī nē inīquus sīs.* I command you not to be unfair.

*Impediō tē quōminus inīquus sīs.* I prevent you from being unfair.

In these Noun Clauses the Subjunctive is ultimately a Subjunctive of Command or Wish:—

*Imperō tibī: aequus sīs.* May you be fair! I command you.

*Imperō tibī: nē inīquus sīs.* May you not be unfair! I command you.

The *ut* (but not the *nē*) is a later addition.

5. **Quīn** with a (Nominative and) **Subjunctive**: e.g.—

*Nōn dubitō quīn inīquus sīs.* I do not doubt that you are unfair.

*Quīn* is a compound of the Old Abl. *quī* (§§ 155, 161) and *ne* (= *nōn*). Thus *quīn* meant originally 'why not?' or 'by which not,' and is so used in Simple Sentences, like *Quīn cōnscendimus equōs?* 'Why not mount our horses?' *Quīn* clauses are, therefore, ultimately Dependent Questions (§ 365) or Relative Clauses (§ 504), but they have come to be equivalent to Dependent Statements or Commands.

## Confusion of the forms of Noun Clause.

The original distinction of meaning between these various forms of Noun Clause have become more or less obliterated, and constructions have been extended by analogy to cases in which they were not originally applicable:

(1) Different meanings may be expressed by the same form: e.g.—

*Dīcō tē esse prūdentem.* I say that you are prudent.
*Jubeō tē esse prūdentem.* I command that you be prudent.

*Fīerī potest ut prūdens sīs.* It is possible that you are prudent.
*Imperō tibi ut prūdens sīs.* I command that you be prudent.

(2) The same meaning may be expressed by different forms. Compare the different ways of expressing 'that you are unfair':

(a) *Dīcō tē esse inīquum.*
(b) *Doleō quod inīquus es.*
(c) *Nōn dubitō quīn inīquus sīs.*
(d) *Fīerī potest ut inīquus sīs.*
(e) *Vereor nē inīquus sīs.*

We have, therefore, to consider what constructions have, in the course of time, come to be connected with particular verbs in the Principal Clause.

### 368a. VERBS OF 'SAYING,' 'THINKING,' 'PERCEIVING,' 'KNOWING.'

*Dīcō mē esse beātum.* I say that I am happy.
*Arbitror tē nōn esse beātum.* I think that you are not happy.
*Simulat sē īnsānīre.* He pretends to be (that he is) mad.
*Constat eōs fuisse beātōs.* It is well known that they were happy.
*Spērō eam ventūram esse.* I hope that she will come.
*Spērābam eam ventūram esse.* I hoped that she would come.
*Pollicētur sē ventūrum esse.* He promises to come.
*Minātus est sē dictūrum esse.* He threatened to tell.

RULE: Verbs of 'saying,' 'thinking,' 'perceiving,' 'knowing,' take the Accusative with the Infinitive (for tenses see § 533). The negative is *nōn*: but 'I say that . . . not' is *negō*.

Verbs of 'saying' { aiō, dīcō, doceō, fateor, negō, nūntiō, respondeō, simulō, scrībō, trādō, polliceor, prōmittō, minor.

'thinking' { arbitror, cōgitō, exīstimō, opīnor, putō, jūdicō, cōnfīdō, crēdō, spērō, suspicor.

'perceiving' audiō, cōgnōscō, discō, intellegō, sentiō, videō.

'knowing' { nōvī, sciō, nesciō, meminī.
Impersonal: appāret, constat.

Equivalent phrases: **certiōrem faciō, certior fīō, accēpimus, auctor sum, fāma est, manifestum est, spēs est, opīniō est.**

☞ The Acc. with Infin. is not, as a rule, employed as Subject of a Passive verb of 'saying' or 'thinking' (*dīcitur, putātur, vidētur;* Impersonal Construction). Here Latin prefers a Simple Sentence with an Infin. (Personal Construction):—

## DEPENDENT STATEMENTS AND COMMANDS. 153

| *Alternative English Constructions.* | *Latin Construction.* |
|---|---|
| It is said that I am mistaken.<br>I am said to be mistaken. } | *Dīcor errāre.* |
| It seems that you are wise.<br>You seem to be wise. } | *Vidēris esse sapiens.* |
| It is thought that he knows.<br>He is thought to know. } | *Putātur scīre.* |

Thus, 'It is said that Homer was blind' is *Homērus trāditur caecus fuisse.* ☞ The Predicate Adjective or Noun agrees with the Subject (cf. *Homērus fuit caecus,* § 325).

**Obs.** But the Acc. with Infin. is used in dependence—

(*a*) On Compound forms like *nuntiātum est, dīcendum est.*

Thus, 'It has been reported that Homer was blind' is *Trāditum est Homērum caecum fuisse.*

(*b*) On a few special phrases, like *vērē (perversē) dīcitur, dīcī potest.*

### Verbs of 'Rejoicing,' 'Grieving,' 'Wondering.'

**365b** *Gaudeō mē valēre.*<br>*Gaudeō quod valeō.* } I rejoice that I am well.

*Indignantur quod spīrātis, quod vōcem mittitis.* They are angry that you breathe, that you speak.

Rule: Verbs of

'rejoicing,' **gaudeō, laetor.** Equiv.: **grātum est**;
'grieving,' **doleō, indignor.** Equiv.: **aegrē (molestē,** etc.) **ferō**;
'wondering,' **mīror.** Equiv.: **mīrum (mīrābile) est,**

take the Acc. with Infin. or (less commonly) *quod.*[1]

So verbs of 'boasting' **(glōrior)**, 'complaining' **(queror)**.

**Obs. 1.** **Piget, pudet, paenitet,** and verbs of 'praising' **(probō, laudō)**, 'blaming' **(reprehendō)**, 'accusing' **(accūsō)**, take *quod :* e.g.—

*Piget mē quod sīc dīxistī.* I am vexed that you have spoken thus.
*Quod adhūc morātus es, valdē probō.* I quite approve of your having ...

**Obs. 2.** *Quum* or *sī* may be used for *quod:* e.g.—

*Gaudeō quum salvus rediistī. Mīror sī haec dīxit.*

---

[1] The Acc. with Infin. and the *quod*-clause are in general used indifferently. But sometimes a distinction may be drawn : e.g. *Gaudeō mājōrēs meōs laudārī.* I rejoice that my ancestors should be praised. (Thought.) *Gaudeō quod mājōrēs meī laudantur.* I rejoice that (at the fact that) my ancestors are praised.—The Subjunctive may be used so as to make a *quod*-clause exactly equivalent to an Acc. with Infin. :—*Mīrābile est quod nōn rīdeat haruspex quum haruspicem vīderit.* It is strange that a soothsayer should (§ 506) not laugh when he sees (§ 507) a soothsayer.

### Verbs of 'fearing.'

**368c** *Vereor nē veniat.* I fear that he **will** come *or* is coming.
*Vereor nē nōn veniat.*  } I fear that he will not come.
   „ *ut veniat.*
*Verēbar nē omnia dīceret.* I feared that he **would** tell all.
*Vereor nē servus meus effūgerit.* I fear my slave has escaped.
*Verēbar nē servus meus effūgisset.* I feared my slave had escaped.

RULE: Verbs of 'fearing' (**vereor, timeō, metuō**. Equiv. **perīculum est**) take *nē* (= 'that') with the Subjunctive. The Negative is *nōn*: but *ut* is often used = *nē . . . nōn*[1] ('that . . . not'); hence 'that no one' is *ut quisquam* (cf. § 350, 2).

### Nōn dubitō. Nōn est dubium.

**368d** *Nōn dubitō quin veniat.* I do not doubt that he is coming.
 „   „ *quin vēnerit.*   „   „ that he has come *or* came.
 „   „ *quin ventūrus sit.* „   „ that he will come.
*Nōn dubitābam quin venīret.* I did not doubt that he was coming.
 „   „ *quin vēnisset.*   „   „ that he had come.
 „   „ *quin ventūrus esset.* „   „ that he would come.

RULE: Negative or Interrogative expressions of 'doubting' (**nōn dubitō, quis dubitat?** Equiv. **nōn est dubium**) take *quin* ('that') with the Subjunctive. Negative *nōn*.

☞ *Dubito*, when used without *nōn* in an affirmative clause, may take (1) a Dependent Question: e.g. *Dubitō quid faciās.* I am in doubt as to what you are doing (are to do). (2) an Infinitive (§ 330): e.g. *Dubitō dīcere.* I hesitate to speak.

### Impersonal verbs of 'happening.'

**368e** *Est ut virō vir lātius ordinet arbusta sulcīs.* It is true that one man arranges his trees in the furrows more widely than another.
*Quī fit ut nēmō suā sorte contentus sit?* How is it that no one is contented with his own lot?
*Fierī potest*       } *ut errāveris.* It is possible    } that you erred.
*Fierī nōn potest*                It is impossible
*Accidit Athēnīs ut ūnā nocte omnēs Hermae dējicerentur.* It happened at Athens that on one night all the Hermæ were cast down.

---

[1] Except when the Principal Clause is itself negative (*Nōn vereor nē nōn . . .*).

*Thrasybūlō contigit ut patriam līberāret.* Thrasybulus had the good fortune to liberate his native land.

*Tantum abest ut nostra mīrēmur ut nōbis nōn satisfaciat ipse Dēmosthenēs.* So far am I from admiring my own works that even Demosthenes does not satisfy me. (The last clause is consecutive: § 352.)

RULE: Impersonal verbs of 'happening' (**est, fit, accidit, ēvenit, contingit, tantum abest**) take *ut* (= 'that') with the Subjunctive. (For Tenses, cf. § 518.) Negative *nōn*.

Obs. Note the similar construction with such expressions as *restat, relinquitur, sequitur, mōs est*; e.g.—

*Restat ut doceam.* It remains for me to show.

*Mōs est ut templum claudātur.* It is customary for the temple to be closed.

Similarly (in dependence on a noun): *Hunc mōrem servant ut captīvōs vendant.* They maintain the custom of selling prisoners of war.

### Quīn (§§ 368d, 369b).

*Fierī nōn potest quīn errēs.* It is impossible that you are not mistaken (= You must necessarily be mistaken).

RULE: *Quīn*, with the Subjunctive, is used for *ut ... nōn* when the Principal Clause is negative or interrogative.

### 'IT IS RIGHT,' 'IT IS WRONG,' 'IT IS NECESSARY.'

**368.** *Aequum erat tē pūnīrī.* It was right that you should be punished.

*Omnibus bonīs expedit salvam esse rempublicam.* It is to the interest of all good men that the State be secure.

*Necesse est mē dīcere.*
„  „ *ut dīcam.*  } It is necessary for me to speak.
„  „ *dīcam.*

RULE: Impersonal expressions denoting

'It is right,' **aequum est (vērum est, fās est**, etc.), **placet, oportet, condūcit, expedit, prōdest, interest;**

'It is wrong,' **turpe est (indignum est, nefās est**, etc.), **displicet;**

'It is necessary,' **necesse est, opus est,**

take (as Subject) the Acc. with Infin.; or, in some cases, the Subjunctive, with or without *ut* (cf. § 367,4).

☞ These verbs also take a Simple Infinitive as Subject (§ 530a), e.g.: *Necesse est mihi dē mē ipsō dīcere* (Simple Sentence: § 452).

## VERBS THAT IMPLY AN ACT OF THE WILL.

### I.

**369a.** *Imperō tibī ut redeās.* I command you to return.
*Imperāvī eī nē redīret.* I commanded him not to return.
*Petō ā tē ut maneās.* I ask you to remain.
*Hortātus est sociōs nē dēficerent.* He exhorted ... not to revolt.
*Permitte mihi ut loquar.* Permit me to speak. (Let me speak: cf. § 333).
*Cavē nē dēcipiāris.* Beware of being deceived.
*Vidērent consulēs nē quid dētrimentī rēspublica caperet.* The consuls ought to have seen (§ 340*) to it that the State should suffer no harm.
*Sōl efficit ut omnia flōreant.* The sun causes the whole world to blossom.

RULE: The following verbs of
'commanding,' imperō (Dat.), mandō (Dat.), ēdīcō (Dat.), hortor;
'asking,' obsecrō, ōrō, precor, rogō; petō (ā), postulō (ā);
'resolving,' dēcernō, statuō, constituō (§ 330);
'granting,' concēdō (Dat.), permittō (Dat.);
'trying,' contendō, nītor. Equiv.: id agō, operam dō;
'taking care,' caveō, cūrō, videō;
'causing,' efficiō, perficiō, committō (*ut*), consequor;
'recommending,' suādeō (Dat.), moneō;
'persuading,' persuadeō (Dat.), impetrō (ā)
take *ut* (= 'that') or *nē* (= 'that ... not') with the Subjunctive (for Tenses, cf. § 518). Sometimes *ut nē* stands for *ut*: cf. § 350, Obs. 2. 'That no one' is *nē quisquam* (cf. § 368c).

Obs. 1. Note the similar construction in dependence on a noun:—
*Vēnit eō consiliō ut adjuvāret.* He came with the design of helping.

Obs. 2. Certain verbs may be used in two senses:—
(i) Implying an act of the will: e.g.—
*Persuāsit jūdicibus (Monuit jūdicēs) nē reum absolverent.* He persuaded (warned) the jury not to acquit the prisoner.
*Dixit (Scripsit) mihi ut venīrem.* He told (wrote to) me to come.

(ii) As verbs of 'saying' (§ 368a): e.g.—
*Persuāsit jūdicibus (Monuit jūdicēs) sē innocentem esse.* He persuaded (warned) the jury that he was innocent.
*Dixit (Scripsit) mihi sē ventūrum esse.* He told (wrote to) me that he would come.

Obs. 3. Note:—*Ōrō veniās.* I entreat you to come. *Fac sciam.* Let me know.
*Hortābantur venīret.* They exhorted him to come. Cf. § 367, 4.

Note the peculiarity of *Cavē dēcipiāris,* Beware that you be **not** deceived = Beware of being deceived = Do not be deceived (Prohibition).

## DEPENDENT STATEMENTS AND COMMANDS.

### II.

**369b** *Impedior quōminus sententiam dīcam.* I am prevented from speaking.
*Sententiam nē dīceret recūsāvit.* He refused to speak.
*Prohibēbō tē nē veniās.* I will prevent you from coming.

RULE: The following verbs of
'preventing,' **dēterreō, impediō, prohibeō, retineō, obsistō** (Dat.), **obstō** (Dat.);
'forbidding,' **interdīcō** (Dat., *nē*);
'refusing,' **recūsō**,
take *quōminus* or *nē* with the Subjunctive. (For Tenses, cf. § 518.)

☞ *Prohibeō* also takes Acc. with Infin. (*Prohibēbō tē venīre.*)

#### Quin (§§ 368d, 368e).

*Germānī retinērī vix poterant, quīn tēla in nostrōs cōnicerent.* The Germans could scarcely be restrained from throwing missiles at our men.

RULE: *Quin* with the Subjunctive is used for *quōminus* or *nē*, when the Principal Clause is negative (or interrogative).

### III.

**369c** *Jubeō tē redīre.* I command that you return.
*Nōlēbat lēgātōs mittī.* He was unwilling that ambassadors should be sent.

RULE: The following verbs of
'commanding,' **jubeō** (§ 333); ☞ also *ut* with Subj.
'forbidding,' **vetō** (§ 333) = 'I command that ... not;'
'permitting,' **sinō, patior** (§ 333);
'willing,' **volō, nōlō, mālō, cupiō**,
take the Acc. with Infin.

Obs. 1. 'I desire to be merciful' may be expressed:—
(1) *Cupiō esse clēmens.*[1] (Third Form of Pred.; § 330.)
(2) *Cupiō mē esse clēmentem.* (Less common.)

Obs. 2. Note the following constructions:—
*Jubeor redīre.* I am commanded to return.
*Vetantur (Prohibentur) dīcere.* They are forbidden to speak (prevented from speaking).

---

[1] This construction is not extended in prose (Latin or English), as it is in Greek and French, to verbs of 'saying' and 'thinking' (ἔφη ποιῆσαι, He said he had done it).

## Dependent Questions and Exclamations.

### Dependent Questions.

370) Quaerō **num** *cantet*. } I ask whether he sings.
    „   *cantet* **ne**.
    „   **nōn**ne *cantet*. I ask whether he does not sing.

*Nescio* **utrum** *vērum sit* **an** *falsum*. } I do not know whether it is true or false.
    „   *vērum***ne** *sit* **an** *falsum*.
    „   *vērum* **an** *falsum sit*.
    „   *vērum sit nec***ne**. I do not know whether it is true **or not**.

*Dīc mihī* **quis** *sīs*. Tell me who you are.
*Nōvī* **quot** *fuerĭtis*. I know how many of you there were.
*Nōn videō in* **utram** *partem amnis fluat*. I do not see in which direction the river is flowing.
*Scīre velim* **quandō** *ventūrus sīs*. I should like to know when you will come.
*Intellegēbam* **quantus** *esset exercitus*. I perceived how great the army was.
*Incertum erat* **cūr** *vēnisset*. It was uncertain why he had come.
*Quaerēbātur* **unde** *profectūrī essent*. It was a question from what place they would start.

### Dependent Exclamations.

*Nōvistī* **quam** *pulchrē cantāverit*. You know how beautifully he sang.
*Mementō* **quantum** *sit praemium*. Remember how great the reward is.

Rules: 1. Dependent Questions and Exclamations take the Subjunctive (Neg. *nōn*).

2. Dependent Questions and Exclamations are introduced in the same way as Independent Questions and Exclamations. 'Or not' in Dep. Quest. is *necne* (Contrast *annōn*, § 584).

Caution. Dependent Questions must be carefully distinguished from

(1) Adj. Clauses introduced by a Relative without an antecedent:
    *Quod dīcis falsum est*. What you say (= That which you say) is false.

(2) Adv. Clauses of Condition introduced by *sīve* ... *sīve* (§ 357):
    *Sīve dīcis, sīve nōn dīcis, falsum est*. Whether you say it or not (= If you say it or if you do not say it), it is false.

## DEPENDENT QUESTIONS AND EXCLAMATIONS. 159

**Test.** Before a Dep. Quest. the words 'the question' or 'the answer to the question' may always be supplied : e.g.—
*Quaerō quid velīs.* I ask the question, 'What do you want?'
*Scio quid velīs.* I know the answer to the question, 'What, etc.?'
Thus a sentence like 'I don't know whether you did it or not, but whether you did it or not you will be punished,' is *Nescio utrum fēcerīs necne, sed sive fēcistī, sive nōn fēcistī, pūniēris.*

    Obs. 1. Note that *ut, nē, sī* may be interrogative words:
    *Rogitant mē ut valeam.* They ask me how I am.
    *Vidē nē mea conjectūra vērior sit.* Consider whether my guess is not truer.
    *Helvētii si perrumpere possent cōnātī sunt.* The Helvetii tried whether they could force their way through. (So, too, with *exspectō.*)
    *Caesar exercitum prōduxit si Pompēius dēcertāre vellet.* Cæsar led out his army to see whether Pompey would fight.
    *Inde domum si forte pedem, si forte, tulisset | mē referō.* Thence I betake me home in the hope, the faint hope, that she had turned her steps thither. (*Aen.* ii., 756 : *si* = 'to see whether.')

    Obs. 2. In the following instances *ut* is exclamatory :
    *Vidēs ut altā stet nive candidum | Sōracte.* You see how Soracte rises glistening with deep snow.
    *Aspice ut antrum | silvestris rāris sparsit labrusca racēmis.* See how the wild vine has scattered the cave with clusters here and there. (Virg. *Ecl.*, v., 7. Note the Indic., which is a survival from the construction of the Simple Sentence.)

    **Nescio quis.** (Some one.) **Haud scio an.** (Probably.)
    *Nescio quis loquitur.* Some one (= *Aliquis*) is speaking.
    *Nescio quid semper abest.* Something (*je ne sais quoi*) is always wanting.
    *Nescio quōmodo fit ut* . . . It somehow happens that . . .
    *Haud scio an nēmō mihī crēdat.* Probably no one believes me.

  RULE : *Nescio quis* (*quōmodo, quandō*, etc.) have no influence on the construction. *Haud scio an* (*Nescio an, Forsitan = Fors sit an*), 'I almost think,' 'Probably,' 'Perhaps,' take the Subj.—*i.e. an* retains its interrogative force.

<br>

DEPENDENT DELIBERATIVE QUESTIONS.

**370†** *Dubitō quid faciam.* I am in doubt what I am to do.
*Nesciēbat quid faceret.* He did not know what he was to do.
RULE : Deliberative Questions take the same form when dependent as when independent (§ 344*).
☞ Note the ambiguity of such sentences : cf. § 370.

# REPORTED SPEECH.

**371** Two methods may be employed in reporting :—

1. The reporter may **quote** words or views in their original independent form (**Direct Speech, Ōrātiō Rēcta**): e.g.—

*Nēmō, inquit Solōn, ante mortem beātus est.* 'No one,' says Solon, 'is happy before death.'

Here we have two Co-ordinate Simple Sentences, one of them parenthetical.

2. The reporter may use the form of a clause, or clauses, **dependent** on a verb of 'saying,' 'thinking,' 'writing,' etc., called the 'leading verb' (**Indirect Speech, Ōrātiō Oblīqua**) : e.g.—

*Solōn negāvit quemquam ante mortem beātum esse.* Solon said that no one is (was) happy before death.

Here we have a Complex Sentence (Principal Clause: *Solōn negāvit*. Subordinate Noun Clause: *quemquam . . . esse*).

In the following passage (a speech of Ariovistus, a German chieftain: adapted from Caesar) the numbers refer to the Rule of Mood (p. 162) :—

*Ōrātiō Rēcta.*

Ariovistus quum Caesaris postulāta cognōvisset : Galli*a inquit, mea* prōvinci*a est.* Nam prius *hūc* vēnī quam Rōmān*ī.* Cūr in *nostrās* possessiōnēs nullā causā allātā ven*ītis ?* Quid fēc*imus ?* Quandō ā *nōbīs* populō Rōmānō injūria *est* illāt*a ?* Sī *ego tibī* nōn praescrībō quemadmodum *tuō* jūre ūt*āris,* nōn oport*et mē* ā *tē* in *meō* jūre impedīrī. Quam indignum *est nōs* haec perpetī ! Nisi ab*ieritis,* nulla *erit hīc* pa*x.* Proinde abdūc exercitum quōcum vēn*istī,* nēve *hodiē* commis*erīs* ut *hīc* locus, ubī con-

*Ōrātiō Oblīqua.*

Ariovistus quum Caesaris postulāta cognōvisset, ita *respondit :* Galli*am* suam prōvinciam esse.(¹) Nam prius *sē illūc* vēn*isse*(¹) quam Rōmān*ōs.* Cūr in *suās* possessiōnēs nullā causā allātā ven*īrent ?* (³) Quid *sē* fēc*isse ?* (⁴) Quandō ā *sēsē* populō Rōmānō injūri*am esse* illāt*am ?* (⁴) Sī *ipse illī* nōn praescrīb*eret*(⁷) quemadmodum *suō* jūre ūter*ētur,* (⁵,⁷) nōn oport*ēre* (¹) *sēsē* ab *illō* in *suō* jūre impedīrī. Quam indignum *esse* (⁶) *sē* haec perpetī ! Nisi abi*issent* (⁷), nullam *futūram esse* (¹) *illūc* pācem. Proinde

# REPORTED SPEECH.

stit*imus*, ex calamitāte populī Rōmānī nōmen cap*iat*. | abdūc*eret* (²) exercitum quōcum vēn*isset*,(⁷) nēve *eō* diē committ*eret* (²) ut *is* locus ubī constit*issent*,(⁷) ex calamitāte populī Rōmānī nōmen cap*eret*.(⁷)

*Translation.*

Ariovistus having learnt the demands of Cæsar, answered *as follows:* "Gaul *is my* province. For *I came here* before the Romans. Why *do you* invade *our* domains without cause assigned? What *have we* done? When *was* an injury ever done by *us* to the Roman people? If *I do* not dictate to *you* how to exercise *your* rights, *I* ought not to be obstructed in *my* rights by *you*. How shameful it *is* that *we* should be treated thus! Unless *you depart*, there *will* be no peace *here*. Accordingly *take* off the army with which *you have* come, and *do* not *to-day* cause *this* spot on which *we stand* to take its name from a disaster inflicted on the Roman people. | Ariovistus having learnt the demands of Cæsar, answered *that* Gaul *was his* province. For *he had come there* before the Romans. Why *did they* invade *their* domains without cause assigned? What *had they* (the Gauls) done? When *had* an injury ever *been* done by *them* to the Roman people? If *he* (Ariovistus) *did* not dictate to *him* (Cæsar) how to exercise *his* rights, *he* ought not to be obstructed in *his* rights by *him*. How shameful it *was* that *they* should be treated thus! Unless they (the Romans) *departed*, there *would* be no peace *there*. Accordingly *let* him *take* off the army with which *he had* come, and *let him* not *that day* cause *that* spot on which *they stood* to take its name from a disaster inflicted on the Roman people.

☞ Before translating a piece of English Oratio Recta into Latin Oratio Obliqua convert it into English Oratio Obliqua: e.g. 'Gaul is my province '='(He said) that Gaul was his province' =(*Dixit*) *Galliam suam prōvinciam esse;* and observe the use of tenses of the Infinitive (§ 533).—For Rules see next page.

## REPORTED SPEECH.

### 1. Mood.

<table>
<tr><td></td><td>Ōrātiō Recta.</td><td>Ōrātiō Oblīqua.</td></tr>
<tr><td rowspan="8">Simple Sent. or Prin. Clauses.</td><td>Statements in Indic.</td><td>Acc. with Infin. (¹)</td></tr>
<tr><td colspan="2">☞ For Moods and Tenses in Conditional Sentences, Class B, see § 357†.</td></tr>
<tr><td>Commands, Wishes, etc. in Imperat. or Subj.</td><td>Subj. (²)</td></tr>
<tr><td>Questions in Indic., 2nd Pers.</td><td>Subj. (³)</td></tr>
<tr><td>     ,,      ,,   1st or 3rd Pers.</td><td>Acc. with Infin. (⁴)</td></tr>
<tr><td>     ,,   Subj. (Deliberative)</td><td>Subj. (⁵)</td></tr>
<tr><td>Exclamations</td><td>Acc. with Infin. (⁶)</td></tr>
<tr><td>Subordinate Clauses in Indic.<br>     ,,     ,,     ,, Subj.</td><td>Subj. (⁷)</td></tr>
</table>

☞ *It will be seen that the Indic. is excluded from O. O. (cf. p. 163, Peculiarities, 3).*

### 2. Tense.

|  |  |
|---|---|
| Pres. | Pres. ⎫ |
| Perf., Past, Imperf., Plupf. | Perf. ⎬ Infin. |
| Fut., Fut. Perf. | Fut.† ⎭ |
| Pres., Impf., Fut. | Impf. ⎫ Subj. |
| Perf., Past, Plupf., Fut. Perf. | Plupf. ⎭ |

☞ *The above rule for the Subj. tenses applies when the leading verb is in a tense of past time.*

### 3. Pronouns and Possessive Adjectives.

Of the 1st Pers. (*referring to the Subject of the leading verb*).     Sē, suus (*in Nom.* ipse *in contrast to another Pronoun*).

Of the 2nd Pers. (*addressed by the Subject of the leading verb*).    Is *or* (*more emphatically*) ille.

☞ *The above rule applies when the leading verb is 3rd Pers. But 'I said that I had given you a book' is 'Dixī mē tibī librum dedisse.'—Note that sē, suus are necessarily* **ambiguous**.

### 4. Adverbs and hīc.

O.R. hīc, nunc, hodiē, herī,    crās, *become in*
O.O. ille, tum, eō diē, prīdiē, posterō diē.

☞ *The above rule applies when the leading verb is a tense of past time.*

---

† Sometimes (in the Passive) the Perf. Part. with *fore* represents the Fut. Perf. Infin.

# REPORTED SPEECH.

## PECULIARITIES.

371* 1. *Ōrābant* ut *sibi auxilium ferret. Properātō opus esse*, etc.

RULE: A Command may be introduced by *ut*, but only when it stands at the beginning of Or. Obl., depending on a verb of commanding, asking, etc. (§ 369a).

2. *Interrogāvit quid factum esset*.

RULE: A Question standing at the beginning of Or. Obl. is always in the Subj. (whether 1st, 2nd, or 3rd Pers.).

3. *Caesarī nuntiātur Sulmōnensēs, quod oppidum ā Corfīniō VII mīlium intervallō abest, cupere ea facere quae vellet.*

RULE: Parenthetical comments of the reporter stand in the Indic.

4. *Themistoclēs dixit Athēniensium urbem prōpugnāculum fuisse barbaris, apud quam bis classēs rēgiās fēcisse naufragium* . . . For upon it the royal fleets had twice suffered shipwreck.

RULE: Relative Clauses in which *quī* = *et is, sed is, nam is* (§ 314) stand in the Acc. with Infin., when dependent on an Acc. with Infin. (cf. § 359, Rule 2, Obs.).

5. *Ariovistus quum Caesaris postulāta cognōvisset, ita respondet: Galliam suam prōvinciam esse. Nam prius sē illūc vēnisse quam Rōmānōs. Cūr in suās possessiōnēs veniat ? Sī ipse illī nōn praescrībat*, quemadmodum *suō jūre ūtātur, nōn oportēre sēse ab illō in suō jūre impedīrī. Nisi abierint, nullam futūram esse illīc pācem. Proinde abdūcat exercitum, nēve committat, ut is locus ubi cōnstiterint*, ex calamitāte *populī Rōmānī nōmen capiat.*

RULE: When Or. Obl. depends on an historical Present (§ 467), the Pres. and Perf. Subj. may stand instead of the Imperf. and Pluperf. So even after a Past (*Dixit*), in the course of a long passage.

6. *Interrogābat cūr paucīs centuriōnibus oboedīrent. Quandō ausūrōs exposcere remedia?* When would they venture to demand redress?

RULE: Rhetorical questions (*i.e.*, questions that do not expect any answer) are generally expressed by the Acc. with Infin., even if of the 2nd Person.

# SYNTAX.—PART II. (cf. § 315).

## USE OF THE CASES.

### The Nominative.

**372** As the Subject of a Finite Verb (§ 316) or Historical Infinitive (§ 339*).

### The Vocative.

**373** The Vocative (Case of Address: § 11) may be used either with or without *ō*:

*Fortūnāte senex! ergō tua rūra manēbunt.* Happy old man! the farm will, then, remain thine.

*Crēdō vōs, jūdicēs, mīrārī.* I fancy you are surprised, jurors (ὦ ἄνδρες δικασταί).

*O fortūnāte adulescens, quī tuae virtūtis Homerum praecōnem invēnerīs.* O happy young man, to have found, etc. (§364).

**374** The Vocative without *ō* is usually inserted in the middle of the sentence, or placed at the end of it: *Dīc, M. Tullī.* Speak, Cicero.

### The Accusative.

**375** I. As the Object of a transitive verb (§ 326, etc.).

**376** OBS. 1. Many English verbs which are used either transitively or intransitively correspond to Latin verbs which are only transitive. The intransitive sense may be conveyed (*a*) by using the Passive; (*b*) by using the Reflexive Pronoun; (*c*) by using a different verb.

(*a*) *Tempestās mūtātur.* The weather is changing.
　　[Compare *Vestem mūtat.* He is changing his dress.]

*Nebula dissipāta est.* The fog broke up.
　　[Compare *Multitūdinem dissipāvit.* He broke up the crowd.]

*Lūna circā tellūrem movētur.* The moon moves round the earth.
　　[Compare *Bracchium movet.* He moves his arm.]

*Lapidēs dēvolvuntur.* The stones are rolling down.
　　[Compare *Lapidēs dēvolvunt.* They are rolling down stones.]

## THE ACCUSATIVE.

(*b*) *Hostēs sē dēdunt.* The enemy are surrendering.
  [Compare *Urbem dēdunt.* They are surrendering the city.]
*Populāribus sē adjunxit.* He has joined the popular party.
  [Compare *Taurōs adjunxit arātrō.* He has joined (yoked) bulls to the plough.]
(*c*) *Dīvitiae tuae crescunt (augentur).* Your wealth is increasing.
  [Compare *Dīvitiās suās auget.* He is increasing his wealth.]

**377** OBS. 2. Many verbs of motion compounded with prepositions take an Accusative :—

### Circum, per, praeter, trans.

*Hostis nōs circumvēnit.* The enemy has surrounded us.
*Hostis agrōs percurrit.* The enemy is overrunning the country.
*Hanc rem praetereō.* I pass by this matter.
*Hostis flūmen transiit.* The enemy crossed the river.
*Caesar exercitum flūmen transduxit (transjēcit).* Caesar led his army across the river. [Two Accusatives: cf. p. 127.]

Some of the above mentioned verbs may be used in the Passive:
*Circumventī sumus ab hostibus.* We were surrounded by the enemy.
*Philippus et Marcellus praetereuntur.* P. and M. are passed over.
*Rhodanus vadō transītur.* The Rhone is crossed by a ford.

### Ad, con, in ob, sub.

**378** Verbs of motion compounded with other prepositions (*ad, con, in, ob, sub*) sometimes take an Accusative. But when the compound verb has distinct local meaning the preposition is generally repeated:

*Deōrum ōrācula adeunt.* They consult the oracles of the gods.
*Multa pericula adeunt.* They are incurring many dangers.
  [But *Ad urbem adeunt.* They go to the city.]
*Convenīre tē volō.* I wish to meet you.
*Iniit magistrātum.* He took office.
*Ingreditur ōrātiōnem (iter).* He is commencing his speech (journey).
  [But *Ingreditur in urbem.* He is entering into the city.]
*Obiit diem suprēmum.* He died, *or* met his fate.
  [Also *Multās regiōnēs obiit.* He travelled over many districts.]
*Maximum labōrem subibō.* I will undergo the greatest toil.
  [But *Sub mūrōs subibō.* I will advance up to the walls.]

Some of the above mentioned verbs may be used in the Passive:

**379** *Praetōrēs adeuntur.* The praetors are consulted.
*Convenīrī sē nōn vult.* He does not wish to be visited.
*Initō magistrātū.* Office having been taken.
*Obitā morte.* Death having been met.

**380**  II. As the Subject of an Infinitive (§ 367,1).
**381**  III. As an Adverb-equivalent :

1. Denoting 'place whither' (§ 435), 'space' (§ 438), 'time how long' (§ 441).

**382**  2. Denoting 'how much' (☞ Only Neuter Adjectives and Pronouns are so used):

*Multum dēmissus homō.* A very abject fellow.
*Quid rēfert ?* What does it matter? (§ 449).

**383**  3. Denoting the *part affected* (**Accus. of Nearer Definition**):
*Tremit artūs.* He trembles in his (as to the) limbs.
*Caput nectentur olīvā.* They shall be bound as to the head with olive.
*Ōs humerōsque deō similis.* In face and figure like a god.

**384**  4. With Passive Verbs (poetical):
*Inscriptī nōmina rēgum.* Inscribed with names of kings (*Virg.* Ecl. 3, 106 ; cf. Aen. II., 273).
On the Accus. in *exuitur cornua*, etc., see § 461.

**385**  IV. As an Adjective-equivalent :
*Alia id genus.* Other things of that kind.

**386**  V. In Exclamations :
*Mē miserum !* Unhappy that I am ! ('Me miserable !' MILTON.)
*Ō (Heū) fallācem hominum spem !* Oh, (Alas,) how treacherous is human hope ! (cf. *Ō fortūnāte adulescens !* §§ 373, 587.)

## The Genitive.

### I. As an Adjective-equivalent

**387**  The Genitive is primarily an adjectival case. The particular way in which it qualifies the noun to which it is joined is shown by the context.

**388**  1. The Genitive may denote 'belonging to,' 'connected with':

*Domus Cicerōnis,* Cicero's house. (**Possessive Genitive.**)
*Benevolentia Cicerōnis,* The benevolence of Cicero.
*Statua Phīdiae,* A statue of (*i.e.* by) Phidias.

*Ēreptae virginis īra,* Anger at the maiden's rescue.

**389**  This Genitive may be used predicatively (§ 302):
*Domus est Cicerōnis,* The house belongs to Cicero (is Cicero's).
*Nōn est victōris arma trādere,* It is not the **habit (mark. part, duty)** of a conqueror to deliver up his arms.
*Nostrae diciōnis est,* It is in our power.

## THE GENITIVE.

**390**  2. The Genitive may denote a *divided whole* (**Partitive Genitive**):

*Pars* (*Multitūdō*) *hostium*, A part (great number) of the enemy.
*Omnium hominum doctissimus*, The most learned of all men.
*Multī* (*paucī*) *nostrum* (*vestrum*), Many (few) of us (of you).
*Alter* (*uter, neuter, quis, quīcumque, quisque*) *eōrum*, One (which of the two, neither, who, whoever, each) of them.
*Quotusquisque sapientium*, How few of the philosophers! § 573.
*Tria mīlia passuum*, Three miles (3,000 paces) : § 124.
*Duo nostrum* (*vestrum*), Two of us (of you) : § 559.

**391**  The partitive Genitive often depends on the Neuter Singular of adjectives and pronouns (used as the Subject or Object of a sentence):

*tantum, quantum, aliquantum,*
*multum, plūs, plūrimum,*
*nihil, minus, minimum,*
*dīmidium, paulum, reliquum,*
*id, quod, quid, aliquid,*
*satis, nimis, parum.*

English generally uses a different construction :

*e.g. Tantum voluptātis*, So much pleasure (lit. of pleasure).
*Satis nivis*, Enough snow.

**392**  Cf. French : *tant de volupté, assez de neige.*
Note the expressions :

*Ubī terrārum?* Where on earth ? (lit. of the lands.)
*Id aetātis*, Of such an age (so old).
*Id temporis*, At that time.

**393**  Instead of the partitive genitive, the prepositions *ex, inter, dē*, are often used with numerals, comparatives, and superlatives :

*Ūnus ex multīs*, One of many.
*Duo dē tribus*, Two of the three.
*Optimus inter eōs*, The best of (among) them.

**394**  The partitive genitive is not used in Latin, except where there is real partition :

*Nōs omnēs*, All of us.  [*Omnēs crēdimus*, All of us believe *or* We all believe].
*Quot estis?* How many are there of you? (How many are you?)
*Paucī sumus*, There are few of us (We are few).

1. Hence we may distinguish:

*Aliquid novi*, Some news. (Something in the shape of news.)
*Aliquid novum*, Something new.

*Tantum molestiae*, So much trouble.
*Tanta molestia*, A trouble so great.

2. The word *uterque* 'both' (properly 'either of two;' § 169) is generally an adjective; but it is also used as a pronoun, and may have a partitive genitive depending on it:

*Uterque consul periit*, Both consuls perished.
*Uterque vestrum audiit*, Both of you have heard (Pron.).
*Utrique audīvistis*, You have both heard (Adj.).

**395** The only adjectives that stand in the partitive genitive are those whose genitives end in *-ī*:

*Quid novī?* What news? *Nihil novī*, No news.
But *Nihil memorābile*, Nothing worth mentioning.
*Nihil aliud*, Nothing else.

**396** 'The whole of,' 'the middle of,' 'the top (bottom) of,' 'the rest of,' are expressed in Latin by adjectives agreeing with nouns (instead of the partitive genitive):

*Tōta insula*, The whole of the island.
*Media insula*, The middle of the island.
*Summus mons*, The top of the mountain.
*Īmus mons*, The foot of the mountain.
*Reliquum iter*, The rest of the march.

**397** 3. The Genitive may denote what might have been expressed as the object of a verb (**Objective Genitive**):

*Interfectōrēs rēgis*, The murderers of the king.
[= *Eī quī rēgem interfēcērunt*, Those who murdered the king.]
*Memoria nostrī*, The recollection of us (cf. § 558).
*Dēsīderium patriae*, The longing for one's country.
*Metus mortis*, The fear of death.

**398** When the Genitive denotes the person who acts or feels, it is sometimes called by contrast the *Subjective Genitive*, e.g.:

*Benevolentia Cicerōnis*, The benevolence which Cicero feels (cf. § 388).
*Amor patris* may mean either 'a father's love' (Subjective Genitive), or 'the love for a father' (Objective Genitive).

## THE GENITIVE.

**399**   4. The Genitive may denote a quality (**Genitive of Quality**):

*Vir magnī ingeniī*, A man of genius (= *Vir ingeniōsus*).
*Puer decem annōrum*, A boy of ten years (ten years old).

RULE: The Genitive of Quality always has an adjective joined to it. Cf. § 434, 2.

**400**   5. The Genitive may define the noun to which it is joined, often answering to an apposition in English (**Appositive Genitive**):

*Vox voluptātis*, The word pleasure.
*Verbum carendī*, The word *carēre* ('to lack').

### II. As an Adverb-equivalent.

**401**   1. Denoting 'how much' (**Genitive of Price**: originally Locative): ☞ Only certain words denoting **indefinite value**, chiefly **Adjectives of Quantity**, are so used, with certain verbs:

(a) With verbs of 'valuing': e.g.

*Magnī (Plūris, Plūrimī) aestimāre.* To value highly (more highly, most highly).

*Parvī (Minōris, Minimī) dūcere.* To consider of little (less, least) worth.

*Tantī (Quantī, Nihilī) esse.* To be worth so much (how much, nothing).

**402**   (b) With verbs of 'buying,' 'selling,' 'costing,' 'hiring'; e.g.

*Emit hortōs tantī quantī voluit.* He bought the garden at his own price. (But *magnā pecūniā*, for a large sum: § 429.)

*Plūris stāre.* To cost more.

*Minōris condūcere (locāre).* To hire (let) for less.

*Quantī vendidit? Magnō. (Parvō.)* How much did he sell it for? For a large (small) sum: cf. § 429.

**403**   (c) With *interest* (e.g. *parvī interest:* § 448) and *rēfert* (§ 449).

**404**   2. With obscured meaning:

(a) Depending on Adjectives that denote 'full,' 'mindful,' 'conscious,' 'desirous,' 'having control,' and their opposites, which in English take 'of':

*Locus plēnus (inānis) hominum.* A place full (empty) of people.

*Memor (Immemor) tuī.* Mindful (Unmindful) of you.

*Mens sibi conscia recti.* A consciousness of rectitude.
*Cupidus (Avidus) laudis.* Desirous of praise.
*Studiōsus vītae umbrātilis.* Desirous of a secluded life.
*Potens suī.* Having control of oneself.
*Compos vōti.* Possessed of one's heart's desire.

**405** Note the Adjectives **perītus, gnārus, particeps**, and their opposites, with Gen. (For **similis, dis-similis** cf. § 417):

*Perītus (Imperītus) bellī.* Experienced (inexperienced) in war.
*Gnārus (Ignārus, Rūdis) pugnandī.* Skilled (unskilled) in fighting.
*Particeps praemiī.* Sharing in the reward.
*Ratiōnis expers.* Without (not sharing in) reason.

**406** OBS. 1. *Plēnus* sometimes takes the Ablative: *plēnus laetitiae* or *laetitiā*.

OBS. 2. Some Present Participles of transitive verbs take a Genitive:
*Vēritātis diligens.* Truth-loving. *Patiens labōrum.* Hard working.
*Patriae amans.* Patriotic.

OBS. 3. The form *animī* (e.g. *anxius animī*, anxious in mind; *animī pendeō*, I waver in mind) is a Locative (§ 59): hence *animīs pendēmus*, we waver in mind.

**407** (*b*) Depending on the verbs:
*Piget, pudet, paenitet, taedet* atque *miseret* (§ 447).

**408** (*c*) Verbs of 'acquitting,' 'accusing,' 'arraigning,' 'convicting,' 'condemning,' take a Genitive of the *charge*, e.g.

**Absolvō** *tē parricīdiī.* I acquit you of murder.
**Accūsō (Incūsō, Insimulō)** *tē furtī.* I accuse you of theft.
**Arcessō (Reum faciō)** *tē mājestātis.* I arraign you for high treason.
**Coarguō (Convincō)** *tē ambitūs.* I convict you of bribery.
**Damnō (Condemnō)** *tē* I condemn you
  *repetundārum.* for extortion.
  *capite, morte; pecūniā.* to death; to pay a fine.
  *capitis, tantī.* to death; to pay so much.

☞ Verbs of 'condemning' take an Ablative of the *penalty* (or a Genitive of *caput, tantum, quantum, quadruplum*, etc.).

### III. AS AN OBJECT.

**409** Depending on the Verbs: *Misereor, meminī, oblīviscor* (§ 327*): *interest* (e.g. *Cicerōnis interest:* § 448).

## The Dative.

**410**  1. Denoting 'to':
(*a*) Depending on verbs of 'giving,' etc. (**Dative of the Indirect Object**: § 331).
(*b*) Depending on *libet, placet, licet, liquet* (§ 450), and *videor:*
*Fortūnātus sibĭ vidēbātur.* He seemed to himself a lucky person.

**411**  2. Denoting 'for':
*Nōn scholae sed vītae discimus.* We learn not for the school but for life. (**Dative of Interest**).
*Domum mihĭ ēmī.* I have bought myself (for myself) a house.
*Receptuī canere.* To give the signal for retreat.

**412**  With *esse* this Dat. may denote possession (**Dative of Possession**):
*Est mihĭ pater.* I have a father. (There is for me a father.)
*Est mihĭ nōmen* **Scīpiŏ** (or **Scīpiōnī**). My name is Scipio.

**413**  With the Gerundive (sometimes, too, with finite verb, esp. Perf. Pass.) this Dative denotes the agent (**Dative of Agent**):
*Hīc tibĭ vītandus est.* This man must be shunned by you. (This man is for you a person to be shunned.)
*Cuī nōn sunt haec audīta?* Who has not heard of this?

**414**  Sometimes this Dative (*mihĭ, tibĭ, nōbīs, vōbīs*) marks a person as interested in a Statement, Question, etc. (so-called **Ethical Dative**):
*Quid mihĭ Celsus agit?* How is Celsus getting on, I should like to know? (cf. Knock *me* at that door, Sirrah!—Shakspere.)

**415**  OBS. 1. The Dative denoting 'for' may be used as an Adjective-equivalent:
*Decemviri lēgibus scrībendīs.* A commission of ten for making laws.
*Signum receptuī.* A signal for retreat.

**416**  OBS. 2. When 'for' means 'in defence of,' 'in place of,' 'as a reward for,' it must be translated by *prō* with the Ablative.
*Prō patriā morī.* To die for one's country.
*Prō beneficiīs tuīs.* In return for your kindness.
When 'for' denotes purpose, it must be translated by *ad:*
*Bōs ad arandum nātus est.* The ox is made for ploughing.

**417**  3. Depending on Adjectives which in English take 'to' or 'for,' together with some Adverbs of kindred meaning:
*Tibi ūtile est, mihĭ erit jūcundum.* It is useful to you; it will be agreeable to me.
*Locus idōneus castrīs.* A place suited for a camp.

*Nigrō simillima cygnō.* Very like a black swan. (But *similis* and *dissimilis* more commonly take the Genitive : § 405.)

*Belgae propiōrēs (proximi) sunt Germānis.* The Belgae are nearer (very near) to the Germans.

But *prope, propius, proximē* takes Accusative or *ab* with Ablative :
e.g. *Habitābat prope litus (prope ā litore).* He used to dwell near to the shore.

*Pār est summis Peripatēticīs.* He is equal to the greatest P.

*Cārus (Inimīcus) est sibī.* He is dear (hostile) to himself.

*Congruenter Nātūrae.* In a manner agreeable to Nature.

418   4. The Dative is used with obscured meaning :
(*a*) Depending on verbs compounded with a Preposition or *bene, male, satis* : e.g.—

*Adsum tibī.* I support (stand by) you.  ⎫
*Dēsum tibi.* I fail (am wanting to) you.  ⎪ Add other
**Praesum** *exercituī.* I command an army. ⎬ Compounds of
**Prōsum** *tibī.* I benefit you.  ⎪ *sum* and a
                                     ⎭ Preposition.

*Assentior (Assentor) tibī.* I agree with (flatter) you.
*Maledīcō tibi.* I speak ill of you.
*Satisfaciō tibī.* I satisfy you.
**Subveniō (Succurrō)** *tibī.* I succour you.
*Hanc rem illī antepōnō.* I prefer this to that.
*Conferō parva magnīs.* I compare small things with great.
*Ēripiō tibī ensem.* I snatch a sword from you.
*Inferō hostibus bellum.* I make war upon the enemy.
*Injiciō tibī catēnās.* I put chains upon you.
*Offerō mē mortī.* I expose myself to death.
*Posthabeō meam ūtilitātem tuae.* I postpone my interests to yours.
*Praeficiō tē exercituī.* I put you in command of the army.
*Subjiciō tē imperiō meō.* I subject you to my authority.

☞ Most verbs (except verbs of motion : § 377), when compounded with a Preposition, become capable of taking a Dative (instead of repeating the Preposition). But *dēficiō, effugiō* generally take the Accusative : e.g. *vīrēs mē dēficiunt* = 'strength fails me' : *mortem effugere nēmō potest* = 'no man can escape death.'

OBS. Some of the above compounds may take a Preposition, especially to express distinct *local* meaning :
*Adsum ad portam.* I am present at the gate.

419     (*b*) Depending on *cŭi*-verbs (§ 328).
420     (*c*) As an equivalent of a Predicate Noun or Adjective (§ 302) with verbs denoting
'to serve as'   *esse*.
'to reckon as'   *dare, tribuere, vertere, habēre, dūcere*.

*Hōc mihī* **sōlātiō** *est*. This is (serves as) a consolation to n.e.
*Cŭi* **bonō** *est?* To whom is it advantageous (of advantage)?
*Hōc tibi* **laudī** *duxistī, sed aliīs* **vitiō** *vertistī*. You have reckoned this as creditable (a credit) to yourself, but made it a reproach to others.

This Dative is called the **Predicate Dative,** and is usually accompanied by another Dative (Dative of person).

OBS. 1. A similar Dative is found with the verbs *dare*, to give, *mittere, accipere, venire, relinquere*.

*Duās legiōnēs castrīs* **praesidiō** *reliquit*. He left two legions as a protection for the camp.
*Venīte nōbīs* **auxiliō**. Come to our aid (as an aid to us).

OBS. 2. *Odiō esse* serves as a Passive of *ōdisse* (cf. **invidiae** *fuisse*, § 329).
*Hōc mihī* **odiō** *est*. This is hateful to me (hated by me).
*Ōdī* **odiōque** *sum Rōmānīs*. I hate the Romans and am hated by them.

421     (*d*) Denoting 'place whither,' for *ad* with Accusative (poetical):
*It clāmor* **caelō**. A shout rises to heaven (cf. ἀνατείνας οὐρανῷ χεῖρας. HOMER).

## The Ablative.
### I. AS AN ADVERB-EQUIVALENT.

422     The Ablative is primarily an adverbial case. The particular way in which it qualifies the Verb, Adjective, or Adverb, to which it is joined, is shown by the context.

423     1. The Ablative may denote 'separation' (**Ablative of Separation**):

*Pellō (Expellō) tē* **urbe**. I drive you from the city.
*Līberō (Levō, Solvō) tē* **cūrā**. I free you from care.
*Cēdō (Ēgredior)* **patriā**. I depart from my native land.

OBS. 1. But Prepositions are employed with the verbs *abeō, exeō, ēvādō*, and sometimes with other verbs of 'separating.'

OBS. 2. This Ablative sometimes denotes 'origin':
*Humilibus parentibus* **ortus**. Of humble parentage.

2. The Ablative may denote 'cause' (**Ablative of Cause**):
   *Ōdērunt peccāre bonī virtūtis amōre.* The good hate to sin through love of righteousness.
   *Inopiā frūmentī.* Through lack of provisions.
   *Jussū ducis.* At the command of the general.
   *Gaudeō (Laetor, Exsultō) hāc rē.* I rejoice at this.

3. The Ablative may denote 'that in respect of which' (**Ablative of Nearer Definition**):
   *Alterō pede claudus.* Lame in one foot.
   *Nātiōne Syrus.* A Syrian by nationality.
   *Meā sententiā.* In my opinion.

4. The Ablative may be used in Contracted Comparative Clauses for *quam* with the Nominative or Accusative (**Ablative of Comparison**): see § 360*.

5. The Ablative may denote 'manner' (**Ablative of Manner**):
   (*a*) With *cum*, if the noun is not qualified:
   *Cum dignitāte cadere.* To fall gracefully.
   (*b*) With or without *cum*, if the noun is qualified:
   *Summā fortitūdine pugnāre.* To fight very bravely.
   *Multīs cum lacrimīs obsecrāre.* To entreat with many tears.

6. The Ablative may denote the 'instrument with which' or 'means by which' (**Ablative of Instrument**):
   *Dente lupus petit.* The wolf attacks with teeth.
   *Secūrī percussus est.* He was beheaded (struck with an axe).
   *Favōrem blanditiīs conciliāvit.* He became popular by flattery.

   But 'by means of a person' is expressed by *per*:
   *Per nuntium certior factus est.* He was informed by messenger.

7. The Ablative may denote 'how much' (**Ablative of Price**), with verbs of 'buying,' 'selling,' 'costing,' 'hiring' (cf. § 402):
   *Aurō patriam vendidit.* He sold his country for gold.
   *Multō sanguine Poenīs victōria stetit.* Victory cost the Carthaginians much blood.

8. The Ablative may denote 'how much more or less' (**Ablative of Measure**):
   *Aliquantō mājor.* Considerably greater. (Greater by a considerable quantity.)
   *Tantō melius.* So much the better.

*Quō plūra habēmus, eō cupimus amplīōra.* The more we have, the more we desire.
*Hibernia est dīmidiō minor quam Britannia.* Ireland is only half as large as Britain.

**431** 9. The Ablative may be used with obscured meaning:
(*a*) Depending on Adjectives that denote
 Worthy, laden, *and* endowed,
 Glad, content, relying, proud,
 and their opposites:
*Dignus (Indignus) honōre.* Worthy (Unworthy) of office.
*Onustus (Refertus) praedā.* Laden (Crammed) with booty.
*Praeditus commūnī sēnsū.* Endowed with tact.
*Orbus (Nūdus, Vacuus) praesidiō.* Reft of defence.
*Laetus prosperō ēventū.* Rejoicing in success.
*Contentus parvō.* Content with little.
*Frētus (Superbus) vīribus suīs.* Relying on (Proud of) his own strength.

**432** (*b*) Depending on verbs of
 'filling,' *impleō, compleō;* add *abundō.*
 'depriving,' *prīvō, spoliō, orbō;* add *vacō.*
 e.g. *Orbō tē vītā.* I deprive you of life.
 *Abundō dīvitiīs.* I abound in wealth.
 *Vacō culpā.* I am free from fault.

For *ā* with the Ablative, denoting the agent, see § 327.
For the **Ablative Absolute** see § 361.
For the Ablative in expressions of Place, Space, and Time, see §§ 435—445.

### II. As an Object.

**433** Depending on verbs that denote *use, perform, lack, need* (including *opus est:* § 451), *enjoy* (§ 329\*).

### III. As an Adjective-equivalent.

**434** The Ablative may be used like the Genitive to denote a quality (**Ablative of Quality**):
*Homō corpore exiguō,* A person of small stature.
*Puer caeruleīs oculīs,* A blue-eyed boy.
*Bonō es animō,* Be of good cheer (Predicate Adj.).

Rules: 1. The Ablative of Quality always has an adjective joined to it.
2. The Ablative rather than the Genitive is used to denote physical qualities (external appearance).

## SUPPLEMENT TO USE OF CASES.
### Expressions of Place.

**435** (*a*) *In urbe erat.*   He was in the city.
*Ex (Ab) urbe profectus est.*   He marched out of (from) the city.
*In urbem contendit.*   He marched into the city.

(*b*) *Rōmae*, at Rome.   *Rōmā*, from Rome.   *Rōmam*, to Rome.
*Samī*, at Samos.   *Samō*, from Samos.   *Samum*, to Samos.
*Carthāgine*, at (from) Carthage.   *Carthāginem*, to Carthage.
*Athēnīs*, at (from) Athens.   *Athēnās*, to Athens.

*domī*, at home.   *domō*, from home.   *domum*, home.
*rūrī*, in the country.   *rūre*, from the country.   *rūs*, to the country.
*humī*, on the ground.   *humō*, from the ground.   (*ad humum*, to the ground).

RULE: 'Place where' is expressed (in prose)
  (*a*) By *in* with the Ablative.
  (*b*) By the Locative (§ 59) of names of towns and small islands, and of the words *domus, humus, rūs*.

'Place whence' is expressed (in prose)
  (*a*) By *ex* (*ē*) or *ab* (*ā*) with the Ablative.
  (*b*) By the bare Ablative of names of towns and small islands, and of the words *domus, humus, rūs*.

'Place whither' is expressed (in prose)
  (*a*) By *in* with the Accusative.
  (*b*) By the bare Accusative of names of towns and small islands, and of the words *domus, rūs*.

OBS. 1. *Ā Rōmā* means 'from the neighbourhood of Rome.'
*Ad Rōmam* means 'to the neighbourhood of Rome.'

OBS. 2. Names of larger islands take Prepositions; e.g. *in Crētā*, in Crete (Κρήτη ἑκατόμπολις): *in Siciliam*, to Sicily.

OBS. 3. Note *domī meae* (Gen.), at my house: *domī Cicerōnis*, at the house of Cicero.

#### PECULIARITIES.

**436**   (*a*) In certain phrases the Preposition is omitted (contrary to the above rule):
*Tōtā urbe.*   In the whole town (throughout the town).
*Iniquō locō.*   In an unfavourable position.
*Meliōre locō.*   In a better position (state).
*Hōc (Hōc in) librō.*   In this book.
*Terrā marique.*   By land and sea.
*Appiā viā proficīscī.*   To march by the Appian road. (Route.)

**437** Note the ways of expressing 'in the city of ——,' 'in the fair city of ——':
*In urbe Milētō.* In the city of Miletus.
*Ex (Ab) urbe Milētō.* Out of (from) the city of Miletus.
*In urbem Milētum.* To the city of Miletus.
*Milēti (§ 435b), in urbe pulcherrimā.*
*Milēti, urbe pulcherrimā.* } In the fair city of Miletus.
*Milētō (§ 435b), ex urbe pulcherrimā.* From the fair city of Miletus.
*Milētum (§ 435b), in urbem pulcherrimam.* To the fair city of Miletus.

## Expressions of Space.

**438**  1. *Sex mīlia passuum progressus est.* He marched six miles.
*Fossa pedēs trecentōs longa.* A trench 300 ft. long.
2. *Distat (Abest) ab urbe sex mīlia (mīlibus) passuum.* It is distant six miles from the city.

RULE: 'Distance' is expressed:
    1. By the Accusative with verbs of motion, and with the Adjectives *longus*, 'long'; *altus*, 'high'; *lātus*, 'broad.'
    2. By the Accusative or Ablative with verbs of rest.

## Expressions of Time.

### TIME WHEN.

**439** *Æstāte diēs longī sunt.* In summer the days are long.
*Īdibus Martiīs interfectus est.* He was murdered on the 15th of March.
*Unō diē sex proelia facta sunt.* On one day six battles were fought.
*Sextā hōrā.* At the 6th hour (12 o'clock, midday).
*Initiō vēris.* At the beginning of spring.
*Eōdem tempore.* At the same time.

RULE: 'Time when' is expressed by the Ablative.

**440** But words which do not themselves denote time generally take *in*; e.g. *in bellō*, in time of war; *in pāce*, in time of peace.

### TIME HOW LONG.

**441** *Trēs annōs regnum obtinuit.* He reigned for three years.

RULE: 'Time how long' is expressed by the Accusative.

**442** *Per* with the Accusative is sometimes used to express 'time how long'; e.g. *multōs per annōs*, for many years.
    Note *quinque et viginti annōs nātus*, twenty-five years old.

### Time within which.

**443** *Urbem bienniō ēvertēs.* You will overthrow the town in (in the course of) two years.
*Hīs decem annīs.* Within the last ten years.
RULE: 'Time within which' is expressed by the Ablative.

**444** Or by *inter, intrā* with the Accusative ; e.g. *inter decem annōs.*

### Time how long before (after): cf. § 430.

**445** *Paucīs diēbus ante mortem ējus.* } A few days before his death.
*Paucīs diēbus antequam mortuus est.*
*Decem annīs post.* } Ten years afterwards. (Not *posteā*.)
*Decem post annīs.*
*Multō ante.* Long before. *Paulō post.* A little while after.
*Hīs tribus annīs.* } Three years ago.
*Abhinc (Ante) trēs annōs.*

## Cases with Impersonal Verbs.

**446** The following impersonal verbs are either used without a Subject expressed, or take as Subject the Nominative of a Neuter Pronoun or an Infinitive (or, in the Complex Sentence, a Noun Clause).

### Piget, pudet, paenitet, taedet, miseret: cf. § 252.

**447** *Piget mē stultitiae meae.* I am vexed at my folly.
*Nōnne tē pudēbat stultitiae tuae?* Were you not ashamed of your folly?
*Paenitēbit eum stultitiae suae.* He will repent of his folly.
*Taedet nōs vītae.* We are weary of life.
*Miseret eōs pauperum.* They pity the poor.
RULE: With the verbs
   *piget, pudet, paenitet* | it vexes, it shames, it repents,
   *taedet* atque *miseret*   | it wearies, it grieves (pities)
the person who feels is denoted by an Accusative ;
that which excites his feeling by a Genitive, except when it is expressed as the Subject (§ 446) : *e.g.*—
*Hōc mē piget.* This vexes me. (I am vexed at this.)
*Taedet nōs eadem audīre.* To hear the same things wearies us.

### Interest.

**448** *Hōc rēgis magnopere interest.* This concerns the king greatly.
*Meā (Tuā, Nostrā, Vestrā) parvī intererat scīre.* It concerned me (you, us, you) little to know.

## CASES WITH IMPERSONAL VERBS.

*Ējus (Eōrum) nihil intererit.* It will concern him (them) not at all.
*Crēdit suā multum interesse.* He believes that it concerns him much.
(Complex Sentence : *suā* is reflexive).

RULE : With the verb *interest,* 'it concerns,'
the person or thing concerned is denoted by a Genitive,
or by the Abl. Sing. Fem. of a Possessive Adjective.

'How much' is expressed
  (*a*) by Adverbs : *magnopere, magis, maximē; parum, minus, minimē.*
  (*b*) by Genitives : *magnī, parvī, tantī, quantī.*
  (*c*) by Accusatives of Neuter Adjectives and Pronouns : *multum, plūs, plūrimum, tantum, quantum, nihil, nōn multum, quid.*

### Rēfert.

**449** *Quid rēfert?* What does it matter?
*Meā (Tuā, Nostrā,* etc.) *parvī rēfert.* It matters little to me (you, etc.).
RULE: *Rēfert* is generally used absolutely (*i.e.* without mention of the person concerned); but it may take *meā, suā,* etc., like *interest* (but not the Gen.). 'How much' is expressed as with *interest.*

### Libet, placet, licet, liquet.

**450** *Libetne (Placetne) tibī introīre?* Is it your pleasure to walk in?
*Hōc mihī facere nōn licuit.* To do this was not permitted me.
*Omnibus liquet eum insānīre.* It is clear to all that he is mad.
RULE : *Libet* and *placet* 'it pleases,' *licet* 'it is allowed' (*licet mihī* 'I may'), *liquet* 'it is clear,' take a Dative of the person.

### Opus est, ūsus est.

**451** *Cīvitātī opus est magistrātibus.* } A state needs officers.
*Cīvitātī magistrātūs opus sunt.* }
*Ea quae mihī opus sunt.* The things which I need.
RULE : With *opus est, ūsus est,* ' there is need '
 the person or thing needing is denoted by a Dative ;
the person or thing needed is denoted by an Ablative, or (with *opus est*) is expressed as the Subject in the Nominative.

### Necesse est.

**452** *Necesse est mihī loquī.* I must (It is necessary for me to) speak.
RULE : *Necesse est* takes a Dative of the person.

### Oportet.

**453** *Oportet mē scīre.* I ought to know. (It behoves me to know.)
*Oportēbat (Oportuit) tē scīre.* You ought to have known *or* should have known : (*i.e.* it behoved you to know : cf. § 356, p. 142, and note).

> **Rule**: With *oportet* 'ought'
> the person who 'ought' is denoted by an Accusative;
> what he ought to do is expressed by an Infinitive.
> (For *Oportet sciās*, You ought to know, see § 368f.)

### Fallit, fugit, praeterit; decet, juvat, dēdecet.

**454** *Nōn mē fallit* (*fugit, praeterit*). It does not escape my notice.
*Ōrātōrem dēdecet īrascī*. It ill becomes a public speaker to get angry.

> **Rule**: With the verbs
> *fallit, fugit, praeterit* | it escapes the notice of
> *decet, juvat, dēdecet* | it beseems, delights, does not beseem
> the person is denoted by an Accusative.

☞ For fierī potest ut . . . 'it is possible that . . .' see § 368e.

## PREPOSITIONS.

**455** Phrases formed with Prepositions are used in Latin chiefly as Adverb-equivalents: comparatively rarely as Adjective-equivalents. Yet we find such phrases as *liber dē amīcitiā*, 'a book about friendship'; *nōbilis ad Trasumēnum pugna*, 'the celebrated battle at the lake Trasimeno'; *mors sine glōriā*, 'a death without glory'; *ad quartum ā Cremōnā lapidem*, 'at the fourth milestone from Cremona': but a Participle is more commonly added, e.g. *ante proelium in Thessaliā factum*, 'before the battle in Thessaly.'

☞ For details as to the meanings of prepositions the dictionary must be consulted.

### 1. Prepositions taking the Ablative.

**456** Dē *monte*, Down from the mountain.
  *Dē hāc rē*, Concerning this matter.
Cum *amīcō*, Together with a friend.
Cōram *jūdicibus*, In the presence of the jury.
Ā *mē*, From me. Ab *urbe*, From the city (cf. Accidence § 300).
Ē *domō*, Out of the house. Ex *urbe*, Out of the city (cf. § 300).
Sine *tē*, Without you.
*Faece* tenus, To (As far as) the dregs.
  [*Tenus* is placed after its case. Sometimes it takes the Genitive in verse, e.g. *labrōrum tenus*, as far as the lips.]
Prō *aedibus*, In front of the house.
  *Prō patre pugnat*, He fights instead of (on behalf of; for) his father.

**Prae** *nōbīs beātī estis,* You are happy in comparison with us.
*Prae lacrimīs loquī nōn possum,* I cannot speak for tears.

RULE: Put the Ablative with *dē,*
*Cum* and *cōram, ab* and *ē,*
*Sine, tenus, prō,* and *prae.*

**457** ☞ On *palam* 'openly' and *clam* 'secretly' see § 300. When used as Prepositions (post-Augustan and poetical) they take the Ablative: e.g. *palam populō,* 'in the presence of the people': *clam vōbīs,* 'without your knowledge.'

### 2. Prepositions taking either Accusative or Ablative.
#### In, sub.

**458** In *urbem eō,* I am going into the city.
In *urbe sum,* I am in the city.
Sub *mūrōs prōgressus est,* He advanced up to the walls.
Sub *mūrīs constitit,* He halted beneath the walls.

RULE: *In* and *sub* denoting *motion towards* take the Acc.
denoting *rest at* take the Abl.

*Sub* with Abl. may mean 'deep in': e.g. *sub antrō.*
*Sub* with Acc. may mean 'just before': e.g. *sub noctem.*

#### Super, subter.

**459** Super *montēs iter fēcit (constitit),* He marched over (halted upon) the mountains.
Super *hāc rē nōn dīcam,* I shall not speak about this.
Subter *moenia flūmen lābitur,* A river flows beneath the walls.

RULE: *Super* denoting *motion towards* or *rest at* takes the Acc.
denoting *about (concerning)* takes the Abl.
*Subter* denoting *motion towards* or *rest at* takes the Acc.

The Abl. with *super* and *subter* is found in the poets, but without distinction of meaning.

### 3. Prepositions taking the Accusative.

**460** Ad *rēgem venit,* He comes to the king.
Adversus *hostem pugnat,* He is fighting against the enemy.
Ante *pugnam glōriātus est,* He boasted before the battle.
Apud *patrem est,* He lives with his father (at his father's house).
Circum *oppidum cucurrit,* He ran round the town.
Circā *secundam hōram vēnit,* He came about the second hour.
Citrā (Cis) *flūmen constitit,* He halted on this side of the river.
Contrā *hostem prōgreditur,* He marches against the enemy.

**Ergā** *eum benevolens es,* You are kindly disposed towards him.
**Extrā** *urbem habitant,* They dwell outside the city.
**Infrā** *mūrōs consēdit,* He sat down beneath the walls.
**Inter** *amīcōs vīvō,* I spend my life among friends.
**Intrā** *urbem habitābat,* He used to live within the city.
**Juxtā** *oppidum est collis,* There is a hill near the town.
**Ob** *hanc rem maeret,* He is grieved on account of this.
**Penes** *hostēs est,* It is in the power of the enemy.
**Per** *silvam errābam,* I was strolling through the wood.
**Pōne** *aedēs arbor est,* There is a tree behind the house.
**Post** *pugnam rediērunt,* After the battle they returned.
**Praeter** *urbem iter fēcit,* He marched past the city.
    *Praeter hanc rem nihil dīcō,* I say nothing except this.
**Prope** *hortōs habitat,* He dwells near the garden (§ 417).
**Propter** *hanc rem gaudet,* He rejoices on account of this.
**Secundum** *flūmen prōgreditur,* He advances along the river.
**Suprā** *caput ējus pendēbat,* It was hanging above his head.
**Trans** *flūmen nāvit,* He swam across the river.
**Ultrā** *montēs habitant,* They dwell beyond the mountains.
**Versus** *orientem spectat,* It looks towards the east.

## VOICES.

**461**    The Passive Voice is sometimes used **reflexively** like the Greek Middle, to denote an action done *to oneself* (chiefly poetical):

*Induor vestem.* I put on a garment. (= *Induō mihi vestem,* or *Induō mē veste.*)

*Exuitur cornua.* She sheds her horns.

*Inūtile ferrum cingitur.* He girds on the useless sword. (= *Accingit sibi ferrum.*)

*Antīquum saturāta dolōrem.* Having sated her ancient grudge.

*Accingor ferrō.* I gird myself with the sword. (= *Accingō mē ferrō.*)

    OBS. 1. The Accusative in such instances denotes an Object, and must not be confused with the Accusative of Nearer Definition (§ 383).

    OBS. 2. In a few verbs the Active may denote an action done to oneself:

    *Accingunt operī.* They gird themselves for the work.

    *Jam verterat fortūna.* The luck had already changed. (cf. § 376c.)

For the **Impersonal Passive Construction** see § 316 *

## MOODS AND TENSES.

### Tenses of the Indicative.

#### Present.

**462** The Present is used :—

1. To describe an action as *now going on*, or a state as *now existing*:

   *Scrībō.* I am writing. *Videō.* I see. *Sciō.* I know.

**463** 2. To describe an action as *recurring habitually* in the present (Habitual Present) :

   *Scrībō.* I write. (I am wont to write = *scrībere soleō.*)

   *Ad quartam jaceō ; post hanc vagor ; unguor olīvō.* Till the fourth hour (*i.e.* 10 a.m.) I lie in bed; after that I take a stroll ; I anoint myself with oil.

   *Lacte, cāseō, carne vescor.* I live upon milk, cheese, and flesh.

**464** By an extension of these senses the Present comes to be used :—

3. To describe an action as merely begun or attempted in the present (though still marked as *in course of accomplishment*) :

   *Consulēs sēdant tumultum.* The consuls begin *or* try to quell (= *sēdāre incipiunt* or *cōnantur*) the tumult.

**465** 4. With adverbial expressions of time like *jam diū, jamdūdum, jampridem, multōs annōs,* etc., to describe an action as begun in the past, but continued up to the present (Eng. 'has been ——ing'). *Jam diū hīc habitō,* I have now been living here for a long time. Compare :—

   " Over the great restless ocean
   Six-and-twenty years *I roam,*"

   where ' I roam ' = ' I have been roaming.'

**466** 5. To denote what is true at all times (including the present) :—

   *Fortūna fortēs adjuvat.* Fortune favours the bold.

   *Bis bīna sunt quattuor.* Twice two is four.

**467**   6. In vivid narration of past events (Historical Present), as a substitute for the Past :

*Affertur nuntius clādis ; rex in publicō· esse nōn audet; inclūdit sē domī.* News is brought of the disaster; the king does not dare to appear in the streets; he shuts himself up at home.

**468**   ☞ Care must be taken in translating such an English form as 'it is written'. This, as a compound tense, is generally expressed by the Latin Present Passive (*e.g.* Many letters are written every day, *Multae epistulae quotīdiē scrībuntur*); but sometimes the same form may be used like the Perfect to denote the result of a past action. In such cases translate by Latin Perfect (*e.g.* The letter is written, = is in the state of having been written, *Epistula scripta est*).

### Imperfect.

**469**   The Imperfect is the Present of the past, *i.e.* has the chief meanings of the Present, transferred to past time. Thus it is used:—

**470**   1. To describe an action as *going on in the past*, or a state as *then existing* (Contemporaneous Imperfect) :

*Archiās eō tempore vīvēbat, et omnia sciēbat,* Archias was living at that time, and knew everything. So often in descriptions of scenery and localities, e.g. *Oppidum erat in colle ; rādīcēs collis duo flūmina subluēbant ; ante oppidum plānitiēs patēbat.* The town stood upon a hill ; two rivers washed the base of the hill; before the town extended a plain.

**471**   2. To describe an action as *recurring habitually* in the past (Habitual Imperfect) :

*Numquam in publicō loquēbātur.* He never spoke (used to speak = *loquī solēbat*) in public. *Rōmae bīnōs consulēs quotannīs creābant.* At Rome they would elect (= used to elect) a pair (§ 126) of consuls yearly.

**472**   By an extension of the contemporaneous sense, the Imperfect comes to be used :—

3. To describe an action as merely begun or attempted in the past (though still marked as *in course of accomplishment*) :

*Consulēs sēdābant tumultum.* The consuls began to (tried to) quell the tumult (cf. § 464). *Exercitum ad urbis praesidium revocābat.* He was for calling back the army to the defence of the city.

4. With adverbial expressions of time like *jam diū, jamdūdum, jampridem, multōs annōs*, etc., to describe an action as begun at some time previous, but continued up to the time spoken of in the past (Eng. 'had been ——ing,' cf. § 465). *Vīgintī annōs illīc habitābam.* I had been living there twenty years.

5. In letter-writing as a substitute for the Present (most frequently at the beginning or end of the letter) :—

*Haec scrībēbam hōrā noctis nōnā.* This I write at the ninth hour of night. (The writer places himself at the point of view of the recipient who, thinking of the action of writing, would say, 'This *he was writing* at the ninth hour.')

6. To express 'sudden discovery' of a fact already existing : *e.g.*—
*Ehem pater mī, tū hīc erās?* Dear me! you here father? [and I did not know it].
*Quantā labōrābās Charybdī!* In what a whirlpool art thou struggling! (HORACE.)

## Chief ways of translating the Imperfect (cf. § 177) :—

*Scrībēbat* { 1. He was writing.
2. He used to write.
3. He began (tried, wanted) to write. }

### Future.

The Future is used :—

1. To describe an action as about to occur (or a state as about to exist) hereafter:

*Diēs veniet.* The day will come. *Crās sextā hōrā cēnābō.* To-morrow at the sixth hour I shall be dining. *Proximō annō Rōmae habitābis.* Next year you will be living at Rome.

Distinguish :—*Moriar.* I shall die. *Moritūrus sum* (§ 491). I am doomed to die. *Mori volō.* I will die.

2. To express command or promise:

*Fīliae salūtem dīcēs.* Greet my daughter.

*Crās dōnāberis haedō.* To-morrow thou shalt be presented with a kid.

### Perfect.

**480** The Perfect is used to describe an action as *now completed*, or a present state as the result of an action now completed (Present Perfect):

> *Graecās litterās didicī.* I have learned Greek. [*Consuēvī.* I have accustomed myself (and, therefore, have the habit). *Nōvī.* I know. *Meminī.* I remember. *Ōdī.* I hate (cf. §§ 244, 245)].

**481** By a slight extension of this sense the Perfect is used:—

1. To signify that something no longer exists:

> *Vixī.* I have had my day (*i.e.* my life is over). *Dīxī.* I have done speaking (*i.e.* my speech is over). *Fuimus Trões.* We are Trojans no more (*i.e.* our existence as a nation is over).

**482** 2. To denote a universal truth (Gnomic Perfect):

> *Nōn aeris acervus et aurī dēduxit corpore febrēs.* A heap of brass and gold removes not fever from the body ('has never been known to remove').

### Past.

**483** The Past (which has the same form as the Perfect: § 177) is used to describe an action as occurring in the past:

> *Mortuus est annō centēsimō post urbem conditam.* He died a hundred years after the founding of the city.

**484** In recounting a number of past actions, which happened in succession, this tense is employed; each action is separately marked as simply past. The Past thus serves as the **narrative tense** of Latin:—

> *Vēnī, vīdī, vīcī.* I came, I saw, I overcame. (*Shakspeare's transl.*)

[By a narrative tense is meant a tense which answers the question, 'What happened next?']

### Past and Imperfect contrasted.

**485** The Imperfect often describes the circumstances attending the actions which the Past *narrates*. Hence the rule of an old grammarian: "In the Past the narrative progresses; in the Imperfect it halts":—

*Verrēs inflammātus furōre in forum vēnit ; ardēbant oculī, tōtō ex ōre crūdēlitās ēminēbat.* Verres, inflamed with passion, came into the forum ; his eyes gleamed (were gleaming), in his whole face barbarity was conspicuous.

**486** ☞ Great care must be taken in translating into Latin the ambiguous Past Tense of English. It may be translated :—

(i) by the Past, *e.g.* I *told* you so (*dīxī*).

(ii) by the Habitual Imperfect, *e.g.* He *spoke* (= *used to speak*) Latin fluently (*loquēbātur*).

(iii) by the Contemporaneous Imperfect, *e.g.* The town was in an uproar ; men *shouted* (= were shouting), women *wept*, dogs *barked* (*clāmābant, flēbant, lātrābant*).

### Pluperfect.

**487** The Pluperfect is used to describe an action as completed at some point of time in the past, or a past state as the result of an action completed in the past :

*Eō tempore bis sex librōs scripserat.* At that time he had written twelve books. [*Consuēveram.* I was accustomed. *Nōveram.* I knew. *Memineram.* I remembered. *Ōderam.* I hated: cf. § 480].

### Future Perfect.

**488** The Future Perfect is used :

1. To describe an action as completed at some point of time in the future, or a future state as the result of an action completed in the future :

*Crās redierō.* To-morrow I shall have returned. [*Consuēverō.* I shall be accustomed. *Nōverō.* I shall know, etc.: cf. § 480].

**489** Sometimes the Future Perfect may be translated by ' will be found to have . . .', or something equivalent :

*Ego certē officium meum praestiterō.* I, at any rate, shall be found to have done my duty (You will find that I have, etc.).

**490** 2. Like the Future (§ 479), to express command :

*Dē hāc rē vīderint sapientiōrēs.* About this matter let wiser people decide (literally, ' will be found to have . . .').

### Future Participle with *est, erat (fuit), erit*.

**491** A prospective action (*i.e.* an action relatively future) may be expressed in Latin, as in English, by the use of the Future Participle with the verb 'to be' (Periphrastic Conjugation):

*Scriptūrus est*, He is about (intending) to write.
*Scriptūrus erat (fuit)*, He was about (intending) to write.
*Scriptūrus erit*, He will be about (intending) to write.

**492** In the Passive no such forms are possible. Say:

*In eō est ut scrībātur*, It is ⎫
*In eō erat (fuit) ut scrīberētur*, It was ⎬ about to be written.
*In eō erit ut scrībātur*, It will be ⎭

### IN SUBORDINATE CLAUSES.

**493** The time of the subordinate clause is in most cases marked more accurately in Latin than in English:

1. In clauses referring to the future:

*Nātūram sī sequēmur ducem, numquam aberrābimus.* If we follow (= shall follow) Nature as our guide, we shall never go astray.
*Ut sēmentem fēcerĭs, ita metēs.* As you sow (= shall have sown), so shall you reap (cf. § 479.)
*Quī adipiscī vēram glōriam volet, justitiae fungātur (fungātur) officiīs.* Whoso desires to gain true glory, will discharge (let him discharge) the obligations of justice.

**494** 2. In clauses subordinate to an Habitual Present or Imperfect:

*Quum gallus cecinit, surgō.* Whenever the cock crows (= has crowed), I get up.
*Quum gallus cecinerat, surgēbam.* Whenever the cock crew, I used to get up.
*Quaecumque audīvī, haerent in memoriā.* Whatever I hear, I remember.
*Quaecumque audierat, haerēbant in memoriā.* Whatever he heard, etc.

**495** The time of the subordinate clause is in other cases marked less accurately in Latin than in English:

1. *Postquam, ubĭ, ut, simulatque* take the Perfect (for Pluperfect) in narrative:

*Ubĭ haec dixit, conticuit.* The moment that he had said this, he became silent. (Cf. § 347, example with postquam.)

**496** 2. *Dum,* 'while,' takes the Present (for Imperfect) in narrative (Ex. in § 347).

## The Subjunctive Mood.

**497** The Latin Subjunctive has to do the work of two moods, which were originally distinct, and which remained distinct in Greek (Subjunctive and Optative). In Latin they have been united so as to form a single **Subjective Mood**, expressing **Will and Thought**. In Simple Sentences and Principal Clauses, and also in some Subordinate Clauses, the Mood has a meaning which may be traced to one of its original meanings; but in some Subordinate Clauses the meaning has become so weakened that the Mood seems purely formal, and may be translated by the English Indicative.

**498**    I. **In Simple Sentences and Principal Clauses.**

(*a*) In Commands (Present), § 341a :
  *Eat.* Let him go.

(*b*) In Prohibitions (Perfect, Present), § 341b :
  *Nē fēcerīs.* Do not do it. *Nē eat.* Let him not go.

(*c*) In Wishes (Present, Imperfect, Pluperfect), § 342 :
  *Moriar!* May I die!

(*d*) In Concessions (Present, Perfect), § 343 :
  *Haec sint falsa sānē.* Granting this to be quite untrue.

(*e*) In Statements as to what ought to have been done (Imperfect, Pluperfect), § 340* :
  *Rem tuam cūrārēs.* You ought to have minded (been minding) your own business.

(*f*) In Deliberative Questions, *i.e.*, questions as to what is or was to be done (Present, Imperfect), § 344* :
  *Quid faciam?* What am I to do?

(*g*) In Modest Assertions or Questions (Present, Perfect, Imperfect), § 340 :
  *Dīcat aliquis.* Some one may say.

(*h*) In Principal Clauses of Conditional Sentences that speak of what *would be* or *would have been* (all tenses), § 355 :
  *Vellem esse Diogenēs.* I should wish to be Diogenes (*nisi Alexander essem*).

     II. **In Subordinate Clauses.**

**499**    (*a*) In Dependent Commands and Statements introduced by *ut, nē, quōminus*, or *quīn* (chiefly Present and Imperfect), § 367, 3-5 :
  *Ōrō ut veniās* (*Ōrō veniās*, §§ 367, 4, 369a, OBS. 3). I entreat you to come.
  *Nōn dubitō quīn errēs.* I doubt not that you are mistaken.

## THE SUBJUNCTIVE MOOD.

(*b*) In Dependent Questions (all tenses), §§ 370, 370†:
   *Nescio quid velīs.* I do not know what you want.
   *Nescio quid faciam.* I do not know what to do (Deliberative).

(*c*) In Final Clauses (Present, Imperfect), § 350:
   *Mīsit lēgātōs ut pācem peterent.* He sent ambassadors to sue for peace.

(*d*) In Concessive Clauses introduced by *quamvīs, licet, ut,* and *quum,* 'though' (all tenses), § 358:
   *Senectūs quamvīs nōn sit gravis, tamen aufert vīriditātem.* Old age though it be not burdensome, yet robs us of freshness.

(*e*) In If-Clauses that imply a negative (all tenses), § 355:
   *Nisi Alexander essem.* If I were not Alexander (*vellem esse Diogenēs*).

For the Subjunctive in other If-clauses cf. § 501.

(*f*) In *ut* or *sī* clauses subordinate to Contracted Comparative Clauses (§ 360):
   *Rīdēs quasi ineptum sit.* You laugh as though it were absurd.

(*g*) In Clauses introduced by *quum* 'as,' 'while,' 'after' (Temporal: Imperfect and Pluperfect), *quum* 'since,' 'because' (Causal: all tenses), *quum* 'though' (Concessive: all tenses), §§ 347, 349, 358:
   *Quum haec dixisset, conticuit.* Having said this, he held his peace.

(*h*) In Consecutive Clauses (Present, Imperfect, Perfect), § 352:
   *Nōn sum ita hebes ut istud dīcam.* I am not so dull as to say what you imply.

(*i*) In Subordinate Clauses of *Ōrātiō Oblīqua,* corresponding to the Indicative of *Ōrātiō Recta*:
   *Eō sibī minus dubitātiōnis darī, quod eās rēs, quās lēgātī Helvētiī commemorassent, memoriā tenēret.* (He said) that he felt the less hesitation, because he remembered the facts which the Helvetian legates had mentioned. ☞ In some dialects of English it would be possible to say 'should remember,' 'should have mentioned.'

# THE SUBJUNCTIVE MOOD.   191

**500**   OBS. In many kinds of Subordinate Clauses which ordinarily take the Indicative, the Subjunctive may be used to mark an action as merely *conceived, contemplated,* or *in prospect:* e.g.—

**501**   (i) In Conditional Sentences that otherwise resemble Class A (§ 354):

*Sī nōn possim dīcere, quid habet admīrātiōnis?* If I be unable to tell, what reason is there for surprise? (CICERO.)

*Sī fractus illābātur orbis, impavidum ferient ruīnae.* Should the welkin crack and fall upon him, the ruins will strike him undismayed. (HORACE, Od. III. 3, 7; cf. II. 2, 4; 14, 6; 17, 14.)

*Quī l faceret?  Sī vīvere vellet, Sējānus rogandus erat.* What was he to do? If he wanted to live, he had to entreat Sejanus. (SENECA: cf. 'If it *were* so, it was a grievous fault'—SHAKSPERE. Other instances in CÆSAR, B.G., VI. 34; B.C., III. 44; CICERO, De Amic., 11.)

☞ Such sentences may be called Conditional Sentences of Class C. Note that the Present Subjunctive refers to present or future time, and the Imperfect Subjunctive to past time: contrast § 355.

**502**   (ii) In Temporal Clauses introduced by *antequam, priusquam, dōnec, quoad, dum* (§ 347). Here the prospective sense becomes more prominent:

*Multa quoque et bellō passus, dum conderet urbem.* Much scourged too in war, till he should found his city. (VIRGIL.)

*Dum (Dummodo)* may be a Conditional Conjunction (= 'provided that'):

*Ōderint dum metuant.* Let them hate so long as they fear. (Neg. *nē.*)

(iii) In Adjective Clauses:

**503**   *Quī huīc pārēre velit, numquam committet ut aliēnum appetat.* He who should will to obey it (*i.e.* the divine law), will never allow himself to covet what is his neighbour's. (CICERO.)

**504**   Such an Adjective Clause often becomes equivalent to a Final, Consecutive, Causal, or Concessive Adverb Clause, or to an If-clause with implied negative (§ 364). In some cases the shade of difference between Indic. and Subj. is so slight that it cannot be rendered in English, e.g.—

*Sunt quī nōn habeant, est quī nōn cūrat habēre.* There are people (*i.e.* an indefinite class) that have nothing; there is one person (*i.e.* the poet himself) that does not care to have. (HORACE.)

*Sunt quī putent* . . . There are people that think . . . (CICERO.)

After a Negative { *Nēmō est quī audeat.* There is no one that ventures.
*Nēmō erat quīn* (= *quī nōn*) *scīret.* There was no one that did not know.

☞ Such clauses cite an act only to exhibit the *character* of the Antecedent, and may be called 'Characterizing Relative Clauses.'

**505**   Note the moods in clauses with restrictive sense: *quod sciam,* 'so far as I know'; *quod meminerim,* 'so far as I remember'; *quantum scio,* 'so far as I know.'

**506**   (iv) In *quod*-clauses: see note on § 368b, and cf. the following example:

*Sed illa palmāria, quod mundum dīxerit fore sempiternum.* But this is the finest (*i.e.* most absurd) thing of all, that he should have declared the universe to be destined to last for ever. (CICERO.)

## THE SUBJUNCTIVE MOOD.

**507** A Subjunctive is often found in clauses subordinate to a Subjunctive or Infinitive (Attractiō Modī):

*Quotusquisque est quī, quum mors appropinquet, nōn moveātur?* ... when death approaches.

*Quid mē prohibēret Epicūrēum esse, sī probārem quae ille dīceret?* ... I approved of what he says *or* said (cf. § 521).

*Dī tibī dent quaecumque optēs.* ... whatever you may pray for.

*Potentis est facere quod velit.* ... what he likes.

*Nōn dēstitit quibuscumque rēbus posset, patriam juvāre.* ... as best he could.

*Vereor nē augeam labōrem dum minuere velim.* I fear I may increase my labour, while I wish to lessen it.

**508** With these examples compare the following (Indic.):—

*Nōn intellegō quamobrem sī vīvere honestē nōn possunt, perīre turpiter velint.* (Here the Subj. might be misunderstood: cf. § 501.)

*Impūnē quae lubet facere, id est rēgem* (§ 530 OBS.) *esse.*

**509** A clause (especially a *quī* or *quod* clause) with a Subjunctive (whether subordinate to a Subj., Infin., or Indic.) is often *equivalent* to a subordinate clause in *Ōrātiō Oblīqua*:

*Aristīdēs ob eam causam patriā expulsus est quod praeter modum jūstus esset.* Aristides was banished for being, as they said, too just.

*Gallī Caesarī grātiās ēgērunt, quod sē magnō perīculō līberāsset.* The Gauls thanked Caesar for having freed them from great danger.

*Sōcratēs accūsātus est quod juventūtem corrumperet.* Socrates was accused of demoralizing the young men.

*Caesar ab Helvētiīs servōs, quī ad eōs cōnfūgissent, poposcit.* Caesar demanded of the Helvetians the slaves who, as he said, had taken refuge with them.

*Paetus omnēs librōs, quōs frāter suus relīquisset, mihī dōnāvit.* Paetus gave me all the books which, as he said, his brother had left. (But *quōs frāter ējus relīquerat* = had left, as a fact.)

*Cōnfīrmātīs mīlitibus nē, quod inīquitās locī attulisset, id virtūtī hostium tribuerent, legiōnēs ēduxit.* Having encouraged the soldiers not to attribute to the valour of the enemy what was due to the unfavourable character of the ground, he led out his legions.

**510** Note a curious idiom in which the idea of 'saying' or 'thinking' is, as it were, expressed twice over (by a verb of 'thinking' or 'saying,' itself in the Subj.).

*Rediit quod sē aliquid oblītum esse dīceret* or *existimāret* = *Rediit quod aliquid oblītus esset.* He returned, because (as he said, thought) he had forgotten something. ☞ So Engl. 'because he said he had forgotten something.'

## Tenses of the Subjunctive.

**511** Each of the four tenses of the Subjunctive may be used—

(1) To denote the same time as the corresponding tense of the Indicative;

**512** (2) As a Future-equivalent, whenever reference to the future is clear from the context. In such cases

the Present Subj. corresponds to the Future Indic.
„ Perfect Subj. „ „ „ Future Perf. Indic.
„ Imperf. Subj. „ „ „ Future Indic. } in past
„ Pluperf. Subj. „ „ „ Future Perf. Indic. } time.

*Vereor nē veniat (vēnerit).* I fear that he will come (will have come).

*Verēbar nē veniret (vēnisset).* I feared that he would come (would have come).

*Pollicentur sē omnia factūrōs, quae Caesar imperet (imperāverit).* They promise to do everything that Caesar shall order (shall have ordered).

*Polliciti sunt sē omnia factūrōs quae Caesar imperāret (imperāvisset).* They promised to do everything that Caesar should order (should have ordered).

**513** But when the reference to the future is not clear from the context, the Future Participle with *sim, essem,* etc., is generally used: *e.g.*—

*Nōn dubitō*          I do not doubt
  *quin scriptūrus sit.*          that he will write.
  *quin futūrum sit ut epistula scrībātur.*    that the letter will be written.

*Nōn dubitābam*       I did not doubt
  *quin scriptūrus esset.*         that he would write.
  *quin futūrum esset ut epistula scrīberētur.* that the letter would be written.

### Sequence of Tenses.

**514** The time of the Subordinate Clause may be either
  (A) adjusted to the point of view of the governing clause: *e.g.*—
    He *does* not know how much twice two *is.*
    He *did* not know how much twice two *was;*
or (B) independent of the point of view of the governing clause:
    He *did* not know how much twice two *is.*

**515** A. The tenses of the Subjunctive[1] for a present or future point of view are the Present and the Perfect (**Primary Sequence**). The tenses of the Subjunctive for a past point of view are the Imperfect and the Pluperfect (**Secondary Sequence**).

**516** The tenses of the Subjunctive are adjusted:—

(i) In Final Clauses (§ 350):

| | |
|---|---|
| **Laud-ō** (-ābō, -āverō) | I praise (I shall praise, etc.) |
| *ut* **lauder.** | that I may be praised. |
| **Laud-ābam** (-āvī, -āveram) | I was praising (I praised, etc.) |
| *ut* **laudārer.** | that I might be praised. |

*Lēgātōs* mittit (Historical Present) *qui pācem* **petant** (or **peterent**).
He sends ambassadors to sue for peace.

**517** (ii) In Dependent Questions (§ 370):

| | |
|---|---|
| **Rog-ō** (-ābō, -āverō) | I ask (I shall ask, etc.) |
| *quid* **faciat.** | what he does (is doing). |
| *quid* **fēcerit.** | what he has done (did). |
| *quid* **factūrus sit.** | what he will do. |
| **Nescit** *quot bis bīna* **sint.** | He does not know how much twice two is. |
| **Nescio** *quidnam causae* **fuerit.** | I do not know what the reason was. |
| **Rog-ābam** (-āvī, -āveram) | I was asking (I asked, etc.) |
| *quid* **faceret.** | what he was doing. |
| *quid* **fēcisset.** | what he had done. |
| *quid* **factūrus esset.** | what he would do. |
| **Nesciēbat** *quot bis bīna* **essent.** | He did not know how much twice two is (*or* was). |

*Nescio quidnam causae* **fuerit** *cūr nullās ad mē epistulās* **darēs.**
I do not know what the reason was why you did not write to me.

**518** (iii) In Noun Clauses introduced by *ut, nē, quōminus*, or *quīn* (§§ 368c, 368d, 368e, 368f, 369a, 369b):

| | |
|---|---|
| **Accidit** *ut* **veniam.** | It happens that I am coming. |
| **Accidit** *ut* **venīrem.** | It happened that I came. (Not *vēnerim*.) |

---

[1] The tenses of Subordinate Indicatives may also be adjusted: cf. Cæsar, B.G., II. 35 (*erant*), I. 6 (*impendēbat*).

## TENSES OF THE SUBJUNCTIVE.

**519** Note the following differences from English :

1. The Latin Perfect with primary sequence is comparatively rare, being found only where emphasis is laid on the *present state* (§ 480) :

> **Nōvistī (Meministī, Oblītus es)** *quid initiō dīxerim.* You know (You remember, You have forgotten) what I said at first.
>
> *Nē* **dubitāverīs** *quin in virtūte dīvitiae* **sint.** Do not doubt that in worth there is wealth.

**520** Far commoner is the Latin Past with secondary sequence, even in cases where English uses a Perfect with primary sequence :

> **Dīxī** *ut* **scīrēs.** I have spoken that you may know.
>
> *Hodiē* **expertus sum** *quam cadūca fēlicitās* **esset.** To-day I have discovered how transitory luck is.

**521** 2. The Imperfect Subjunctive in Conditional Sentences referring to present time takes secondary sequence :

> *Forsitan et pinguēs hortōs quae cūra colendī* | **ornāret, canerem.** Perchance I should tell also how husbandry decks the luxuriant garden (cf. § 507).

**522** We may, therefore, give the following general RULE FOR SEQUENCE IN ADJUSTED CLAUSES : Avoid the Imperfect and Pluperfect Subjunctive in dependence on a **Present, Future, or Future Perfect.** Avoid the Present and Perfect Subjunctive in dependence on an **Imperfect, Perfect, Past, or Pluperfect.**[1]

**523** OBS. Clauses depending on Participles and Infinitives are as a rule adjusted to the principal verb :

> *Verēns nē* **dēdātur, discēdit.** Fearing that he may be surrendered, he is going away.
>
> *Verēns nē* **dēderētur, discessit.** . . . might . . . went away.
>
> **Cupiō** *scīre quid* **velīs.** I desire to know what you want.
>
> **Cupiēbam** *scīre quid* **vellēs.** I desired . . . wanted.

**524** But a clause dependent on a Perfect Infinitive is adjusted to that Infinitive :

> *Dīcitur* **quaesīvisse** *quid* **agerem.** He is said to have asked what I was doing.

---

[1] In *Ōrātiō Oblīqua* beginners should use only Secondary Sequence (§ 515

## THE IMPERATIVE MOOD.

**525** B. The tenses of the Subjunctive in Consecutive Clauses are independent of the point of view of the governing clause:

*Tantum pecūniae in aerārium intexit, ut ūnīus imperātōris praeda fīnem attulerit tribūtōrum.* He brought so much money into the treasury, that the booty of one general put an end to the payment of tribute.

**526** The tenses of the Subjunctive in Dependent Questions are sometimes independent of the point of view of the governing clauses:

*Hic quantum in bellō fortūna possit, cognosci potuit.* On this occasion might be learnt what influence fortune has in war.

**527** So too in many Concessive and Causal Clauses.

## VERB-NOUNS AND VERB-ADJECTIVES.

**528** Verb-Nouns and Verb-Adjectives retain their verbal nature:

1. They take the same case as the verb to which they belong (though the Gerund and Supine with Acc. are, as a rule, avoided; § 536):

*Ars occāsiōne ūtendī.* The art of using an opportunity.

**529** 2. They are qualified by Adverbs (not Adjectives):

*Eadem totidem audīre.* To hear the same things so often.
*Armīs frequenter ūtī.* To employ armed force constantly.
*Lēgibus constanter pārendō.* By steadily obeying the laws.
*Vir magnopere colendus.* A person to be highly respected.
*Callidē nactus occāsiōnem.* Having skilfully found . . .

## The Infinitive.

**530** The Infinitive is used:

(a) As Subject (Neuter Gender, § 203) of *est (erat, fuit)*, and many impersonal verbs (§ 446):

*Eadem totid m audīre taedet.* To hear (Hearing) the same things so often is wearisome.
*Dulce et decōrum est prō patriā mori.* It is sweet and seemly to die for one's country.

OBS. When *esse* or *fieri* stands as Subject, with a Predicate Adjective or Noun belonging to it, the Pred. Adj. or Noun stands in the Accusative:
*Esse bonum magna laus est.* It is a great praise to be good.
*Consulem fieri magnificum est.* To be made consul is a splendid thing.
But after *licet* with the Dative, the Dative is used (cf. RULE, § 330 ☞ p. 127):
*Licet mihī esse beātō.* I am free to be happy.

(*b*) As a Predicate Noun :
*Vīvere est cōgitāre.* To live is to think.

(*c*) As Object, depending on certain verbs, § 330 :
*Nōlō eadem totidem audīre.* I am unwilling to hear the same things so often.

(*d*) As one of two Objects, depending on certain verbs, §333 :
*Doceō tē Latīnē scīre.* I am teaching you to understand Latin.

(*e*) As an Adverb-equivalent, qualifying Adjectives (chiefly poetical) :
*Dignus amārī.* Worthy to be loved (= *Dignus quī amētur*).
*Perītus cantāre.* Skilled in singing (= *Perītus cantanai*).

☞ 'The time to eat' etc. (Adjective-equivalent) is *tempus edendī* (§ 534).

(*f*) As equivalent to a finite verb :
  (i) In a Simple Sentence (Historical Infin.), § 339* :
    *Fors omnia regere.* Chance directed all.
  (ii) In a Noun Clause of a Complex Sentence (Accusative with Infin.), § 367, 1 :
    *Dīcō eum Latīnē scīre.* I say that he knows Latin.

**531** The Accusative with Infinitive is also used as an Exclamation or indignant Question : *Tē hōc dīxisse !* That you should have said this ! *Mēne inceptō desistere victam ?* What, I abandon my purpose baffled ?

**532** The same sense may be expressed by *ut* with the Subjunctive :
*Tū ut umquam tē corrigās !* To think of your ever reforming
*Egone ut cantem !* What, I sing !

## Tenses of the Infinitive.

**533** The three tenses of the Infinitive, called Present, Perfect, and Future, mark an action as **not completed, completed,** or **in prospect**:

{ *Constat eum scrībere.* It is well known that he **is** writing.
{ *Constābat eum scrībere.* It was well known that he **was** writing.

{ *Constat eum scrīpsisse.* It is well known that he wrote (**has** written).
{ *Constābat eum scrīpsisse.* It was well known that he **had** written.

{ *Constat eum scrīptūrum esse.* It is well known that he **will** write.
{ *Constābat eum scrīptūrum esse.* It was . . . that he **would** write.

*Spērō fore ut epistula scrībātur* (§ 368e). } = *Spērō* (*Spērābam*) *epistulam*
*Spērābam fore ut epistula scrīberētur.* }    *scrīptum īrī*.

## The Gerund and Gerundive.

**534.** The oblique cases of the Gerund supply a Genitive, a Dative, an Ablative, and (chiefly after *ad*) an Accusative, of the Present Infinitive Active:

*Discere jūcundum fierī potest.*  Learning may become pleasant.
*Cupit discere.*  He desires learning (cf. § 330).
*Prōpensus est* **ad discendum.**  He is inclined to learning.
*Studiōsus est* **discendī.**  He is desirous of learning.
*Operam dat* **discendō.**  He devotes himself to learning.
*Mens alitur* **discendō.**  The mind is nurtured by learning.

But instead of the Gerund with a dependent Accusative, a construction with the Gerundive (Adjectival form of the Gerund) is generally preferred, especially after a Preposition:

*Prōpensus est* **ad artem discendam** (to learning a craft).
*Studiōsus est* **artis discendae** (of learning a craft).
*Operam dat* **artī discendae** (to learning a craft).
*Mens alitur* **arte discendā** (by learning a craft).

☞ The dependent Noun stands in the Case in which the Gerund would have stood, and the Gerundive (for Gerund) agrees with it, as an Adjective. [*Discendī* **artem** becomes *artis discendae*.]

**535.** The Nominative of the Gerund with *est, erat, erit*, etc., assumes the meaning of 'must' or 'ought'; so, too, the Gerundive, as a Predicate Adjective, e.g.—

**Discendum** *est nōbīs.*  { Learning is for us.
　　　　　　　　　　　　　　We have to learn (§ 412).
　　　　　　　　　　　　　　We must (ought to) learn.

*Nunc est* **bibendum.**  Now we (one) must drink.

**Ars** *nōbīs* **discenda** *est.*  { A craft is for us to-be-learnt.
　　　　　　　　　　　　　　　　　　A craft must be learnt by us (§ 413).
　　　　　　　　　　　　　　　　　　We must (ought to) learn a craft.
　　　　　　　　　　　　　　　　　　[For *Discendum est nōbīs artem.*]

**536.** Thus we have the GENERAL RULES:

1. Avoid the Gerund with a dependent **Accusative**.
2. With the Gerund and Gerundive the person who 'must' or 'ought' is denoted by a Dative.

## THE SUPINES.

**537** But clearness or euphony demand:
*Studium* aliquid inveniendī. The desire of finding something.
Agendī grātiās *causā*. For the sake of expressing gratitude.
Hostī ā mē *parcendum est*. I ought to spare the enemy (§ 538).

**538** Note **Oblīvīscendum** *est injūriārum*. We ought to forget wrongs (§ 327*).
Hostī parcendum *est*. One ought to spare an enemy (§ 328).
Vī ūtendum *est*. We must use violence (§ 329*).

RULE: Use the Gerund (not Gerundive) of verbs which take a Genitive, Dative, or Ablative. [Yet the Gerundive of verbs which take an Ablative is used instead of the Gerund in -ī or -ō with a dependent Ablative: e.g.

*Nōn opus est* vī ūtendā. There is no need to use (of using) violence.
Occāsiō vītae fruendae. An opportunity of enjoying life.

☞ These verbs originally took an Accusative (for Ablative)].

**539** The Gerund and Gerundive never depend on *sine*, 'without':

'I did it without noticing (without knowing)' is *Imprūdēns (Ignārus, Īnscius) fēcī*.
'He returned without accomplishing his purpose' is *Rē infectā rediit*.
'You cannot do good to another without doing good to yourself' is
    *Alterī nōn potes prōdesse quin (ut nōn:* § 352*) tibi ipsī prōsīs*.
'You blame without understanding' is *Culpās neque intellegis*.

**540** The Gerundive is also used

1. In a Predicate of the 5th Form, with *dō, trādō, cūrō, mittō, concēdō, suscipiō, locō, condūcō*: e.g.

*Trādidit urbem dīripiendam*. He handed over the city to-be-plundered.
*Pontem faciendum cūrāvit*. He had a bridge made.

**541** 2. As an Attribute: e.g.

*Rēs magnopere expetendae*. Things earnestly to-be-desired.
*Homō vix ferendus*. An unendurable fellow.

But 'an incurable disease' (' a disease which cannot be cured') is *morbus quī sānārī nōn potest*.

## The Supines.

**542** The Supine in *-um* is used with verbs of motion, to denote purpose: e.g.

*Missī sunt pābulātum*. They were sent a-foraging (to forage).

For other (commoner) ways of expressing purpose, see § 351.

**543** The Supine in *-ū* is found only in a few phrases: e.g.

*mīrābile dictū*, strange to tell.
*incrēdibile (difficile, nefās) memorātū*, incredible (difficult, unlawful) to tell.
*optimum factū*, the best thing to do.

## The Participles.

**544** Participles are used :—

1. As Predicate Adjectives (Perf. Part., Fut. Part.): e.g.—
   *Gladiātor mortuus est.* The gladiator is dead (cf. §§ 188 483).
   *Gladiātor moritūrus est.* The gladiator is bent on death (§ 491).

2. As Attributes (Pres. Part., Perf. Part.): e.g.—
   *Gladiātor moriens.* A dying gladiator.
   *Gladiātor mortuus.* A dead gladiator.

☞ The Future Part. is not used as an Attribute in classical prose: except *futūrus*, e.g. *rēs futūrae*, 'the future.'

3. In the Ablative Absolute construction (§ 361).

**545** Many Participles have assumed the character :—

1. Of independent Adjectives :
   *Praesens pecūnia.* Ready money (cf. § 215).
   *Certa poena.* Certain punishment.

2. Of Nouns:
   *Amans.* A lover.        *Adulescens.* A young man.
   *Factum.* A deed.        *Candidātus.* A candidate.
   *Senātūs consultum.* A resolution of the Senate.

**546** The Present Participle is used in a Predicate of the 2nd Form only when it has acquired the meaning of an independent Adjective or Noun : e.g.—
   *Dictō sum audiens.* I am obedient to command.

### Ways of Translating the Participles.

**547** The Participle may be equivalent to a

Temporal Clause : *Servius regnans*[1]  'Servius, while he is (was) king . . .'

Causal Clause :         „        „     'Servius, because he is (was) king . . .'

Conditional Clause :    „        „     'Servius, if he is (was, were, etc.) king . . .'

Concessive Clause :     „        „     'Servius, though he is (was) king . . .'

Co-ordinate Sentence: *Urbem captam incendērunt.*  'They captured the city and fired it.'

Note that in this use the Participle has no separate Subject of own. (Contrast Ablative Absolute, § 361.)

---

[1] *e.g.* in *Servius regnans populō cārus est (erat).*

**548** The Participle and Noun may often be translated together by a Noun followed by *of* . . . :

*Ocāsus Caesar multīs pulcherrimum facinus vidēbātur.* The slaying of Cæsar seemed to many a glorious deed.
*Post urbem conditam.* After the foundation of the city.

### Temporal Meaning of the Participles.

**549** The three Participles called Present, Perfect, and Future mark an action as **not completed, completed,** or **in prospect**:

{ *Legens saepe obdormiō.* While I **am** reading, I often fall asleep.
{ *Legens obdormīvī.* While I **was** reading, I fell asleep.
{ *Locūtus taceō.* I **have** said my say, and am silent.
{ *Locūtus tacēbam.* I **had** said my say, and was silent.
{ *Reditūrus sum.* I am about to return.
{ *Reditūrus eram.* I was about to return.

**550** OBS. 1. The Perfect Participle of many Deponent and Semi-deponent Verbs is used with the sense of the Present Participle, e.g. *veritus*, 'fearing'; *ratus*, 'thinking'; *ausus*, 'daring'; *confīsus*, 'trusting'; *diffīsus*, 'distrusting,' etc.

**551** OBS. 2. The Present Participle occasionally has habitual sense:
*Dīxit eum capācem sed aspernantem.* He called him able but a scoffer.

**552** The want of a Perfect Participle Active (§ 201) is variously supplied. 'Having said this, he departed,' may be translated:

*Quum haec dīxisset* (§ 347) *abiit.*
*Hīs dictīs* (Passive Construction : Abl. Abs., § 361) *abiit.*
*Haec locūtus* (Deponent Verb, § 221) *abiit.*

**553** The want of a Present Participle Passive (§ 201) is variously supplied. 'Being distressed by want of provisions, the enemy surrendered,' may be translated as follows:

*Hostēs quum inopiā frūmentī premerentur* (§ 347), *sē dēdidērunt.*
*Hostēs, quī inopiā frūmentī premerentur* (§ 364). *sē dēdidērunt.*
*Inopiā frūmentī labōrantēs* (*labōrō*, 'I am distressed') *hostēs sē dēdidērunt.*

**554** CAUTION 1. The English (but not the Latin) Pres. Part. is often used loosely with completed sense. 'Mounting his horse, he galloped off to Rome' is *Quum equum cōnscendisset* (*Equō cōnscēnsō*) *Rōmam āvolāvit.* Contrast ' (While) mounting his horse, he heard the news,' *Equum cōnscendens nuntium accēpit.*

**555** CAUTION 2. 'Those standing by,' etc., is a peculiarly English idiom (= *Adstantēs* or *Quī adstābant*): cf. § 567.

## PRONOUNS AND ADJECTIVES CONNECTED THEREWITH.

**556** **Personal Pronouns and Possessive Adjectives.**

'Of me,' 'of you,' 'of him,' etc., are generally expressed, *not* by the Genitives in -*i* and -*um* of the Personal Pronouns (cf §§ 558, 559), but by a Possessive Adjective or Pronoun (§ 135), or by the Genitives *ējus, eōrum, eārum* (§ 131), *illīus, illōrum, illārum*:

*Amīcus meus.* My friend. ('A friend of mine' is *Ūnus ex amīcīs meīs* or *Amīcus meus.*)
*Quae anteā patris fuērunt, nunc mea sunt.* What once belonged to my father is now mine.
*Benevolentia tua.* Your kindness.
*Hōc est consilium ējus.* This is his plan.
*Consilium suum mūtāvit.* He has changed his plan (cf. § 562).
*Nōn est nostrum arma trādere.* It is not our habit (cf. § 389) to yield up our arms.
*Aut vestrō aut Hennensium sanguine Henna inundābitur.*

**557** OBS. The Genitive implied in the Possessive Adjective may be qualified by an Adjective:
*Meā ūnīus operā.* By the agency of me alone.

**558** The **Genitives in -ī** of the Personal Pronouns (*meī, tuī, suī, nostrī, vestrī,* § 128), are used chiefly as Objective Genitives (§ 397):
*Mementō meī (Memor es meī).* Remember me.
*Amor suī.* The love of oneself. 'Amour propre.'
*Odium vestrī.* The feeling of hatred against you.

**559** The **Genitives in -um** of the Personal Pronouns (*nostrum, vestrum,* § 128) are used only as Partitive Genitives (§ 390), and in connection with the Genitive *omnium*:
*Multī nostrum (vestrum).* Many of us (of you).
*Patria est commūnis omnium nostrum parens.* Our country is the common mother of us all ('of all of us': § 394).

**560** Thus we have the following summary of results:—

|  | generally. | in objective sense. | in partitive sense. |
|---|---|---|---|
| of me | *meus* | *meī* |  |
| of him | *ējus* or *suus* | *ējus* or *suī* |  |
| of us | *noster* | *nostrī* | *nostrum* |

## PRONOUNS AND ADJECTIVES CONNECTED THEREWITH. 203

**561** The Possessive Adjectives are frequently omitted when the sense would be clear without them:
*Oculīs cernimus.* We see with our eyes.

**562** Sē (sēsē), suī, sibī, and suus generally refer to a **Subject**:
Either (1) to the Subject of the same sentence or clause:
*Sē amat.* He loves himself.

**563** Or (2) to the Subject of the governing clause (so especially in Noun Clauses, and in Clauses subordinate to Noun Clauses):
*Sciēbat sē errāvisse.* He knew that he had been wrong. (He knew himself to have been wrong.)
*Orāvit ut sē dēfenderem.* He entreated me to defend him.

Here ambiguity may easily arise:
*Hortātur sociōs: recēdant et sē ad meliōra tempora reservent; sibī cum Spartānīs fortūnam experiendam.* He exhorts his allies to retire and reserve **themselves** for happier days: that he had to try his fortune with the Spartans.

**564** OBS. 1. But suus, in the sense of 'his own,' sometimes refers to some word which is not the Subject:
*Scipiŏ Syrācūsānīs suās rēs restituit.* Scipio restored to the people of Syracuse their own property.

**565** OBS. 2. 'The general and his soldiers fled' is *Dux militēsque ējus fūgērunt.* Here *dux militēsque ējus* is the Subject; 'his' does not *refer* to the Subject, but is part of it.

**566** 'One another' is expressed in Latin
(1) By a phrase formed with *inter*:
*Frātrēs inter sē amāre dēbent.* Brothers ought to love one another.
*Prōdesse inter sē.* To be mutually helpful.
*Rēspublica nōs inter nōs conciliat.* The state reconciles us one to the other.

(2) By *alter ... alterum*, when two persons are spoken of; *alius ... alium*, when more than two persons are spoken of:
*Frātrēs alter alterī prōdesse dēbent.* Two brothers ought to help one another.
*Gallī alius alium cohortātī sunt.* The Gauls exhorted one another.

(3) By repetition of the Noun:
*Cīvēs cīvibus parcere aequum est.* It is right that fellow-citizens should spare one another.

**567** The **Demonstrative** *is, ea, id* is omitted in Latin examples like the following, where English has 'that' or 'those':
1. *Terentiī fābulīs minus dēlector quam* **Plautī**. I take less pleasure in the plays of Terence than **in those of Plautus**

2. *Adstantēs.* **Those** standing by. (= Those who were standing by, *Eī quī adstābant.*) ☞ *Eī adstantēs* would mean 'They, standing by': cf. § 555.

**568** Note the frequent use of *tam, tot, tantus* with a Demonstrative:
*Hōc tam turpe bellum.* This disgraceful war.
*Hic tantus vir.* This great man.
*Haec tot exempla.* These many instances.

**569** **Relative Pronouns and Adjectives.** Contrast Latin and English usage in such examples as the following:

**Quam** *quisque nōrit* **artem**, *in hāc sē exerceat.* Let each man practice himself in **the craft which** he understands. (Literally, What craft each man understands, in that, etc.)
*Centum talenta*, **quae pecūnia** *maxima est.* A hundred talents, **a sum of money which** is very great.
*Themistoclēs dē servīs suīs* **quem** *habuit* **fidēlissimum** *mīsit.* Themistocles sent **the most trusty slave that** he had.
*Quā es prūdentiā.*    ⎱ Considering your foresight,
*Quae est prūdentia tua.* ⎰ = *prō prūdentiā tuā.*

For *quī* = *et is, sed is, nam is,* see § 314\* : cf. § 371\* (*Ōrātiō Oblīqua, Peculiarities,* 4).

**570** OBS. 1. Note *quod sī,* 'but if'; *quod quum,* 'but since.'

**571** OBS. 2. Sometimes the Relative serves to link to a Principal Clause a group consisting of two clauses:

*Errāre mālō cum Platōne,* **quem** *quantī faciās* **sciō.** I prefer to err with Plato, and I know how highly you think of him.
*Nōn est polītus iīs artibus,* **quās quī** *tenent ērudītī appellantur.* He is not accomplished in those arts, the possessors of which are called cultured.

**572** Carefully distinguish the **Indefinite Pronouns and Adjectives** (1) from one another:

*Negō ante mortem* **quemquam** *esse beātum.* I deny that **any one at all** is happy before death.
*An* **quisquam** *Croesō dīvitior erat?* Was **any one at all** richer than Croesus?
*Sine* **ullā** *spē.* Without **any** hope **at all.**
**Quīvīs (Quīlibet)** *istud facere potest.* **Any one you like** can do that.
*Est hōc* **aliquid,** *tametsī nōn satis.* This is **something,** though not enough.
*Nōn sine* **aliquā** *spē.* Not without **some** hope.

# CONJUNCTIONS.

Sī quis haec dīcat ... If **any one** were to say this.
Athēniensis **quīdam**. **A certain** Athenian.
Suum **cuīque** incommodum ferendum est. **Each** man must bear his own burden.

☞ *Quisquam* and *ullus* are used where the sense is negative. For *quis, quī*, see § 152.

**573** OBS. Note the use of *quisque* with Superlatives and Ordinals :
Optimus quisque. Every good person. The good (as a class).
Decimus quisque. Every tenth man. Quotusquisque. How few.

**574** (2) from the Relative Pronouns and Adjectives :
**Quisquis (Quīcumque)** hōc dīcit, errat. Whoever says this is mistaken.

**575**
### TABLE OF CORRELATIVES.

| Interrogative. | Demonstrative. | Relative. |
|---|---|---|
| *Pronouns and Adjectives.* | | |
| quis? *who?* | is, *that* | quī, *who* |
| uter? *which (of two)?* | alter { the one (of two) / the other (of two) } | uter, *whichever (of two)* |
| quālis? *of what kind?* | tālis, *such* | quālis, *as* |
| quantus? *how great?* | tantus, *so great* | quantus, *as* |
| quot? *how many?* | tot, *so many* | quot, *as* |
| *Adverbs.* | | |
| quotiens? *how often?* | totiens, *so often* | quotiens, *as* |
| quam? *how?* | tam, *so* | quam, *as* |
| quandō? *when?* | tum, *then* | quum, *when* |
| ubĭ? *where?* | ibĭ, *there* | ubĭ, *where* |
| unde? *whence?* | inde, *thence* | unde, *whence* |
| quō? *whither?* | eō, *thither* | quō, *whither* |
| quā? *along what line?* | eā, *along that line* | quā, *along which (line)* |

# CONJUNCTIONS.

### CO-ORDINATING CONJUNCTIONS.

**576** Co-ordinating Conjunctions link similar words or groups of words: *e.g.* two nouns, two adverbs, two sentences of the same kind, two clauses of the same kind. For list see § 314.

**577** Sentences are frequently introduced by Adverbs, such as *itaque, igitur*, 'therefore'; *tamen,* 'nevertheless'; *etiam, quoque,* 'also'; *quidem,* 'indeed.'

**578** Note that 'and' is frequently not expressed:
*Vēni, vīdī, vīcī.* I came, I saw, I overcame.
*Eumenēs omnēs cūrā, vigilantiā, patientiā vincēbat.* Eumenes surpassed all men in industry, watchfulness, and endurance. (= *Eumenēs omnēs cūrā* et *vigilantiā* et *patientiā vincēbat.* Note that in Latin, if one member of a series is linked by *et*, all must be linked.)

**579** *Atque* (= *ad* + *que*, 'and in addition,' 'and what is more') may stand before a vowel or a consonant: *āc* only before a consonant. *-que* (and *-ve*) are rarely attached to words that end with a short *e*.

**580** *An* introduces a Co-ordinate ..uestion:
*Audītis, an mē lūdit amābilis Īnsānia?*     Hear ye? or does a sweet frenzy mock me?

**581** Contrast: *Vinceris aut vincis.* You are conquered or conquer.
*Homō minimē malus, vel potius optimus.* A person by no means bad, or rather very good.

☞ *Aut* is used when one of the alternatives must be rejected: *vel* when either alternative may be accepted.

**582** *Neque, nec,* and *nēve, neu* are compounded of a Co-ordinating Conjunction (*-que* 'and,' *-ve* 'or') and a negative particle ('nor' = 'and not'). *Nēve, neu* introduce a Co-ordinate **Prohibition** or Co-ordinate Clause of Purpose:
*Memoriam pristinae virtūtis retinēte, nēve perturbātī sītis animō.* Retain the memory of your former valour and be not alarmed.
*Nē dixerīs, neu crēdiderīs.* Do not say so, and do not believe it.
Contrast: *Multum labōrat, nec respirandī fit cōpia.* He toils energetically, nor is there opportunity of taking breath.
*Nōn vīdērunt neque sciunt.* They have not seen, nor do they know.

**583** *Neque, nec* occasionally introduce a Co-ordinate Prohibition, or Co-ordinate Clause of Purpose.

'Both . . . and,' 'Either . . . or,' 'Whether . . . or,'
'Neither . . . nor.'

**584.** *Et dīcō et sentiō.* I both say so and think so.
*Aut vērum aut falsum est.* It is either true or false.
*Peccāvit igitur, pāce vel Quirīnī vel Rōmulī dīxerim.* He sinned therefore, I am inclined to say (§ 340) with all deference to either Quirinus or Romulus (i.e. *sīve deus est sīve homō*.)

☞ On *sīve . . . . sīve* see §§ 357, 370 Caution.

*Utrum vērum est an falsum ?*  }
*Vērumne est an falsum ?*       } Is it true or false?
*Utrum vērum est an nōn (annōn) ?* Is it true or not? (cf. § 370).
*Neque vērum est omnīnō, neque omnīnō falsum, sed aliquā ex parte vērum.* It is neither altogether true nor altogether false, but partially true.

**585.** Notice *neque . . . et,* 'not only not . . . but':
*Nec mīror et gaudeō.* Not only am I not surprised, but I rejoice.

## SUBORDINATING CONJUNCTIONS.

**586.** A list of Subordinating Conjunctions is given in § 346 (Adverb Clauses). Some of these are also used (with slightly different sense) in Noun Clauses (see §§ 367, 2–5).

For *quamquam* 'and yet,' Co-ordinating Conjunction ( =*atqui*), see § 314.*

## INTERJECTIONS.

**587.** *Ō mē miserum.* Oh! unhappy that I am. (Acc. of Exclamation: § 386.)
*Ō formōse puer.* Ah! fair boy. (Vocative: § 373.)
*Heū mē miserum.* Alas! unhappy that I am. (☞ Not with Dat.)
*Ēheū fugācēs, Postume, Postume,* Alas! Postumus, dear Postumus,
  *Lābuntur annī.* the fleeting years glide past.
*Heī mihī.* Ah me! }
*Vae victīs.* Woe to the conquered! } Dat. of Interest (§ 411).
*Heūs Syre, ubi es ?* Ho! Syrus, where are you?
*Ecce nuntius.* Behold the messenger! (Here is the messenger.)
*Ēn Priamus.* Look! there is Priam.
*Prō dī immortālēs.* Ye immortal Gods!
*Prō deum hominumque fidem.* By all that is holy! (☞ Acc. with *prō* in this phrase only.)

## ORDER OF WORDS.

**588** The order of words in a Latin sentence is not rigidly fixed; but the following differences from English should be noted.

#### Normal Order.

**589**  1. The **Verb** stands at the end of the sentence or clause:

*Caesar Gallōs* **dēvīcit.**   Cæsar subdued the Gauls.
*Caesar proficiscī* **constituit.**   Cæsar determined to march.
*Gallī eō annō ā Caesare* **dēvictī sunt.**   The Gauls were subdued by Cæsar in that year.
*Caesar quum Gallōs* **dēvīcisset,** *in Italiam rediit.*   Cæsar having subdued the Gauls, returned to Italy.
*Constat Caesarem Gallōs* **dēvīcisse.**   It is well known that Cæsar subdued the Gauls.

**590**  But the verb *sum* frequently stands in other positions:
**Erant** *in illā urbe multi hominēs.*   There were many people in that town.

**591**  2. **Adjuncts,** including Negatives, precede the part of the sentence which they qualify:

**Vehementer** *gaudeō.*   I rejoice greatly.
**Glōriae** *cupidus.*   Desirous of fame.
**Urbem** *capere* **nōn** *potuit.*   He could not take the city.
**Urbem nōn** *capere potuit.*   He might have avoided taking the city.
**Nōn** *pulchrē cantāvit.*   He did not sing well.  (He sang badly.)
*Ex animī sententiā tū uxōrem habēs?*  **Nōn** *ex animī sententiā uxōrem habeō.*   Have you a wife, to the best of your belief?  I have a wife, not to my liking.  (A joke on the two meanings of *ex animī sententiā.*  'I have not a wife, to the best of my belief,' would have been *Ex animī sententiā uxōrem* **nōn** *habeō.*)

**592**  3. *Nē ... quidem,* 'not even,' 'not ... either,' takes the negatived word in the middle:

*Nē* **jocō** *quidem mentīrī dēbēmus.*   We ought not to lie even in fun.
*Nē* **hōc** *quidem vērum est.*   This is not true either.

**593**  4. No general rule can be given for **Attributes;** but note that in many common phrases the Adjective stands after the word which it qualifies: e.g.

*cīvis* **Rōmānus,** *populus* **Rōmānus,** *fēriae* **Latīnae,** *aes* **aliēnum,** *jūs* **cīvīle**, *Carthāgō* **Nova**, *pecūnia* **publica**, *dī* **bonī**, *pontifex* **maximus**, *vir* **fortis** (or **fortis** *vir*), *vir* **fortissimus**.

**594** So also do Predicate Adjectives, and Adjectives which are qualified by an Adjunct (as in English):

*Vercassivellaunus* **vīvus** *comprehenditur.* Vercassivellaunus is caught alive (cf. § 324, Obs. 1).
*Pugna ad Cannās* **commissa.** The battle fought at Cannæ.

**595** So also do Possessive Adjectives (§ 135) and *ējus, eōrum, eārum*:

*Amīcus* **meus.** My friend. *Amīcus* **ējus.** His friend.
*Patriam* **suam** *aurō vendidit.* He sold his country for gold.

**596** On the other hand, Demonstrative Adjectives (§§ 138-150), Interrogative Adjectives (§ 151), Numeral Adjectives (§ 122), and Adjectives denoting quantity, generally stand before the word which they qualify (as in English):

**hīc** *homō*, **ea** *cūra*, **vīgintī** *nāvēs*, **magna** *pars*, **magnō** *opere*, **parvum** *carmen*, **multī** *hominēs*.

**597** 5. One clause is frequently inserted in another (☞ The Principal Clause is printed in **clarendon type**):

**Datis** *etsī nōn aequum locum vidēbat suīs*, **tamen confligere cupiēbat.** Although Datis saw no favourable ground for his men, yet he desired to engage.
*Ōrātor* **metuō** *nē languescat senectūte.* I fear that the speaker may grow feeble in old age.

**598** But a sentence like the following, with several clauses inside one another, like Chinese boxes, is to be avoided:

**At hostēs** *quum*, **quī**, *quae in castris gererentur*, cognoscerent, *misissent*, **ad flūmen contendunt**.

Say: **At hostēs** *quum misissent*, **quī**, *quae in castris gererentur*, cognoscerent, **ad flūmen contendunt**.

**599** 6. The following words stand after some other word:
  (i) *-que, -ve* (§ 314), *-ne*.
  (ii) *autem, vērō, enim* (§ 314), *igitur, quoque, quidem*, and sometimes *tamen*.
  (iii) The Indefinite *quis, quī* (§ 151), *aliquis, quispiam* (§ 340). *quō*, 'any whither,' *quā*, 'along any line.'
  (iv) On *mēcum, sēcum*, etc., see § 134.

### Variations of Normal Order.

**600** The normal order may be varied for the sake of **emphasis** or **rhythm**.

1. To put words in an unusual position (especially at the beginning or end of the sentence) is to make them emphatic:

**Gallōs** *Caesar dēvīcit.* Caesar subdued *the Gauls* (not the Spaniards).
*Gallōs dēvīcit* **Caesar.** *Caesar* (not Pompey) subdued the Gauls.
**Dēvīcit** *Caesar Gallōs.* Caesar *subdued* (not merely attacked) the Gauls.
*Aliud iter habēmus* **nullum.** Other road we have none.
**Tuus** *pater haec nōn crēdit.* Your own father does not believe this.

**601** When two similar groups of words are contrasted, the order may be either (i) the same, or (ii) the opposite.

(i) **Aliō** *locō*, **aliō** *tempore.* At another place, at another time. (Anaphora.)

(ii) *Multōs*   $\chi$   **dēfendī,**   Object—Verb. ⎫
      **laesī**       *nēminem.*   Verb—Object. ⎬ (Chiasmus.[1])

*Ōrātiō* (Subject) **pugnat** (verb), **repugnat** (verb) *ratiō* (Subj.).

**602** Anaphora and Chiasmus have been called 'the two chief forces which control the order of the Latin sentence.' (NÄGELSBACH.)

**603** 2. Prose has its rhythm as well as verse; but the rhythm of prose must be learnt by ear. Note, however, that the rhythm of verse should be avoided in prose; therefore avoid $-\cup\cup-\cup$ (end of hexameter), $-\cup\cup\stackrel{\cup}{-}$ (end of pentameter). Prose writers are fond of such endings as *esse videātur* ($-\cup\cup-\cup$), *comprobāvit* ($-\cup-\cup$), *auxerant* ($-\cup-$).

## PROSODY AND METRE.
### Prosody.

**604** Prosody teaches the quantity of syllables.

☞ (i) In the following rules the sign $\cup$ is used for syllables declared to be short. (ii) The rules do not apply to words borrowed from the Greek (§§ 20, 50).

---

[1] From χιδ{εω, 'to place in the form of the letter χ,' *i.e.* in cross order. So too in English: 'Fell it alone; alone it fell' (ROKEBY).

GENERAL RULES. (Cf. Accidence, §§ 2-6.)

**605** 1. A syllable is long when it contains
   (*a*) a naturally long vowel or diphthong;
   (*b*) a naturally short vowel followed by two consonants or a double consonant (*x* or *z*), even when the one consonant stands at the end of a word and the other at the beginning of the next. But when the two consonants are a mute (*p, b; t, d; c, g*) or *f*, followed by a liquid (*l, r*), the syllable may remain short.

**606** 2. A vowel standing before another vowel or *h* in words of Latin origin is generally short. (So, too, *prae-* in compounds: e.g. *prăeesse*.)

*Exceptions.*

(i) Genitives in *-ius*: e.g. *ūnīus, illīus* (§ 166).
(ii) Vocatives in *-āī, -ēī*: e.g. *Gāī, Pompēī* (§ 27).
(iii) *fīō, fīēbam, fīam*, etc.; but *flerem*, etc.; *fīeri* (§ 239): e.g. *Omnia jam fīent, fīeri quae posse negābam.*
(iv) In the 5th Decl. *-ēī* when a vowel precedes (*faciēī*), *-ĕī* when a consonant precedes (*spĕī*): (cf. § 56).

**607** 3. **Elision.** A final vowel or *-am, -em, -im, -om, -um* is not counted as forming a separate syllable in verse, when the next word begins with a vowel or *h* (cf. p. 111, note 3), but is said to be **elided** (*i.e.* 'struck out').

**608** 4. **Hiātus** means the non-elision of a final syllable in this position. Hiātus is allowed before and after an Interjection (e.g. *hĕū ŭbĭ pactă fĭdēs:* 7 syllables), and exceptionally under other circumstances (e.g. *Ter sunt cōnāti impōnĕrĕ Pēlĭō Ossam:* 14 syllables).

**609** 5. The contraction of two vowels in the same word is called **synīzēsis** (e.g. *dĕinde, dĕōram, antĕit:* 2 syllables each). *I* and *u* before a vowel in the same word sometimes become *j* and *v*, the two consonants then make the previous syllable long (cf. § 605. 1*b*): e.g. *flŭctōrum* becomes *flŭvjōrum, ăbĭĕtĭ* becomes *abjĕtĭ, tĕnŭĭs* becomes *tenvĭs*. Conversely *v* sometimes becomes *u*: e.g. *sĭlvae* becomes *sĭlŭae* (cf. p. 111, Obs. 1).

SPECIAL RULES.

## Words of One Syllable.

**610** Words of one syllable are long: e.g. *ā, āc, nē, rē* (add the compound *quārē*), *fās, pār, ōs (ōris), nōn, vīs* (Noun and Verb: add compounds, e.g. *māvīs*), *sīs* (add compounds, e.g. *adsīs, possīs*).

## Exceptions.

**611**  1. All words of one syllable ending in *b, d, t*:
e.g. *ăb, ŏb, sŭb; ĭd, quĭd, quŏd, sĕd; ăt, ĕt, ŭt, quŏt* (thus all 3rd Persons Singular, like *stăt, dĕt, fĭt*).

2. The following Pronouns and Adjectives: *ĭs, quĭs, quă* (Indef.: § 153); *hĭc* (very rarely short, cf. § 139).

3. *-quĕ, -vĕ, -nĕ.*

4. *ĕs,¹ făc, fĕr;*
   *vĭr, cŏr, fĕl;*
   *cĭs, ĭn, pĕr;*
   *ŏs,² văs,³ mĕl;*
   *bĭs and tĕr;*
   *ăn, nĕc, vĕl.*

## Words of more than One Syllable.

**612**  1. Final *-i, -o, -u, -as, -es, -os* are generally long: e.g. *vōcī, laudāvī; puerō, virgō, laudō; gradū, diū; mensās, aetās, moneās, monēbās; vōcēs, nūbēs, laudēs, monēs; dominōs, custōs.*

### Exceptions.

**613**  -**I**: *nĭsĭ, quăsĭ.*
  *mihĭ, tibĭ, sibĭ, ubĭ, il.ĭ.* (But *ubīque, ibīdem.*)
-**ŏ**: *egŏ, duŏ, citŏ, modŏ, quōmodŏ, dummodŏ, tantummodŏ.*
  *sciŏ, nesciŏ, putŏ, volŏ.* (☞ This *ŏ* is not found in other Verbs in the best period.)
  *Polliŏ, Scīpiŏ, Virrŏ* (and other proper names of 3rd Decl.).

-**ĕs**: (i) in Nom. Sing. of 3rd Decl. when Gen. has *-ĭtis, -ĕtis, -ĭdis*: e.g. *milĕs, segĕs, obsĕs* (except *abiēs, ariēs, pariēs*).
  (ii) in the Preposition *penĕs.*

-**ŏs**: *compŏs, impŏs.*

**614**  2. All other final syllables are generally short: e.g. *mensă, bellă; dominĕ, vōcĕ, laudārĕ; vōcĭs, cīvĭs, tristĭs, magĭs; dominŭs, genŭs, vōcibŭs, priŭs.*

### Exceptions.

**615**  -**ā**: (i) in Abl. Sing. of 1st Decl.: e.g. *mensā, dūrā.*
  (ii) in Imperative of 1st Conj.: e.g. *laudā.* (But *pută.*)
  (iii) in all words that do not admit of changes of form: e.g. *anteā, frustrā, extrā.* (But *ită, quiă.*)

-**ē**: (i) in Abl. Sing. of 5th Decl.: e.g. *faciē, diē* (*hodiē*).
  (ii) in Imperative of 2nd Conj.: e.g. *monē.* (But *vidĕ, carĕ.*)
  (iii) in Adverbs formed from Adjectives in *-us*: e.g. *dūrē.* (But *benĕ, malĕ*, § 170.)

---

¹ Thou art *or* be thou. (Add compounds, e.g. *adĕs, potĕs.*)
² i.e. *ŏs* (*ossis*), a bone: but *ōs* (*ōris*), see § 610.
³ i.e. *văs* (*vădis*), a surety: but *vās* (*vāsis*).

**-Is**: (i) in Dat. and Abl. Plur.: e.g. *mensis, pueris, nōbis, vōbis.* (Add the Adverbs *grātis, foris.*)
 (ii) in Nom. Sing. of 3rd Decl. when Gen. has *-itis, -inis*: e.g. *Samnis, Salamis.*
 (iii) in 2nd Sing. Pres. Ind. Act. of 4th Conj.: e.g. *audis.*
 (iv) *velis, nōlis, mālis.*
 (v) *fueris, laudāveris,* etc.

**-Us**: (i) in Gen. Sing. and Nom. and Acc. Plur. of 4th Decl.: e.g. *gradūs.*
 (ii) in Nom. Sing. of 3rd Decl. when Gen. has *-ūtis, -ūdis, -ūris*: e.g. *virtūs, palūs, tellūs.*

## Metre.

**616** Verses are made up of feet, just as music is made up of bars. The commonest feet are:—

1. The dactyl: | ♩ ♪ ♪ | e.g. *scrĭbĕrĕ, currĕrĕ.*
2. The spondee: | ♩ ♩ | e.g. *nōlī, nōlunt.*
3. The iamb: | ♪ ♩ | e.g. *dŏmōs, dŏmant.*
4. The trochee: | ♩ ♪ | e.g. *vōcĕ, mentĕ.*
5. The anapaest: | ♪ ♪ ♩ | e.g. *mĭsĕrōs, ăbĭgunt.*

Trochee trips from long to short;
From long to long in solemn sort
Slow Spondee stalks; strong foot ! yet ill able
Ever to come up with Dactyl trisyllable.
Iambics march from short to long:
With a leap and a bound the swift Anapaests throng.
COLERIDGE.

**617** The **dactylic hexameter** consists of 5 dactyls and a spondee.[1] In the 1st, 2nd, 3rd and 4th foot a spondee may be substituted for a dactyl. The verse accent (*ictus*) falls on the first syllable of each foot.

**618** Occasionally the 5th foot is a spondee; the verse is then called 'spondaic.'

**619** To scan a verse is to divide it into feet:—

| ♩ ♪ ♪ | ♩ ♪ ♪ | ♩ ♪ ♪ | ♩ ♪ ♪ | ♩ ♪ ♪ | ♩ ♪ |
|---|---|---|---|---|---|
| Quadrŭpĕ- | dantĕ pŭ- | trem sŏnĭ- | tū quătĭt | ungŭlă | campum |

---

[1] The last syllable of this and other kinds of verse may be shortened or lengthened.

## METRE.

♩♪♪ | ♩♪♪ | ♩ ♩ | ♩ ♩ | ♩♪♪ | ♩ ♩
Armă vĭ- | rumquĕ că- | nō Trō- | jae qui | prīmŭs ăb | ōris

♩ ♩ | ♩♪♪ | ♩ ♩ | ♩ ♪♪ | ♩♪♪ | ♩ ♩
Carthā- | gō Ĭtălĭ- | am con- | trā Tĭbĕ- | rĭnăquĕ | longē

*The last syllable of Carthāgō is elided (§ 607).*

**620** The ends of words ought not to coincide throughout with the ends of feet. When a foot is *divided* by a word, it is said to have *caesūra* ('cutting').

**621** Caesūra after a long syllable is called 'strong,' after a short syllable *weak*. Either the 3rd or the 4th foot of the hexameter ought to have strong caesūra. The verse *Arma virumque*, etc., has two strong and three weak caesūrae.

**622** The **dactylic pentameter** (2 × 2½ feet) consists of two halves, each of which is formed of two dactyls followed by a long syllable (cf. note on § 617); in the first half a spondee may be substituted for either dactyl, but not in the second half.

♩♪♪ | ♩ ♪♪ | ♩ 𝄽 ‖ ♩♪♪ | ♩♪♪ | ♪ 𝄽
Frĭgĭdĭ- | us glăcĭ- | ē ‖ pectŭs ă- | mantĭs ĕ- | răt

♩♪♪ | ♩ ♩ | ♩ 𝄽 ‖ ♩♪♪ | ♩♪♪ | ♩ 𝄽
Nīl mĭhĭ | rescrī- | bās ‖ attămĕn | ipsĕ vĕ- | nī

**623** The pentameter is used only alternately with the hexameter (elegīac verse):

Dōnĕc ĕris fēlix, multōs nŭmĕrābĭs ămīcōs;
Tempŏră sī fŭĕrint | tristĭă, sōlŭs ĕrĭs.

In the hexameter rises the fountain's silvery column;
In the pentameter aye falling in melody back.
                                                COLERIDGE.

**624** The **iambic trimeter** consists of six iambs.

♪♩ | ♪♩ | ♪♩ | ♪♩ | ♪♩ | ♪♩
Beā- | tŭs il- | lĕ qui | prŏcul | negō- | tiīs

**625** For an iamb may be substituted:

(i) a tribrach ♪♪♪ in any foot. ⎫
(ii) a spondee in the 1st, 3rd, or 5th foot. ⎬ So in Horace and Catullus.
(iii) a dactyl in the 1st or 3rd foot. ⎪
(iv) an anapaest in the 1st foot. ⎭

## THE CALENDAR.

Names of the months (Adjectives: § 46):—*Jānuārius, Fĕbruārius, Martius, Aprīlis. Māius, Jūnius, Quīnctīlis* (July: called *Jūlius* after Julius Cæsar), *Sextīlis* (August: called *Augustus* after Augustus), *September* (Gen. *-bris*), *Octōber, November, December.* ☞ We retain the number of days of the Roman months.

The 1st day of each month was called *Kalendae* (f., Pl., 1st Decl.).
, 5th ,, most months ,, *Nōnae* ,, ,,
,, 13th ,, ,, ,, ,, *Idūs* (f., Pl., 4th Decl.).
But :— In March, July, October, May,
The Nones were on the 7th day,
(and the Ides on the 15th).

The intervening dates were expressed as so many days *before* the Nones, Ides, or Calends. In reckoning backwards the Romans were accustomed to count the 'terminus ā quō' as well as the 'terminus ad quem.' Thus *Nōnae* means the 9th ( = 8th) day before the Ides. (A good practical rule is to add one in subtracting from Nones or Ides, and two in subtracting from the number of days in the month, for dates before the Calends of the next month.)

Instead of the regular expression, e.g. *diēs quartus ante* with Acc., it was usual to say *ante diem quartum* with Acc. *Pridiē,* 'on the day before,' also generally took the Acc. The expressions *ante diem* ... and *pridiē* ... may themselves depend without change of form on a Preposition (e.g. *ex ante diem quartum Nōnās Jūniās, in pridiē Kalendās Decembrēs*).

### Examples.

'On the 1st of January,' *Kalendīs Jānuāriis* (Abl.; § 439).
,, 2nd ,, *ante diem quartum Nōnās Jānuāriās* (a. d. IV. Non. Jan.).
,, 3rd ,, *ante diem tertium Nōnās Jānuāriās* (a. d. III. Non. Jan.).
,, 4th ,, *pridiē Nōnās Jānuāriās* (prid. Non. Jan.).
,, 5th ,, *Nōnis Jānuāriis* (Non. Jan.).
,, 14th ,, *ante diem undēricēsimum Kal. Fēbruāriās* (a. d. XIX. Kal. Febr.).

In leap year a day was intercalated after February 24th (a. d. VI. Kal. Mart.), and called *diēs bis sextus ante Kalendās Martiās* (a. d. bis sextum Kal. Mart.).

## WEIGHTS AND MONEY.

The Roman pound weight (*libra* or *libra pondō,* or simply *pondō*[1]) and also the pound of copper (*ās,* m., gen. *assis,* the unit of money) were divided into twelve ounces (*unciae*). Fractions were expressed as follows:—

| | | | | | | | |
|---|---|---|---|---|---|---|---|
| *uncia* | 1/12 | *triens* | 1/3 | *septunx* | 7/12 | *dextans* | 5/6 |
| *sextans* | 1/6 | *quincunx* | 5/12 | *bēs* | 2/3 | *deunx* | 11/12 |
| *quadrans* | 1/4 | *sēmis* | 1/2 | *dōdrans* | 3/4 | | |

[1] A by-form for the Abl. of *pondus, ponderis.* 1 lb. of silver = *argentī pondō;* 10 lbs. of gold = *aurī pondō X.*

Thus ' an heir to a third of the estate ' was *hērēs ex triente*.
Money (even in large sums) was reckoned as so many sesterces (*sertertius*[1] or *nummus*).
Numbers of sesterces below a million were expressed by cardinal numerals : *e.g.*—

    *decem sestertii*              = 10 sesterces (HS X)
    *ducenti octōgintā sestertii* = 280 sesterces (HS CCLXXX)
    *decem milia sestertium*[2] (§ 28) = 10,000 sesterces (HS $\overline{\text{X}}$).

Numbers of sesterces above a million were expressed as so many times 100,000 sesterces, by numeral adverbs : *e.g.*—

    *deciēs sestertium* for *deciēs centēna milia sestertium* (§ 124)
        = 1,000,000 sesterces (HS | $\overline{\text{X}}$ | )

    *viciēs sestertium* = 2,000,000 sesterces (HS | $\overline{\text{XX}}$ | )
    *sestertium triciēs trecenta trigintā tria milia trecentōs trigintā trēs nummōs accēpi* = I have received 3,333,333 sesterces.

## ABBREVIATIONS.

### Praenōmina.

| | | | |
|---|---|---|---|
| A. | = Aulus | MAM. | = Mamercus |
| APP. | = Appius | N. *or* NUM. | = Numerius |
| C. *or* G. | = Gāius | P. | = Publius |
| CN. *or* GN. | = Gnaeus | Q. *or* QV. | = Quintus |
| D. | = Decimus | S. *or* SEX. | = Sextus |
| K. | = Kaesō | SER. | = Servius |
| L. | = Lūcius | SP. | = Spurius |
| M. | = Marcus | T. | = Titus |
| M'. | = Mānius | TI. *or* TIB. | = Tiberius |

### Other Abbreviations.

| | | | |
|---|---|---|---|
| A.U.C. | = annō urbis conditae | PRO C. | = prō consule |
| AED. | = aedīlis | PRO PR. | = prō praetōre |
| COS. | = consul *or* consule | PRO Q. | = prō quaestōre |
| COSS. | = consul *or* consulibus | Q. | = quaestor |
| D. | = dīvus | Q.B.F.F.S. | = quod bonum, fēlix faustumque sit |
| D.D. | = dōnō dedit | | |
| D.D.D. | = dat, dicat, dēdicat | S. | = salūtem |
| D.M. | = dīs mānibus | S.C. | = senātūs consultum |
| DES. | = dēsignātus | S.D.P. | = salūtem dīcit plūrimam |
| F. | = fīlius | | |
| IMP. | = imperātor | S.P.Q.R. | = senātus populusque Rōmānus |
| N.L. | = nōn liquet | | |
| O.M. | = optimus maximus | S.V.B.E.E.V. | = sī valēs bene est, ego valeō |
| P.C. | = patrēs conscriptī | | |
| P.M. | = pontifex maximus | V.R. | = utī rogās |
| PR. | = praetor | | |

---

[1] The sestertius [*sēmis tertius* = 2½ *assēs*] was worth rather more than 2*d.*; sesterces may be roughly converted into pounds sterling by dividing by 100 : *e.g.*—
    100,000 sesterces = £1,000 (more exactly £885 8*s.* 4*d.*).

[2] Also *decem sestertia*, 'sestertium' being converted into a Neuter Singular.

# INDEX TO SYNTAX.

The References are to Sections, except where p. stands (page).

abhinc, 445
Ablative, 422-434; Abl. Abs., 361
āc, 314, 359
Accusative, 375-386; with Infin., 333; 367, 1; 368 a, b; 368 f; 369 b, c; 531
Adjective as Noun-equiv., 309 (3); 325, p. 121; transl. by Adv., 324, Obs. 2; with Gen. 404-406; with Dat. 417; with Abl. 431
Adjective Clause, 313; 362—364
Adverb Clause, 313; 346—361‡
Agent, 327; 413
Agreement of Verb, 317; 319—323; of Pred. Adj. or Noun, 325—325†; 335; dep. on Infin., 330 ☞, 333 ☞, 530 Obs.; of Pronoun, 325, p. 121; of Attribute, 336; 337; of Relative, 363
aliquis, 572
an, 370; 580; 584
Anaphora, 601; 602
animī, 406
annōn, 370; 584
Antecedent, 362; 363, Obs. 2, 4
antequam, 347
Apposition, 337; 366, 3
atque, 314; 359
Attractio Modi, 507
aut, 314; 580; 581

Caesura, 620; 621
"can" "could," 330; 340 Caution; 356 (a)
Causal Clause, 349
Chiasmus, 601; 602
clam, 457
Cognate Object, 326*
Commands, 341 a
Comparative Clause, 359
Comparison, 360*; 426
Complex Sentence, 312; 346—371*
Compound Verbs, 377; 378; 418
Concession, 343
Concessive Clause, 358
Conditional Sentences, 353—357†; 501
Conjunctions, 576—586; Co-ord, 314; Subord., 346;—Relative, 362, Obs. 1
Consecutive Clause, 352

Constructio ad sensum, 318; 322*
Correlatives, 575
Cui-verbs, 328
cum=et, 322†

Dative, 410—421
dēficiō, 418
Deliberative Questions, 344*; 370†
Dependent Statements and Commands, 365; 367—369 c
Dependent Questions and Exclamations, 365; 370
domī, 435
dōnec, 347
dubitō, 330; 368 d
dum, 347; 496; 502

effugiō, 418
Elision, 607
et . . . et, 584
etsī, 358
Exclamations, 345

fierī potest ut, 368 e
Final Clause, 350
"for" prō or ad, 416
fore with Perf. Part. Pass., p. 162 note
forsitan, p. 159
Future Participle with esse, 357†; 491; 544 ☞;= Final Clause, 351 -

Genitive, 387—409
Gerund and Gerundive, 534—541 English Gerund depending on Prepositions, 369 b; 534; 539
Gnomic Perfect, 482

Habitual action, 463; 471; 494
haud scio an, p. 159
Hexameter, 617
Hiatus, 608
Historical Infin., 339*

Iambics, 624; 625
Ictus, 617
id aetātis, 392
id genus, 385
id quod, 363, Obs. 1
id temporis, 392
Imperative, 341 a, b, Obs, 1, 2; 343

# INDEX TO SYNTAX.

Imperfect Subj. referring to past time, 340; 340*; 344*; 352; 355, Obs. 2; 360; 501; referring to present time, 342, 355; referring to future time, 347 (*antequam*, etc.); 512
Impersonal Verbs, 446—454; 368 e, f
Impersonal Passive Constr., 316 *☞*
Indefinite 2nd Pers. Sing., 316*; 340
Indicative for Subj., 356; 500—510
Indirect Object, 331
Infinitive, 530—533; English Infin. and Gerund, as Subject, 530 (*a*); as Pred. Noun, 530 (*b*); as Object, 330; as one of two Objects, 333; in Noun Clause, 367 (368 a, 369 a, b, c); in Exclamations, 531; 532; expressing purpose, etc. (with 'to'), 350; 351; 364; 530 (*e*); 540—543
Interjections, 587
invidiae fui, 329
ita (limiting), 352, Obs.

Kinds of Sentences, 338

licet, 450, 358, 530 Obs.
Local Clause, 348
locō, 436
longum est, 357*

"may," "might" = 'am (was) permitted,' 450; = "can," "could," 356 (*a*), cf. 330; as auxiliary of mood, 340, 342, 343, 350, 358
mē miserum, 386
Metre, 616—625
Modest Assertions, 340
multum, 382, 448
"must," 452; 535

nātus, 442
ne, 344†; 370
nē, 340*; 341 b; 342; 343; 350; 368 c, 369 a, b;—"whether," p. 159, Obs. 1
nē . . . quidem, 592
nē quis, 350, Obs. 3
necne, 370
necque, nec, 314; 582; 583
"need," 451; 452
nescio an. p. 159
nescio quis, p. 159
nēve (neu), 314; 341 b; 350 Obs. 1; 582
nisi, 357
Nominative, 372

nōnne, 344†; 370
nōn quod (quō), 349, p. 138
nōn quin, 349, p. 138
Noun Clauses, 365—370
num, 344†; 370

Object, Case of, 326; 327*; 328; 329*; 330*, 330**
"one" (Indef. Pron.),572; 340; 341 a, Obs., 341 b, Obs. 3
Oratio Obliqua, 371
Oratio Recta, 371
Order of Words, 588—603
"ought (to)," 330; 453; 535; 340*; 356 (*a*)

palam, 457
Participles, 544—555; with Gen., 406
Passive — Greek Middle, 461
Passive construction, 327; 329; 330*; 330** Obs. 2; 332; 377; 379
Pentameter, 622
per, 460, 428, 442
Place, 435—437
Position, Rule of, 605
postquam, 347; 495
Potential Subj.; see Modest Assertions, 340
Predicate Adjective or Noun, 302; 324; 325—325†; 330 ☞; 334; 367, 1; 368 a, p. 153; 530, Obs.
Predicate Dative, 420
Predicate Genitive, 389
Prepositions, 455—460 (cf. 300)
Pres. Subj. referring to present time, 349; 352; 355, Obs. 3; 358; referring to future time, 342, 347 (*antequam*, etc.), 355, 512
Price, 401, 429
priusquam, 347
prō, Prep. 456; Interj., 587
Prohibitions, 341 b
prope, 417
Pronouns, etc., 556—575
Prosody, 604—615
Prospective action, 347, 352, 491, 500, 502

quā es prūdentiā, 569
Quality, 399; 434
quam, 345; 359
quamquam, 358; 314*
quam omitted, 360 †
quam ut, 360
quamvīs, 358
quasi, 360

## INDEX TO SYNTAX. 219

quemadmodum, 359
Questions, 344—344 †
quī, 569—571
quia, 349
quīcumque, 574, 364 note
quid, "how much," 382 ; 449
quīdam, 572
quīlibet, 572
quīn = quī nōn, 504
quīn, 367, 5 ; 368 d ; 368 e ; 369 b
quis, (Indef.) 572
quisquam, 572
quisque, 572, 573
quisquis, 574, 364 note
quīvis, 572
quō, 348 ; 350 ; 359
quoad, 347
quod, 'because,' 349
quod, 'that,' 367, 2 ; 368 b ; 506
quōminus, 367, 4 ; 369 b
quod dīceret, 510
quod sciam, 505
quod sī, 357
quum = quod, 368 b
quum, 347 ; 349 ; 358

Reflexive Pronoun, 562 ; 563 ; 376
Relative Clauses, 363 ; 364
Reported Speech, 371

sē, 562 ; 563
Sequence of Tenses, 514—526
"shall," in Commands, 341 a ; 479 ;
  369 a ; as auxiliary of tense, 477
"should" = "ought to,', 340 * ; 453 ;
  as auxiliary of tense, 347 ; 368 a,
  c ; 512 ; 513; as auxiliary of mood,
  355 ; 368 b, note ; 368 f ; 369 a,
  c ; 501—504
sī, 353—356 ; 501
 „ = quod, 368 b Obs. 2
 „ = "whether," 370, p. 159 Obs. 1
sīcut, 359
similis, 417
simulatque, 347 ; 495
sīve, 357, 370 Caution (2)
Space, 438
Spondaic lines, 618
Subject, Case of, 316
Subjective Genitive, 398
Subjunctive, Uses of, 497—510
sunt quī putent, 504
Supines, 542 ; 543
suus, 562—565
Synizēsis, 609

tametsī, 358
tamquam, 360
 " sī, 360
tam, tot, tantus, 568
temperātum est mihī, 329
Temporal Clause, 347
Tenses of Indicative, 462—496
 „  „ Infinitive, 533
 „  „ Participle, 549
 „  „ Subjunctive, 511—526
"that " (ways of translating), 350 ;
  352 ; 367, p. 152; 368 ; 369
Time, 439—445
Transitive or Intransitive ? 376

Ubī, 347 ; 348 ; 495
 „ terrārum, 392
ullus, 572
ut, 346 ; 347, p. 137; 350 ; 352 ;
  358 ; 359 ; 367, 3, 4 ; 368 c;
  368 e ; 368 f ; 369 a ; 495 ; 532
 „ = 'how,' 344† II (ut valēs?) ; 370,
  p. 159 Obs. 1, 2
 „ = nē nōn, 368 c
ut nē, 350, Obs. 2 ; 369 a
uterque, 394 ; 584
utrum . . . . an, 370 ; 584

vacō, 328 B ; 432
Verbs of 'fearing' 368 c ; 'happening ' 368 e : 'rejoicing.' etc., 368
  b : 'saying.' 'perceiving,' etc.
  368 a ; ' willing,' 369 a—c
Verb-nouns and verb-adjs., 528—555
Verbs taking Gen., 327 * ; 407 ; Dat.,
  328 ; 418 ; Acc. or Dat., 328 * ;
  Abl., 329 * ; 432 ; 451 ; Infin.,
  330 ; two Accusatives, 330*;
  330 ** : Acc. and Gen., 408 ;
  Acc. and Dat., 331 ; Acc. and
  Abl., 423 ; Acc. and Infin., 333 ;
  334, Obs. 2 ; 367 ; 368 a ; 369 b, c
vel, 580 ; 581
velutsī, 360
videor, 368 a ☞, p. 153 ; 410 (b)
Virtual Oratio Obliqua, 509
Vocative, 373, 374

"will," "would," expressing resolve,
  330 ; as auxiliary of tense, 477 ;
  368 a, c ; 512 ; 513. "Would"
  as auxiliary of mood, 355 ; =
  "used to," 471
Wishes, 342

'Yes,' 344 † ☞

"Almost every grammatical system has its *rationale*, capable of being comprehended by the mind, if the mind is kept steadily to it, and of serving as a clue to the facts; but . . . every one of the grammars following a different system" the student "masters the *rationale* of none of them; and in consequence, after all his labour, he often ends by possessing of the science of grammar nothing but a heap of terms jumbled together in inextricable confusion."—MATTHEW ARNOLD.

The PARALLEL GRAMMAR SERIES includes the following volumes:

**ENGLISH GRAMMAR**, by J. HALL, M.A., Head Master of the Hulme Grammar School, Manchester; A. J. COOPER, F.C.P., Head Mistress of the Edgbaston High School for Girls; and the Editor of the Series.

**ENGLISH EXAMPLES AND EXERCISES.** Part I., by M. A. WOODS, Head Mistress of the Clifton High School for Girls. Part II. by A. J. COOPER, F.C.P., Head Mistress of the Edgbaston High School for Girls.

**FRENCH GRAMMAR**, by L. M. MORIARTY, M.A. (Oxon.), Assistant Master in Harrow School; late Professor of French in King's College, London; Taylorian Scholar in French.

**FIRST FRENCH READER AND WRITER**, by R. J. MORICH, Chief Modern Language Master in the Manchester Grammar School, and W. S. LYON, M.A. (Oxon.), Assistant Master in Manchester Grammar School.

**GERMAN GRAMMAR**, by KUNO MEYER, PH.D., Lecturer in German in University College, Liverpool.

**FIRST GERMAN READER AND WRITER**, by E. A. SONNENSCHEIN·

**GREEK GRAMMAR**, by F. HAVERFIELD, M.A. (Oxon.), Sixth Form Master in Lancing College. [*In active preparation.*]

**LATIN GRAMMAR**, by E. A. SONNENSCHEIN, M.A. (Oxon.), Professor of Classics in the Mason College, Birmingham.

**FIRST LATIN READER AND WRITER**, by C. M. DIX, M.A., Assistant Master in the Oratory School, Birmingham.
[*This book contains the essential rules of Elementary Syntax, and thus forms, together with the Latin Accidence, a Complete Course for Beginners.*]

**SECOND LATIN READER AND WRITER**, by C. M. DIX.

**SPANISH GRAMMAR**, by H. B. CLARKE, B.A. (Oxon.), Taylorian Scholar in Spanish. [*In active preparation.*]

**ITALIAN GRAMMAR**, by C. M. C. BÉVENOT, Professor in the Mason College, Birmingham, late Assistant Master in Clifton College, Taylorian Exhibitioner in Italian. [*In active preparation.*]

☞ *Other "READERS and WRITERS" to follow the above will be shortly produced.*

SWAN SONNENSCHEIN & CO.

www.ingramcontent.com/pod-product-compliance
Lightning Source LLC
Chambersburg PA
CBHW021810230426
43669CB00008B/701